SENSITIVE BY NATURE

Understanding Intelligence and the Mind

By

James V. Luisi

© 2002 by James V. Luisi. All rights reserved.

No part of this book may be reproduced, stored in a retrieval system, or transmitted by any means, electronic, mechanical, photocopying, recording, or otherwise, without written permission from the author.

ISBN: 1-4033-0039-9

This book is printed on acid free paper.

1stBooks - rev. 05/20/02

Inside The Cover

Different perspectives can be useful for different things. By analyzing the mind, with a somewhat different perspective of ourselves, we can attempt to penetrate many of the barriers that have kept us from understanding what we are all about. The demystification of the human mind opens a world of new possible solutions to human limitations, and new interpretations of who we are as individuals, and a species.

From this day on it is a race, not to a finish line, but to a new starting line, which may initiate the most powerful technological revolution of the new millenium. It is a race to develop new beings, devoted and eager to please, that are a new and improved version of man's best friend.

Business Information
1st Edition, 2001

Dedication

I dedicate this book to my daughter Olivia, whose striking cleverness, remarkable people skills, cheer, and good sense of humor provides me with an example of what endearing qualities to strive for in myself.

Table of Contents

I. Prologue xv
   Background xvi
   Requirements xvi
   Conceptual Design xvii
   General xvii
   Summary & Questions xviii

II. Forward xix
   Summary & Questions xix

III. The Main Characters xxi
1 General Background 1
   1.1 Evolution of Physical Characteristics 1
   1.2 Evolution of Intellectual Characteristics 2
   Summary & Questions 3

2 The Beginning 5
   2.1 A Little About Quantum Mechanics 6
   2.2 Back From a Little Science 7
   2.3 A Little Experimentation 8
   2.4 What Was Brewing? 8
   2.5 Life 8
   2.6 DNA 10
   2.7 Molecular Evolution 10
   2.8 Evolution of Parts 12
   2.9 Entire Organisms Evolve 12
   2.10 Cycles of Organisms 14
   2.11 More Complex Organisms 14
   Summary & Questions 15

3 Hominids 16
   3.1 Upright 19
   3.2 Lifestyle of Being Upright 20
   3.3 Social Skills 21
   3.4 Evidence of Life Style 21
   3.5 Nakedness 22
   3.6 Primate Intelligence 22
   3.7 Sharing 22
   3.8 Ancestors of Homo sapiens 23
   3.9 Technology Outpaces Evolution 26
   Summary & Questions 26

4 Homo sapiens 28
   4.1 Introduction 28
   4.2 Effects of Agriculture 28

4.3 Human Characteristics 29
4.4 Spoken Language 29
4.5 Concepts 31
4.6 Behavior 31
4.7 Complex Behavior 32
4.8 Gatherer/Hunter 33
4.9 Reproductive Behavior 34
Summary & Questions 35

5 Physical Brain 37
5.1 Reasons for a Brain 39
Summary & Questions 40

6 Introduction to Computers 41
6.1 Natural Tools 41
6.2 Manufactured Tools 41
Summary & Questions 42

7 Software Limits 43
7.1 Formal Systems 44
7.2 Context of Rules 45
7.3 Processing Power 46
7.4 Informal Systems 47
7.5 Analogies 47
7.6 Notion of Requirements 48
Summary & Questions 50

8 Requirements - Physical Body 51
8.1 Supporting Frame 52
8.2 Musculature 52
8.3 Nervous System 55
8.4 Circulatory System 56
8.5 Respiratory System 56
8.6 Digestive System 57
8.7 Excretory System 58
8.8 Skin 58
8.9 Peripherals 59
8.10 Sensory Components 60
8.11 The Brain 62
Summary & Questions: 64

9 Requirements – Thinking 66
9.1 Origins of Intelligence 66
9.2 Intelligence 66
9.3 Thinking[2] 67
9.4 Self Awareness 68

9.5 Perception 69
9.6 Context of Information 71
9.7 Paradigm 73
9.8 Paradigms of Humans 75
9.9 Paradigms of Humans, Level Ones 76
9.10 Paradigms of Humans, Level Twos 79
9.11 Paradigms of Humans, Level Threes 82
9.12 Imagination 85
9.13 Sleep 87
9.14 Dreams and Dreaming 88
9.15 Memory 89
9.16 Internal Representation of Knowledge 90
9.17 Retrieval of Knowledge 92
9.18 Organizing Information 93
9.19 Brain Management 94
9.20 Attention and Focus 95
9.21 Attention Span 96
9.22 Importance Determination 96
9.23 Bubble-up Importance 98
9.24 Levels of the Mind 98
9.25 Recursion 100
9.26 Infinite Loops 101
9.27 The Nature of Insanity 103
9.28 Theorizing 106
9.29 Strategy 107
9.30 Original Thought 107
9.31 Artistic Ability 109
9.32 Free Will 110
Summary & Questions 111

10 Requirements – Learning 113
10.1 Learning 114
10.2 Role Playing 117
10.3 Positive and Negative Reinforcement 118
10.4 Hormones 119
10.5 Knowledge 120
10.6 Chunking 121
10.7 Association 122
10.8 Degrees of Certainty 125
10.9 Generalizations 126
10.10 Culture 128
10.11 Common Sense 130
Summary & Questions 134

11 Requirements - Psychological Effects 135
11.1 Humor 136

11.2 Motivation 138
11.3 Emotions 139
11.4 Love 141
11.5 Appreciation of Beauty 143
11.6 Personality 144
11.7 Self-esteem 145
11.8 Novelty 146
11.9 Subliminal Messages..147
11.10 Politics 150
11.11 Competing Wills 150
Summary & Questions 151

12 Requirements - Judgment and Problem Solving 153
12.1 Problem Solving...155
12.2 Deciphering 156
12.3 Spatial Problems..158
12.4 Holistic versus Reductionistic 160
12.5 Analogies...161
12.6 Isomorphism..162
12.7 Logic and Reasoning - Deductive versus Analogical Reasoning...162
12.8 Handling Contradictions 166
12.9 Fairness 166
12.10 Judging 'Good' Versus 'Bad' 167
Summary & Questions 171

13 Requirements – Beliefs 172
13.1 The Soul 174
13.2 Superstitions..176
13.3 Theology 179
13.4 Religion 181
Summary & Questions 183

14 Requirements – Communication 185
14.1 Language 186
14.2 Meaning 190
14.3 Literary Forms...193
14.4 Colloquialisms and Figures of Speech 193
14.5 Metaphors..194
14.6 Conceit 195
14.7 Anticlimax 195
14.8 Climax 195
14.9 Antithesis...196
14.10 Apostrophe 196
14.11 Euphemism 196
14.12 Exclamation...196
14.13 Hyperbole 197

14.14 Irony	197
14.15 Litotes	198
14.16 Metonymy	198
14.17 Oxymoron	198
14.18 Paradox	198
14.19 Onomatopoeia	199
14.20 Personification	199
14.21 Synecdoche	199
14.22 Rhetorical Question	199
14.23 Simile	200
14.24 Puns	200
14.25 Summarizing Communication	202
Summary & Questions	203
15 Requirements - The Philosophical	**205**
15.1 Control of Robots	207
15.2 Fundamental Rights	208
15.3 Moral Dilemmas	209
15.4 Rules For Mechanically Intelligent Beings	212
15.5 Tests for Intelligence	214
15.6 Physical Advantages for Survival	218
15.7 Survival and Mechanical Intelligence	219
15.8 Successfulness	220
15.9 Closure on Philosophy	221
Summary & Questions	221
16 Managing Requirements	**223**
16.1 Defining What Requirements Are	224
16.2 Organizing Requirements	227
16.3 Reorganizing Requirements	228
16.4 Logical Design	229
16.5 Physical Design	229
16.6 Implementation	230
16.7 Integration Testing	231
Summary & Questions	232
17 General Design – Introduction	**234**
17.1 General Approach	234
17.2 The Eliza Effect	237
17.3 Quantum Series Conceptual Design	238
17.4 Language of the Brain	239
17.5 Components of the Brain	241
Summary & Questions	242
18 Symbol Generation	**243**
Summary & Questions	249

19 Pattern Recognition 250
   19.1 Introduction 250
   19.2 Pattern Recognition Components 253
   Summary & Questions 254

20 Integrating Segments of Stimuli 256
   20.1 World of Fabricated Stimuli 258
   Summary & Questions 258

21 Symbol Activation 259
   21.1 Role of Symbols 259
   21.2 Symbol Activation 259
   21.3 Interpretive Centers 260
   21.4 Types of Activation Requests 262
   21.5 Prioritizing Symbol Activation 262
   21.6 Introducing Levels 263
   Summary & Questions 264

22 Importance Determination 266
   22.1 Some Important Background 266
   22.2 Conceptual Design 267
   22.3 Setting Levels of Importance 270
   22.4 Setting Thresholds 270
   Summary & Questions 271

23 The Imagination 273
   23.1 Integrating Segments of Stimuli 277
   23.2 Consciousness 277
   23.3 Thought Management 278
   Summary & Questions 280

24 Analogical Engine 281
   24.1 Role of Analogies 283
   24.2 Simple Analogies 285
   24.3 Proportional Analogies 286
   24.4 Predictive Analogies 287
   Summary & Questions 287

25 Metaphorical Engine 289
   25.1 The Metaphorical Engine 291
   Summary & Questions 293

26 Paradigms 294
   Summary & Questions 298

27 Architecture of the Mind 299
27.1 System Architecture 299
27.2 Software Architecture 300
27.3 Hybrid Information-Control System 301
Summary & Questions 302

28 Cognitive Database 304
Summary & Questions 305

29 Conclusion 306
29.1 Chance and Probabilities 306
29.2 Intelligence Born 307
29.3 Credit to the Leakey Legacy 308

30 Epilogue 310
30.1 Content 312
30.2 Presentation 312
30.3 Philosophy 313
30.4 Logic and Reason Revisited 314
30.5 Religion Revisited 316
30.6 Next Steps 317
Bibliography 321
Index 325

I. Prologue

Many books, research papers, and articles have been written about artificial intelligence, the majority of which tend to be quite technical and unimpressive. Research scientists have become so unsettled by the published research that they have attempted to separate themselves from it by renaming their field of specialty from artificial intelligence to cognitive science.

When we look at the level of progress that researchers have achieved in the various areas of science, such as physics, chemistry and biology, we get the sense that new discoveries are proportional to the investment in research. In striking contrast, there is a surprising lack of progress in artificial intelligence, especially when one considers the combined efforts of the academic, government, and commercial communities over several decades.

In order to achieve success, a new approach will be necessary. If it can be determined how the characteristics of the artificial intelligence challenge differs from every other area of research, then given those differences we must determine the most appropriate method to proceed.

In short, this manuscript addresses this very issue. Not only is an understanding of the functions that comprise intelligence surprisingly interesting, but it is applicable toward understanding oneself, as well as the people one interacts with everyday. It is more effective than a primer in psychology.

Using terms that are easily understood these concepts are discussed in a manner that requires no previous training and only an interest in science. It does not assume technical knowledge regarding logic, biology, chemistry, computer science, mathematics, psychology or philosophy. In the 'Background' section, we set the stage for discussing the mind by evaluating the path of scientific discovery to reveal the origins of intelligence. This section introduces the reader to the theme of evolutionary effects and identifies the fundamentals of intelligence, which are further explored in later chapters.

The 'Requirements' section that follows encompasses about half of the manuscript. It discusses a selection of the most difficult and controversial topics that have concerned psychologists, philosophers and cognitive researchers in simple terms. Using a unique paradigm, the functions that comprise intelligence are presented in a manner such that they actually lend themselves toward automation.

In conclusion, the 'Conceptual Design' section discusses, without technical jargon, a practical model that reflects the functional capabilities of the mind. The goal of this section is to identify a framework of high level concepts to allow the reader to appreciate how intelligent processes can be supported using a mechanical approach.

Background

The 'Background', section develops two themes concurrently. At a rudimentary level it identifies how evolutionary forces, including the development of animal intelligence, has influenced survival. Ultimately these forces contributed to the development of a vast number of species equipped with brains, including our own. Many of the evolutionary advancements that have resulted identify new or improved intellectual capabilities.

The backdrop of information provided by paleoanthropologists Louis and Mary Leakey, and their son Richard illustrate many of these evolutionary advancements and provide valuable insight into the development of the human brain. By describing our origins through evolutionary stages, the Leakey's help us understand how we compare to others in the animal kingdom.

Another theme is the role that natural mechanical processes play in creating biological intelligence. This also supports an analogous view toward man-made processes creating a mechanical form of intelligence. Mechanical forces have caused the brain to develop additional functions to process streams of information. As these functions and streams of information grow in complexity, it does not change the fact that they were built upon a foundation consisting of rather fundamental information and processes.

Requirements

The 'Requirements' section defines the major intellectual functions that comprise the mind. Topics discussed include: what thinking is and how it is performed, what awareness is, what the different aspects of learning are, and how psychological effects participate in the thought process. However, in order to appreciate the inter-relationship of these functions, the scope of requirements cannot be narrowly based. The intent throughout this section is to repeatedly demonstrate that these functions have aspects in common, no matter how disparate they appear. Ultimately, what these functions have in common forms the foundation of how the mind works.

A continuing theme in this section is the notion that individuals have intellectual capabilities in varying strengths. Such differences can affect the likelihood of survival and influence an individual's ability to appreciate the intellectual aspects of things in different ways.

Typically, the intellectual capabilities of the mind are thought to influence one's success as an individual and as a participant in society. Success, however, is not necessarily money or power, but rather, a state of mind, whether an individual uses their intellect to invent, implement, cooperate, lead, motivate, negotiate, understand or communicate, their perceived level of success can only be determined by how they interpret their world and make decisions.

In observing that the greedy can never have enough, or the generous too little, one realizes that everything is dependent upon your paradigm. Since paradigms are at the core of how individuals interpret their universe, understanding how paradigms participate in the thought process becomes a critical aspect to understanding the requirements for any advanced form of intelligence.

Conceptual Design

The 'Conceptual Design' section defines the various functions of the intellect as being comprised of parts, many of which are used in different combinations to make other functions.

> For example, just as there are many electrical tools, each of them is manufactured from a combination of parts, such as power supplies, motors, fans, resistors, diodes, transistors, transformers, capacitors, and relays.

To decompose functions into their component parts, a variety of challenges must be met. The most important, however, is that the requirements must be reasonably complete, and must be characterized to render them as implementable, as opposed to preferences, vague ideas and notions, which are not implementable.

> For example, large business system development efforts often co-mingle non-requirements with requirements. Consider the difference between the requirement that each bank transaction must comply with the tax code of the federal, state and local jurisdictions, and the requirement that each bank transaction should comply with the organization's standards on ethics.
>
> What could a mandate to conduct only ethical business mean?

Once the requirements have been separated from the 'mumbo-jumbo', they must be distilled into sets of functions that are implementable. Therefore, the role of the 'Conceptual Design' section is to show that once the functional requirements of the mind are properly defined and reduced into their parts, the resulting components can be used to recreate various intellectual capabilities.

General

There is extensive use of quotes throughout the book. While many of the ideas contained within the quoted material could have easily been paraphrased, and in a few cases made easier to read, it was considered important to give credit to the specific authors using their words as often as possible. The trade off may have left a slightly more challenging manuscript to follow, as the writing style of the authors quoted differs somewhat from the manuscript itself. On the other hand, the reader may benefit by realizing that misinterpretations are less likely to occur when using the original words of a literary source.

Summary & Questions

Depending upon the perspective that is brought to the subject matter, one may find that the questions at the end of each section are quite challenging. The way that the topics are presented facilitates the emergence of interesting new perspectives hence, it is important for even the most knowledgeable individual to progress through the material in the sequence that it is covered. The objective is for the reader to gain new perspectives on many topics that they may already familiar with.

This is a good point in time, before continuing further, to identify your present understanding and perceptions about artificial intelligence. Briefly explain:

1. What is artificial intelligence?
2. What areas of science does artificial intelligence combine?
3. What are the challenges facing artificial intelligence?
4. What are some of the opinions of experts on artificial intelligence? (i.e., Bill Gates of Microsoft, Marvin Minsky of MIT)
5. What approaches have been attempted to develop artificial intelligence?
6. Is there an approach for artificial intelligence that you would like to recommend?
7. What information about intelligence would you recommend research scientists begin with?
8. How should researchers organize the vast amount of information they gather?
9. Once the information is gathered, how should they proceed?
10. What are some of the reasons why individuals encounter difficulty when thinking about thinking?

II. Forward

This is a true story. It consists of concepts that when put together in a particular sequence, light the path to a new discovery. As we travel along this winding path, we will share an adventure that will give rise to new ways of thinking about ourselves, and potentially change our world for the better.

Whenever we acquire knowledge, we find various ways to incorporate it with the things we believe to be true. The better that all the pieces fit together, the more useful the newly acquired information is likely to be. Although many engage in the educational contest to acquire as many facts as possible, simply discovering ways of applying the knowledge one already has, is what true intelligence is all about.

The approach we have taken, to understand human psychology, is to first demystify the development of the human mind by looking at the functions that have evolved within animal minds in general. Although we start from a conventional scientific perspective, we gradually nudge the reader through a requirements gathering phase, which involves identifying the parts needed to discuss the thinking capabilities of the entire being.

After all, having a complete understanding of any problem, is what allows an appreciation of its solution. And understanding the solution, is what will allow those intelligent individuals among us, to prepare to take full advantage of it.

It is highly likely that, when many individuals realize where this trail actually leads, their reaction will be that it is not possible. But as it is with many inventions, when they say it is impossible, good inventors know that they must be on the right track.

Some segments of humanity are prepared to undertake this journey. And if we don't choose to embark upon it, others eventually will, potentially long after we are gone.

Summary & Questions

The most influential factors that can lead to new discoveries are usually a combination of hard work and a new way of looking at things. However, in order to proceed on a solid foundation, it is critical to reevaluate the facts that are known and why they are believed to be true.

Regarding any problem solving effort, briefly explain:
1. What are the first steps that should be taken in problem solving?
2. How should researchers treat the advice that they receive from those outside their specific research effort and or research team?
3. What are some of the things that should be required of the members of a research team?

4. What are the most important things for a research team to record?
5. How would you propose recording this information?
6. What things will require naming conventions, why are naming conventions required, and how should they be determined?
7. What are the various representations that can be used to record information?
8. Provide an example of the types of information that should be recorded.
9. What are some of the ways in which to organize the information?
10. What tools may be required to manage the information?

III. The Main Characters

You have these things inside of yourself that are always doing something. Whether you are eating breakfast, concentrating on an exciting book, staring at a television screen, or in a deep sleep, you just can't stop them. Not only that, but you can't control them, you can't influence them, nor can you even communicate with them. On the other hand, they control you, they influence you and they communicate with you. What are they? Or better yet, what are you?

- - -

Neuron Story: *"Do you think they're aware of us?"*
"They're only aware of what we let them become aware of."

- - -

1 General Background

"If at first the idea is not absurd, then there is no hope for it."
Albert Einstein

1.1 Evolution of Physical Characteristics

Frequently discoveries and scientific breakthroughs are chained together in a sequence of events, in which each discovery is built upon some aspect learned from the preceding one.

For example, the story of how traits are passed through a species as they evolve is the 'chain of discovery'. An exciting trail was blazed by Charles Darwin setting sail on the Beagle to the Galapagos Islands, where he studied the traits of various plant and animal species. The focus of his trip was to observe the different species that had evolved in isolation after being cut off from the population on the mainland for such a long period. This discovery is what led Charles Darwin to write his landmark treatise on natural selection, which asserted that mankind was a part of nature, rather then being above or separate from it, and that all life was related through a common ancestral link from the remote past.

The sequence of discovery then continued with an Augustinian monk, Gregor Mendel, who experimented with garden peas in order to understand how physical traits were expressed. Although the envelop Mendel sent Darwin containing his research sat unopened on Darwin's desk in 1882, Mendel's research proved a number of assertions that were core to Darwin's theories.

Mendel worked for Abbot Napp, who was part of the Catholic Church in Moravia that was attempting to modernize, in opposition to the Italian pope.

For example, "One of the ways in which the church was straining to modernize was through the pursuit of natural sciences. Witness the scientific undertakings of the brethren of the St. Thomas monastery and of other clerics throughout the Hapsburg Empire: the formed the core of a progressive, democratic Catholic intelligentsia in Moravia that managed to ask scientific questions unfettered by Christian dogma. These enlightened clerics, Abbot Napp prominent among them, helped contribute to the unprecedented flourishing of science in Vienna, the hub of the empire, in the second half of the nineteenth century." (The Monk in the Garden, Robin Marantz Henig, pg. 65)

Through controlling which plants interbred, Mendel observed the patterns of heredity. It was because of Mendel's quantitative approach and inquisitive nature that he discovered that some of the individual traits in pea plants were either dominant or recessive, thus contributing to the fundamental principles of inheritance.

Many more important contributions were made by the scientific community including those in the analysis of more complex molecules through advancing technology.

> For example, the study of DNA strands by Watson and Crick determined that the foundations for the chemical basis for inheritance were to be found in the double helix structure. These discoveries then paved the way for others to journey farther into the mysteries of life.

As the chemical foundation of life unfolds, we realize that, like human discovery, which builds step by step upon each prior discovery, so it is with the evolutionary process. This chemical foundation builds step by step upon each prior change, propelling life forward from its beginnings, advancing through an extensive period of time.

Throughout the history of the human race, discoveries have been developing at an increasingly rapid pace. The rate at which discoveries progress, even outpace the rate of growth in the human population. With information rapidly traveling the globe through the Internet, the length of time for one breakthrough to pave the way for the next has, in some cases, become a matter of days and weeks. Consider the difference when it was a matter of months in the 1980's, years in the early industrial revolution, and decades to centuries during the first sixteen hundred years of recorded history.

1.2 Evolution of Intellectual Characteristics

Along with physical characteristics, intellectual characteristics have also been progressing by means of an internal force, perhaps a demonstration of Darwin's 'survival of the fittest' at its best.

While genetic evolution is credited with the passing of instinctual knowledge, it is also responsible for establishing the ability to learn. As an animal learns how best to use its increasing adaptability, so does the length of time in which it takes to learn, thus leading to the improvement of its offspring. With this greater knowledge there is also the drawback of the increased amount of time a young animal is dependent on its parents. There is direct correlation between the level of intelligence of a particular species and the amount of time before it is suitable to be on its own.

Learning is regarded as more of a process made up of many small steps building upon one another, and each having the potential to greatly influence the survivability of a particular animal or species. Specifically, animals may learn what materials are beneficial to consume, how to cure what ails them, how to hunt, and where shelter can be found with regard to climate or geography.

The degree to which learning occurs is related to the brain's size in proportion to the entire animal. The capabilities and knowledge of the brain are established by either the ability to learn from observation and experience, or the ability of genetic materials to pass on instinctual behavior from generation to generation in order to promote the survival of the species. As such, the proportionally larger brain offers many advantages over lessor equipped animals.

For example, chimpanzees, which belong to the ape family with larger brains, have the intelligence to adapt better to a changing environment than any New or Old World monkeys.

The point of this discussion is that the study of intelligence, including brain theory, should not be limited to humans, or even their close relatives. Rather it should include any animals blessed with a brain. Therefore, as it is possible to become easily overwhelmed, it may suit us to start with those animals with the smallest brain, no matter how limited we might consider their capabilities to be.

Using this approach, we will see how function upon function has been linked together, developing first in the simplest of brains to those more advanced. As we see how each new layer of function is built upon preceding ones, we can now begin to look at nature's role in the construction of the human mind.

There are, in fact, many contributions to the understanding of the formation of the brain and intellect to be found in animals both with and without brains. Protozoans, insects, plants and surprisingly parasites, supply us with pieces to the puzzle.

So let's go back to the ocean, long after the soup cooled down, to the time after a single mass of land pushed its way up through the liquid surface. Let's look at the first life forms that carried their own liquids with them, allowing them to emerge from the ocean.

Summary & Questions

Just as evolutionary forces build successive improvements upon one another, scientific breakthroughs advance in an analogous manner. However, similar to the success or failure of a new species, major scientific discoveries are sometimes lost or simply not accepted by the very community that could benefit the most.

Regarding new discoveries, briefly explain:
    1. What factors have contributed to the acceleration of discoveries?

2. What are the factors that challenge the survival of a new discovery?
3. Identify a few interest groups that facilitate the dissemination of new discoveries.
4. What are the interest groups that have obstructed new discoveries in the past?
5. How do you recognize an interest group that is likely to obstruct a new discovery?
6. What recommendations would you make for overcoming such obstructions?

2 The Beginning

If you take a moment to consider the universe as we know it, we are but a tiny speck well within a little section we have named the Milky Way galaxy. On this tiny speck that we call Earth, we use everything our minds have to offer, such as our imaginations, observations, belief systems and scientific theories, in an attempt to explain where everything comes from.

There are many views as to how the universe came into existence. One such theory, which is called the 'Big Bang Theory', depicts the formation of the universe as a result of a catastrophic event. One explanation refers to an energy fluctuation within a vacuum, causing the explosion, another predicts an endless cycle of an expanding and collapsing universe. Also, other theories argue a different method for the creation of the universe. For our purposes, we will start with the assumption that there was a 'big bang'. Scientists generally agree that this event would have taken place approximately nine billion years ago, although some believe that the universe is significantly older than that. At minimum, it gives a point from which to begin.

The universe immediately following the last 'big bang' was believed to contain the initial soup of quantum particles. This soup of sub-atomic particles ultimately led to the formation of atoms, molecules, stars and galaxies. Hence, scientists feel that it is important for them to understand the mechanics behind the Big Bang and what immediately followed.

For example, as a result of the advent of computer modeling, there's more known about the first few seconds of the initial phases of the Big Bang, such as temperatures and particle ratios, than is known about the next several million years.

From the moment that the first stars were created, to the point in time when our solar system formed, something critical to the formation of life occurred. Larger atoms, those with an atomic number greater than twelve were produced, including all of the elements heavier than magnesium, such as calcium and potassium.

The only natural process with enough energy to generate these elements occurs when stars violently explode in an event called a 'super nova'. This explosion, which for certain types of stars occurs as a normal part of their lifecycle, manufactures and disperses these heavy elements, specifically all elements above the atomic number of twelve, out into neighboring clouds of matter.

After becoming enriched with the heavy elements, these clouds of matter eventually evolved into new stars and planets. Without a 'super nova', all of the elements found on Earth above the atomic number of twelve would never have been brought into existence. Therefore, at some time before the Earth could have formed, a nearby star had to explode creating a super nova. This explosion seeded the area with the material that formed our planet, which consisted particularly of the atomic elements that were absolutely necessary to establish life.

Scientists believe that approximately four and a half billion years, the formation of our planet and solar system benefited from such an event. Although there was neither life nor intelligence when this event occurred, the building blocks that were necessary to eventually create them were present for the first time.

After our planet formed, its entire surface was an extremely, hot soup, comprised of atoms and simple molecules where today's species could never exist. Intense heat permeated a hostile atmosphere with oceans of liquid toxins below. Tidal actions caused by the gravitational forces of the sun and moon churned this horrible brew repeatedly as the milleniums passed.

2.1 A Little About Quantum Mechanics

Approximately a hundred years ago, scientists thought that the smallest unit of matter in the universe was the molecule. The molecule was the smallest piece of something that still retained the properties of the larger mass of material, but the discovery of the atom disproved those theories.

The discovery of the atom was an incredible breakthrough, identifying a finite set of building blocks that, when put together in different combinations, created new molecules. It seemed all too perfect until it was realized that not just any combination of atoms was able to create new molecules. There were numerous rules to the possible combinations. All of the patterns and theories that were developed in an attempt to explain these findings failed, that is, except for one.

A scientist by the name of Niels Bohr defined a model, called the 'Bohr atom', where he was able to predict the outcome, of repeated experiments. In his model there existed shells of electrons that orbited a densely packed nucleus of protons and neutrons. These protons and neutrons accounted for the atomic weight of specific atoms, where the number of protons matched the number of electrons maintaining a neutral charge. Protons were assigned a positive charge of one, while the electrons were assigned a negative charge of one.

With credit to Bohr's findings, the proton, neutron and electron were now identified as the smallest units of matter, the building blocks from which all else is created.

With this understanding of matter, science progressed quickly, especially in the fields of chemistry, physics and even mathematics. But new observations were beginning to reveal limitations to the atomic model, and there had to be something else. The geometry of matter, as well as crystals, the make-up of compounds and certain combinations of atoms and molecules, became increasingly difficult to explain using the model of the 'Bohr atom'.

One of the additional problems was that the properties of light could not be applied to protons, neutrons and electrons. Scientific theories at that time could not explain how light displayed the duality of particle and wave properties. It eventually became apparent, that matter could not be considered as being completely separate from energy, and hence, the theory of quantum mechanics was born, and with it, came a whole new family of particles.

Quantum mechanics explained that all matter acted simultaneously as a particle and as a wave. As every particle moves through space, it travels its path in the pattern of a wave. The ability to perceive the wave properties was simply a function of the size or mass of the object. Photons or electrons, which are extremely small, display more of a wave property because they have nearly a zero mass. Baseballs and rocks, on the other hand, primarily display their particle properties because of their relatively large mass.

The essential point in the behavior of atoms is that electrons traveling within the shell of an atom, not only behave like particles that orbit heavily attracting nuclei, but they also behave like fields of charge. Therefore, electrons not only act like particles, but they also act like a standing wave of charge. Additionally, with electron clouds acting as standing waves, various probabilities exist that a specific electron will be found in one physical location versus another, thus creating the potential for chemical bonds.

When a larger atom bonds to a smaller one, an area of the normally shielded large atom becomes exposed with a positive charge. The exposure of a positively charged area opens the door to the formation of ionic bonds. Therefore, it is the reduced probability of electrons shielding a large nucleus from another atoms' electron clouds, a key aspect of quantum mechanics, which permits ionic bonding to occur.

An important aspect to remember is that specific angles of chemical bonds, hence the geometry of molecules, are determined by the relative sizes of the atoms involved in conjunction with this effect of 'quantum mechanics'.

2.2 Back From a Little Science

Before taking our excursion into the quantum world, we were discussing the primordial soup that was left to brew for millions of centuries. We are now ready to continue, since you have been armed with a few quantum mechanical facts with which to use in our discussion.

2.3 A Little Experimentation

A great deal of analysis has been performed on the chemical compounds that play a role in genetics. These molecules range from simple amino acids to complex chemical chains called DNA and RNA.

Experiments involving the production of a particular type of RNA (ribonucleic acid), (e.g., messenger RNA), have shown that when simple molecular building blocks, called amino acids, are combined with one another, certain pairs of these building blocks always attach together for no obvious reason.

It turns out that these building blocks have specific geometries that are predicted by quantum mechanics, and as a result, they fit much more snugly in some positions than in other positions. When these pieces fit well together, they become extremely difficult to break apart, however, when they are not tightly fitted together, applying small amounts of heat will cause them to separate.

When the process of heating and cooling is applied repeatedly, eventually all of the molecules find a snug position, even if poorly fitting pairs had previously occupied the same positions.

2.4 What Was Brewing?

The experiments we have discussed help to exhibit that during the early period on Earth, when there was a continuous mixing of simple atoms and molecules something much greater was actually going on. The mixing, which was assisted by the tidal action of the moon, as well as, the heating and cooling effects of the sun, contributed to the building of more complex molecules. These newly formed molecules followed the same mechanical laws that govern molecules today.

Within this warm organic soup, molecules continued to grow, either by utilizing energy from the sun or by utilizing geological heat sources present in the Earth's own abundant internal energy.

At some point, these molecules formed natural communities. Concentrations of building blocks would promote the proliferation of complex organic chains, with the domino effect creating still more complex formations, all without the aid of any intelligence, or life, as we know it. The only forces present were the relentless mechanical forces of the quantum world.

2.5 Life

From a certain point of view it becomes interesting to consider the question of what exactly constitutes life, especially since molecules were absorbing energy, growing and reproducing themselves long before what scientists call 'living cells' came into existence. The components of 'pre-cell molecules' existed in a type of symbiosis to effectively increase their numbers by combining simple parts together into more complex ones. The only organic molecules capable of replicating themselves, however, began with the first molecular forms of DNA and RNA. No other molecules capable of replicating themselves have ever been identified.

Although it can be debated that the first molecules of DNA and RNA could be categorized as a form of life, for our purposes we will accept the definition of 'life' as organizations of molecules into packages called cells.

The first cellular life forms, existing approximately 3.4 billion years ago, were primitive plant cells. These primeval prokaryotes, which were precursors to algae and bacteria, fed on the 'organic broth', which then covered the planet. Between 570 and 700 millions years ago a burst of evolutionary diversification occurred as multi-cellular plants and animals, such as jellyfish and primitive worms, begin to appear in the fossil record.

> For example, "beginning just before 570 million years ago, skeletons developed independently in a number of animal lineages. One worm-like lineage that pursued a swimming mode of life evolved a stiff dorsal cord and eventually an articulated internal skeleton that supported the body to improve swimming efficiency; thus, fish arose from the early invertebrates." (Microsoft, Encarta 98)

The primitive plant cells now permeating the environment with new molecules, supplied nutrients for other life forms that had adapted into being able to process this new type of food.

One of the molecules of early plants that contributed to the environment was oxygen (O_2). During the period that oxygen began polluting the environment, no other form of life could utilize it. Its existence, however, made it possible for the evolution of new organisms that could thrive on it. Newer types of plant cells, and eventually animal cells, came into existence with not only the ability to consume oxygen, but the dependence on it for life.

As plants evolved with the ability to store energy from the sun, new life forms were able to take greater advantage of the abundant nutrients. Many new organisms evolved which no longer needed to directly store the sun's energy. These animals did not acquire energy from direct sources, such as the sun or geothermal heat, but instead acquired energy from the ability to remove energy from other life forms, through a process called 'digestion' and subsequent absorption. The food chain rapidly developed, bridging the gap from raw radiated energy, into more specialized forms of food.

At this point, molecules were reaching new heights of complexity. The various precursors of life were all established within the means of mechanical laws, which operated over millions of centuries.

James V. Luisi

2.6 DNA

The smallest units of life, whether plant or animal, are units we refer to as cells. Living cells are unique in that they make complete replications of all their parts into new cells. The only organic molecules that facilitate this are DNA and RNA. The blueprint for all of the genetic information is encoded into these unique structures, whether they are for simple life forms, such as amoebae, or highly complex, such as humans.

The genetic blueprint is always stored as a sequential string of simple amino acid building blocks, snugly bonded together in distinct sequences. Each individual string translates into the instructions for building all of the cells of the entire organism. The more complex the life form, the longer the string. In order to gain a perspective as to the length of an individual DNA string, lets explore the following.

> For example, "DNA molecules are always folded up very tightly so that they may fit into the tiny size of a living cell. While simple life forms have rather short strings, if an individual string of DNA for a human, or for a primate, were laid out in a straight line, it would measure a distance of approximately 180 centimeters, which exceeds the height of most humans." (In Search of the Double Helix, Gribbin, 1977, pg. 298)

2.7 Molecular Evolution

Lengthy molecules have a number of advantages, aside from helping to keep us alive, they also increase the chance of mutations. The longer the molecule, the more information it contains, not only about its biological purpose, but also about its evolution. The more we know about the evolution of the molecule, the more we know about the evolution of the organism that it is part of.

The relative closeness of species can be determined by the degree of molecular variation in their protein molecules such as hemoglobin, DNA or RNA. Molecular comparisons of distant species, such as plant 'leghemoglobin' and vertebrate animal 'hemoglobin', give valuable insight into the path of life and evolution.

One technique for determining molecular age is referred to as the statistical rate of variation, which is dependent upon the length of the molecule. Smaller differences in larger molecules indicate a closer proximity in time and relationship.

Using a statistical rate of variation, determining the time period that the 'globin' molecules of baboons, gorillas and humans came into existence, confirms the geophysical dating of fossil evidence, such as in East Africa, which represents the descent of 'Old and New World' primates.

> For example, "One factor that has made the East African sites particularly important is that the fossils

discovered there can be dated reliably, and the means by which this is done is the ash that periodically tumbled out of the Rift Valley's many volcanoes. All the fossil-rich deposits from Olduvai in the south to the Hadar in the north are interlayed with volcanic ash, just like many layers of jam in a multiple sponge cake. We can determine when the ash spewed out of the volcanoes by a number of sophisticated geophysical techniques."

"So, if we find a fossil entombed in deposits underneath a layer of ash that is two million years old but above another layer that was laid down two and a quarter million years ago, then we know that the bone was buried between these two dates. In practice we can usually be much more specific than this because the extremely active volcanoes belched out their gas and ash more frequently than every quarter of a million years. During many a Pliocene evening the hominids on the shore of Lake Turkana would have gazed with wonderment at the staggeringly beautiful sunsets enhanced by gas and dust from volcanic eruptions, eruptions that in the future would help us reconstruct their family tree!" (People of the Lake, Leakey and Lewin, p66)

Even though fossils are being discovered at a higher rate, the findings are still considered to be rare, and they continue to become even less abundant. Although rain, wind and running water may expose new fossils, when they are exposed to the weather they rapidly disintegrate, and disappear forever. When one considers the number of animal skeletons that would have been consumed by scavengers, few remain to become fossilized. Once they vanish below the surface, few ever appear above the surface again and found in time.

As the gaps are filled by even greater paleoanthropological efforts, every attempt is being made to utilize alternative sources of information, such as the incredible details that molecular studies have begun to reveal.

The mounting evidence of molecular evolution clearly indicates that our own immediate ancestor was also that of the chimpanzee and gorilla. The research into the relationship between species has continued at a rapid pace ever since the 1970's, and includes the plant, as well as the animal kingdom.

With these molecular techniques, we learn the evolutionary path of molecules, the evolutionary path of the organisms comprised of these molecules, and therefore, the evolutionary path of life, and therefore intelligence.

2.8 Evolution of Parts

Molecules may have formed plant cells as a more efficient technique for collecting and harnessing energy from the sun or geothermal energy sources. The reason for the change, however, could not have been to gain efficiency.

Can efficiency be the sole explanation for the formation of cells from cooperative sets of complex molecules promoting their own proliferation?

Certainly not. That would imply a conscious effort on the part of molecules to improve their ability to collect energy.

Is it likely that complex molecules improved the proliferation of future generations of molecules by constructing complex systems, where they could go out into the world to produce future generations of their own kind?

Certainly not. That would imply a conscious effort on the part of molecules to promote their own existence.

For that matter, can any advanced life form make a conscious effort to improve or promote their existence at a molecular level?

Certainly not. Animals cannot apply any conscious effort in promoting their own evolutionary success. For that matter, plants and protozoans do not possess the capacity to apply a conscious effort either.

Cells have evolved for mechanical reasons. If by chance a new symbiotic relationship of complex molecular structures evolved, in order to survive they would have to possess mechanical benefit.

> For example, it would have to be more efficient at collecting energy, more capable of utilizing abundantly available molecules, or more efficient at replication.

In any event, the formation of a selectively permeable membrane that supplied an organizing structure to cells had to provide mechanical advantages to free-floating molecules. Whether it provided protection, or simply an increased probability that components with a symbiotic relationship would be readily available, cellular life not only propagated itself better than its previous free-floating predecessors, but these new cells probably utilized their free-floating predecessors, as a readily available source of nutrition.

2.9 Entire Organisms Evolve

Cells would continue to evolve as the molecules did before them. They would mechanically evolve into organisms with varying degrees of mechanical advantage. Determined by the forces of 'quantum mechanics', evolution has been determined by successful amino acid combinations, collections of molecules, and organisms that could benefit the most from the resulting mechanical outcome of probability and chance.

The mechanical evolution of molecules preceded the evolution of single cell organisms, which existed before multi-cell organisms. Sexual reproduction then accelerated the process even further. Errors in copying longer molecules increased as well, with mutations adding a greater degree of variation. Complex molecules, and the imperfect mechanisms for their replication, were rapidly helping to evolve organisms that were increasingly complex. However, mutations originated from other sources as well.

For example, mutations can occur at a faster rate with the help of genetic parasites. Wondering genetic material, called 'genetic parasites', use the genes of their hosts to get themselves replicated by inserting themselves into random places in the genome, which get passed to offspring. "As it hops from chromosome to chromosome within a cell, or as it leaps from species to species, it can wedge itself into the middle of a new gene." "But every now and then, the disruption turns out to be a good thing, evolutionary speaking. An interrupted gene may suddenly become able to make a new kind of protein that does a new sort of job."

"And once a genetic parasite has established itself in a new host, it can disrupt the unity of the entire species. The typical fate for a genetic parasite is to explode through its host's genome during the succeeding generations, wedging itself into thousands of sites. As time passes, the hosts that carry it will diverge on their own into separate populations – not distinct species, but groups that tend to breed among themselves", although the separation of the groups has the effect of encouraging the groups to eventually split into a new species.
(<u>Parasite Rex</u>, Carl Zimmer, p. 188)

After hundreds of millions of years, different types of cells were created, and many of them became increasingly specialized.

- - -

Neuron Story: "The neurons started to handle data transfer better than any other cell. The technique of throwing many little messages in bottles into the ocean, all bearing the same code, was just not doing the job. Besides being too slow and too much effort, clearing out the old message to make way for the new one was more difficult than sending it out in the first place."

"Eventually, these neurons started connecting to one another. Inventing the ion pump, these were the first cells to discover a new technology, called 'electricity', and with it, they then invented their own form of 'Morse code', which traveled along an evolving information highway of living cells."

2.10 Cycles of Organisms

Collections of cells fed off of others, each finding a niche for itself, or becoming extinct. The niche in which an organism survived was primarily due to the availability of materials that it required. Eventually a closed ecological system was developed. The life cycle of each type of organism could only proceed, as its raw materials for survival became available.

Plants collected solar energy, animals ate plants and other animals, and then bacteria decomposed all of these organisms back into their basic building blocks. Today we identify the categories of this cycle as (1) the producers, (2) the consumers, and (3) the decomposers.

'Producers' have the ability to (1) absorb raw energy, such as electromagnetic radiation or heat, and (2) to convert a percentage of it into chemical energy as a means of storing the energy. 'Consumers', on the other hand, do not have the ability to use raw energy at all, but instead must rely upon their ability to digest 'producers' to meet their energy requirements, and some consumers meet some or all of their energy requirements by consuming other 'consumers'.

The 'decomposers' are at the end of the cycle and they meet their energy requirements by feeding off the energy released in the breaking down of complex molecules, built up by the 'producers' and 'consumers', into simple molecules. These simple molecules are then transformed again by the 'producers', into energy storing molecules that support consumers, thus allowing the cycle to repeat.

2.11 More Complex Organisms

As organisms evolved, so did their sensory systems. Organisms that could seek out energy had an advantage. Plant cells developed so that they could bend and grow towards the sun. Animal cells developed the ability to detect and eventually move toward their food. Organisms that could detect an enemy had an advantage in that they were sometimes able to flee from danger. Organisms with sensory systems had the ability to process information and reveal things about their environment. Information became power. The more an organism could detect, the better positioned it was to react with the best of its capabilities.

From hydra to sea insects, as well as other sea creatures, sensory systems continued to advance. Plants, on the other hand, were doing quite well on both the land and the sea. Organisms from the sea, and eventually the land, continued to evolve improved sensory systems.

Organisms may not have understood the basic factors involving survival of the fittest, but they lived it. Like so many of us, they didn't concern themselves with where they came from, what made them function, or why they existed. They had no concept of themselves, any more than the free-floating molecules had. They simply lived.

Neuron Story: "The neurons kept building communication networks. Making connections and transmitting data became their specialty."

"They had no idea of what they might possibly develop into. They were simply the handlers of information."

Summary & Questions

When beginning any effort, it is important to place everything in its proper perspective, beginning with its origin on through it various evolutionary stages. Equally important, however, are the various interpretations that the scientific community may have previously employed. It may become apparent that the present interpretations may be steppingstones to a more useful paradigm, which in turn may reveal a variety of new perspectives that facilitate a greater level of understanding.

Regarding how well we actually understand various phenomena, briefly explain:

1. What are examples of scientific breakthroughs that were a direct result of new paradigms facilitating a greater level of understanding?
2. How have new paradigms led to additional scientific breakthroughs?
3. In what instance did a theoretical area of science lead to a major discovery?
4. Describe the types of information that nature might need to store.
5. How does nature store information?
6. What vocabulary does nature use to store information?
7. What are the limitations of this vocabulary, if any?
8. What are the limitations of nature's method of storage, if any?
9. What types of information have humans been able to extract from the information stored by nature?
10. How does nature communicate information among the components of an organism?

James V. Luisi

3 Hominids

When animal life first exited the ocean there was only one landmass for them to occupy, Pangaea. Hence, for hundreds of millions of years, this single continent cradled all life on the land, with evolution leading to such inhabitants as insects, amphibians, reptiles, and dinosaurs.

> For example, "Land plants appeared about 400 million years ago, spreading from lowland swamps as expanding greenbelts. Arthropods (some evolving into insects) and other invertebrate groups followed them onto land, and finally land vertebrates (amphibians at first) rose from freshwater fish nearly 360 million years ago. In general, the subsequent radiations of land vertebrates made them increasingly independent of water and increasingly active." (Microsoft's, Encarta 98)

As we travel backward in time, the first primitive small mammals appeared just seventy-five million years ago, the dawn of the 'Age of Mammals'. Although there is some debate as to whether there were dinosaurs that could partially regulate their body temperature, the main difference between mammals and all life that preceded them was that mammals were homothermic, maintaining a constant body temperature. With this evolutionary adaptation, animals could now maintain a steady level of activity in varying climates, as opposed to slowing down, or potentially becoming dormant in cooler temperatures, which was the case with animals such as reptiles.

> For example, "Most zoologists believe that mammals evolved from a group of extinct mammal-like reptiles, Theriodontia, which existed during the Triassic period. The earliest animal fossils that have definitely been identified as mammals, were found in rocks from the Jurassic period." (Microsoft's, Encarta 97)

> By this time, an incredible variety of dinosaurs had long dominated the Earth. Within a small fraction of that period, consisting of just a few million years, the dinosaurs disappeared from the planet, which would now be dominated by mammals. During that same time, seventy-five percent of all invertebrate species were rapidly obliterated by a mass extinction.

About seventy million years ago, just as the dinosaurs died off, a shrew-like creature adapted to life in the trees, possibly to find refuge from its reptilian predators. Molecular strings governing the genetic blueprint were quickly evolving as they continued to grow in both their length and complexity. Then about sixty-five million years ago, early prosimians, which were an early group of nocturnal primates, dwelled in trees and moved about with the aid of claws.

A few million years later, just over sixty million years ago, primate characteristics evolved from the prosimians. These included grasping hands, which would be a great advantage to hold onto branches, separately moving fingers, which improved manual dexterity of the hands to feed on tiny insects, and forward facing eyes, making depth perception possible. Depth perception provided a great advantage to living in the trees while grabbing and jumping to branches.

As the sensory systems of predators improved, so did the survival pressures for more refined senses. Still, primitive primates faired rather well, as the dense forests that carpeted Pangaea sheltered the growing number of mammals for over the next fifty million years.

About twelve million years ago great changes occurred in the environment. Mountain ranges formed as the continent of Pangaea gradually split into six separate parts; temperatures continued to drop worldwide; grasslands encroached upon the great forests; and new lakes were formed as old ones disappeared forever. All the while, molecular strings were rapidly evolving.

Manual dexterity in primates improved with the opposable thumb, involving the freedom to move the thumb across the palm of the hand in a swinging action, gradually becoming an evolutionary characteristic among primates. This characteristic only became fully developed in *Homo sapiens*, which permits us to form our perfect precision grip of index finger tip to the tip of the thumb.

> For example, "Later, as the larger primates became more active during the day, the nerve network at the back of their eyes became even more sophisticated, further refining their discrimination of light and dark to the perception of color." (Origins, Leakey and Lewin, 1977)

With more developed senses, some animals had a great advantage. This was not only because they were better equipped than competitors, but also because their brain was receiving a more detailed set of input about the world and they were developing the ability to process this additional information. As the brain evolved, the neurons were developing longer and more sophisticated pathways.

- - -

Neuron Story: "We neurons are busier than ever. We process more and more information, and we've devised a "three dimensional" interpretation of the world."

"And there's this new thing called "color", which allows us to make even better pictures in our heads by distinguishing among the various frequencies of light"

"It's amazing how we keep finding ways to use these new streams of stimuli."

- - -

After the continent of North America split off from Pangaea, the primates that went with it, some New World monkeys, became stranded and eventually became extinct some fifty-five million years ago. The remains of these North American monkeys have been uncovered at various excavation sites in Montana.

In South America, which separated from Pangaea much later than North America, a mere two million years ago, many New World monkeys still prosper.

The surviving primates in South America, however, did not advance significantly. As a result, these 'New World' monkeys have become significantly more primitive than their 'Old World' cousins, who remained on the masses of land that became the continents of Africa and Asia.

The explanation for the lack of progress in the South American monkeys is that the climate remained rather tropical, resulting in an abundant food supply as these primates advanced from an insect diet to fruits and vegetables. In contrast, the Old World primates had to compete for diminishing resources as grasslands continued to replace tropical forests.

As noted in People of the Lake, with the extinction of primates in the North American continent and the lack of evolutionary progress in the South American continent, there were no hominids in the Americas until humans entered a few ten thousand years ago.

It is no coincidence that this period of constant change in the environment and increased competition among the Old World monkeys corresponds to the period during which the most rapid evolution of primates occurred. These developments were influenced over a long stretch of time by the changing environment. This time period allowed the chemical composition, that of complex molecules, to change enough through purely mechanical actions, to be a factor in the outcome. Enough variation resulted to permit advantageous traits to emerge, which played a role in the success of survival for the best adapting primates, as well as, other groups of organisms.

For example, less than twelve million years ago, the ancestor to apes and hominids, "dryopithecine", could be characterized into three major categories. *Dryopithecus*, was the dryopithecine from which all modern apes have evolved, *Gigantopithecus*, from which the now extinct, large terrestrial apes of Asia evolved, and *Ramapithecus*, the first of the hominids.

> As noted in People of the Lake, *Ramapithecus* was the smallest, about three feet tall, with *Dryopithecus* next in size, and *Gigantopithecus*, which was larger than a gorilla until disappearing around a half a million years ago.

3.1 Upright

In the time period, from between eight and five million years ago, there is a gap in the fossil record.

> As noted in People of the Lake, one of the most important events during the fossil void was for *Ramapithecus* to learn how to walk upright. While no one knows how it occurred, its locomotion may not have resembled contemporary primates, since it is thought that its evolution may have been unique. However it occurred, by three million years ago, hominids walked around the Pliocene landscape in a manner quite similar to humans.

To *Ramapithecus*, this effect was to become the first significant departure from his ancestors. Evolution had provided a distinction that would forever affect the entire planet. The primary advantage of habitual bipedal locomotion, as opposed to occasional bipedalism found in apes, was to make the hands free for other uses, such as carrying, and throwing.

Of the future generations of *Ramapithecus*, (1) *Homo*, (our ancestral line), (2) *Australopithecus africanus*, and (3) *Australopithecus boisei*, were the only hominids that walked upright, habitually striding on two legs leaving the two front limbs completely free. (It should be noted that there may well have been a fourth remnant *Ramapithecus* that also coexisted for some time with these three lines. The only names we know it as, is Don Johanson's 'Lucy', or catalogue number AL-288.)

> As noted in People of the Lake, once the *australopithecines* died off around one million years ago, our lineage was the only hominid remaining to stride on two limbs.

According to the work of Owen Lovejoy, an anthropologist who specializes in biomechanics, it was the *australopithecines* that actually were more efficient walkers on two legs, and it was *Homo* who actually had a hard time walking upright because our ancestors had larger heads.

It was the mechanics that resulted from a wider pelvis that gave *Homo* the added difficulty in upright walking resulting in greater stresses and balance problems than that of its *australopithecine* cousin.

Although there are crucial advantages to bipedalism for the further development of hominids, (e.g., the higher 'vantage point' for vision and the ability to carry food and implements), that quadrupedalism would not have, bipedalism suffered the drawback that it was more energy expensive.

Whatever disadvantages there may have been to upright walking, for *Homo* or for any of the upright walking descendants of *Ramapithecus*, we must conclude that the natural benefits of upright walking outweighed the costs, or the process of natural selection would have seen to their demise. Even though *Homo* didn't have the preferred skeletal structure for upright walking, the other advantages of the larger head must have been much more advantageous, as *Homo* was the only surviving hominid leaving distant cousins to slip into eventual extinction.

As noted in Origins, five or six million years ago, when *Ramapithecus* underwent a rapid diversification, the evidence reveals that other creatures also underwent diversification at a rapid pace, supporting the theory that changes in the environment created a need to rapidly adapt in order to survive.

3.2 Lifestyle of Being Upright

With the grasslands expanding, the animals that could stand upright had the ability to spot the possibility of danger from a much greater distance. Simply standing on two legs, however, was quite different from walking on two legs. Walking efficiently on two legs required different feet, feet that would no longer be ideal for tree climbing. The animals that became well adapted to the grasslands, as the forests receded, are the ones that we will focus on.

However, among the more than twenty varieties of apes on the African continent, the forces of survival favored the unusual ape that could walk upright because bipedalism was far more energy efficient than quadrupedalism among apes.

For example, "Previously, people who studied walking in this context had compared human bipedalism with quadrupedalism in conventional quadrupeds, such as dogs and horses. Humans came out second in any measure of the efficiency of energy used for locomotion. But as Rodman and McHenry point out, humans evolved from apes, not from dogs. Not a novel observation, but one that has been overlooked in these kinds of calculations. Chimpanzees are not particularly good quadrupeds energetically, especially over long distances, because their style of locomotion is a compromise between walking on the ground and climbing in the trees." (Origins Reconsidered, Leakey and Lewin, 1993, pg. 90-91)

Sensitive by Nature

Hence, whenever food became scarce and dispersed, demanding more travel, the apes with bipedalism had a distinct advantage not only to get to the food, but to carry it back, as well.

Many of the animals in the grasslands improved their survival skills by forming groups. A few animals of the group could stand and look out for signs of danger, while others ate, drank, rested or played. Their group living increased survival rates and led to the development of social skills. The more social the animal, the greater the probability that members of the group would survive by helping one another.

3.3 Social Skills

There are a number of survival benefits in being a social animal. Although the protection offered by a group is one, the most significant benefit is group learning. The transfer of knowledge from one animal to the next, from each generation forward, represents an efficient building block approach to knowledge, and is a powerful method for improving survival. Animals can learn which plants to eat, avoid and which to use for healing. Some can learn better ways to hunt, where to find water, and how to adapt to the changing seasons.

Another significant aspect to intellectual development is the length of time that offspring rely upon adult members for support. Compared to other primate populations, hominids have a significantly longer childhood, in which they are dependent upon their parents, as compared to apes and/or monkeys.

Dependency ranges from a year for monkeys, upwards to three to four years for apes, and up to fourteen or so years for hominids, and *Homo sapiens*. It is during this period that learning occurs at the most accelerated pace. Although the mechanism for acquiring knowledge is primarily observed through example, the transfer of knowledge can also be accomplished through various forms of communication. These forms of communication are not only comprised of spoken or written words, but would also include any sounds of approval for positive or negative reinforcement, body language, motions of limbs and hands, as well as facial expressions that may indicate a source of possible danger.

3.4 Evidence of Life Style

Typically, people think that bones are the only remains that provide clues into the past. Richard Leakey, in his book Origins, points out that behavior is yet another way to study our ancestors.

While first hand observation of our ancestors is well out of the question, we can still study group populations, tools, available food, water sources, shelter, and social organizations of our closest evolutionary relatives. This, with an analysis that various social behaviors have within a population, can all assist in generating the probable details of our past.

3.5 Nakedness

While there is much variety in body hair among humans today, it can be readily agreed upon that we are naked, especially when compared to the other surviving primates.

> As noted in People of the Lake, the forces of evolution propelled Homo into nakedness. The combination of a mode of locomotion that consumes more energy, and the hot sun, may have favored any variety of methods for keeping cool, such as the shortening and sparseness of body hair, as well as the development of countless sweat glands.

3.6 Primate Intelligence

The degree of intelligence that a primate has, or that any animal has, is manifested in its thoughts, and the communication of these thoughts to others. For this reason, it is critical to support the research efforts involving Chimpanzees learning sign language. With this we can observe how effectively it may be passed onto offspring and how the language might evolve from one generation to the next.

Our ancestors were social animals. The relatively high degree of sociability may well have been the one real advantage that *Homo* had over the other hominids, *Australopithecus africanus* and *Australopithecus boisei*.

> As noted in Origins, the gibbon is probably the least social of all primates, and as a consequence, it is probably one of the least intelligent.

Hence, social animals are better equipped to take advantage of their intellect. The more knowledge that could be passed down through the generations, the more prepared the animal group would be to survive and adapt to their environment. This knowledge could then be integrated into the group securing its future survivability.

3.7 Sharing

In a social community, whether large or small, the importance of sharing is great. If it is a common behavior for one to help another, then the chance of survival increases for all in the group. Likewise, if there is seldom any reciprocation, then the likelihood of survival for the entire community decreases. Therefore, it is through selectivity of communities that the traits of 'sharing' can be promoted.

Sharing among herbivorous primates is extremely rare. Troops of primates tend to pick and eat their food on site. Mostly all examples of sharing involve the omnivorous (meat-eating) primates. Hunting animals, especially those that hunt together, tend to share their catch with other members of their community.

It is thought that, for primates, meat was more a symbol of power than a staple of food. The little meat that was acquired was likely to be handed out by the successful hunter in priority of those he favored. Most of the food supply, however, probably consisted of fruits, nuts, berries and seeds. Even the extremely selfish Chimpanzee can be found sharing a rare morsel of meat if another persistently begs for a long enough period of time.

The act of 'sharing' has a number of great implications, as it represents the beginning of an organized economy, and hence, impacts the social organization.

3.8 Ancestors of Homo sapiens

As mentioned earlier, the first of the hominids was *Ramapithecus*. This early hominid existed in Africa about nearly twelve million years ago. By around four million years ago there were a variety of up to three other hominids that shared the environment with our particular hominid ancestor, and they were all variations of *Ramapithecus*. For one reason or another, these close relatives of ours did not escape extinction, as our hominid ancestors did.

We can only theorize what may have contributed to this outcome. It may have been due, in part, to the extinct hominids' inability to share and/or cooperate as compared to our successful hominid ancestor, or perhaps it was because of their failure to rapidly adapt to increased competition in a changing environment.

Of these hominids, it was determined that our ancestor had the largest brain. Its brain was approximately two thirds the size of a *Homo sapiens*. Admittedly, brain size alone is not a measure of intelligence. From among the late *Ramapithecus*, Australopithecus africanus, Australopithecus boisei and early *Homo habilis*, early *Homo habilis* had the largest skull of all the hominids.

With the advent of *Homo habilis*, modern hominids were present about three million years ago. Within two million years, following the evolutionary stage of *Homo habilis*, many hominids became extinct. An evolutionary stage following *Homo habilis*, *Homo erectus* and *Neanderthals* emerged first from Africa, spreading out well beyond the continent of Africa. They moved up into Asia and Europe, leaving their trail of unwritten history throughout the landscape of the continents they inhabited.

When *Homo sapiens* emerged from Africa, it traveled the same path, eventually replacing the other species of hominids.

Unlike *Ramapithecus*, *Homo erectus* and *Neanderthalis*, would have looked and moved similarly to humans today. They may also have used fire for warmth and cooking, since fire was found to be in use as far back as a half a million years ago. As advanced as *Homo erectus* was, it still wasn't the first modern hominid to use stone tools.

For example, from Leakey's research we learned that the tools from the Hadar site in Ethiopia indicate that hominids had been using choppers and cutting flakes as far back as three million years ago. Tools at the 'KBS site' at Lake Turkana indicate that hominids had been doing the same at two million years ago.

Mary Leakey had noted gradual improvements in stone tool technology at Olduvai, but it wasn't until the advent of the Acheulian teardrop-shaped hand ax about one and a half million years ago that stone technology advanced to a new level. Hominids were developing the intellectual ability to conceptualize new tools.

Although the use of fire was relatively recent, at only a half a million years ago, it was just about one hundred thousand years ago that stone technology began to accelerate with new techniques for making tools. New tools began to emerge with still a greater acceleration occurring about forty thousand years ago. This would have been during the last fifty thousand year reign, leading up to '*Homo sapiens sapien*', with the rapid acceleration only occurring with '*Homo sapiens sapien*'.

For example, "Applying a rough time scale, we can say that the step from erectus to sapiens occurred around half a million years ago, and the refinement to sapiens sapiens perhaps fifty thousand years ago. These transitions must have occurred not just once, through some kind of omniscient predestination, but many times and in many places, as the built-in evolutionary momentum propelled erectus towards sapiens in a biologically unstoppable way. Certainly, isolated populations of Homo erectus must have been left behind in the process of evolutionary advancement. And occasionally, too, some sapien populations would seem to have veered along ill-fated evolutionary routes from which they could not retreat; the stocky ice-adapted Neanderthalers (more properly called Homo sapiens neanderthalensis) of Western Europe are an example."

(Origins, Leakey and Lewin, 1977)

There are two competing theories pertaining to the evolutionary path of *Homo sapiens*. One states that *Homo erectus*, who was the only hominid to venture outside the African continent through the Middle East into Asia and Europe, evolved toward *Homo sapiens* in a number of different geographic locations and in various ways. As that theory goes, some groups were successful, such as those groups that evolved into *Homo sapiens sapien*, while other groups were less successful, and faced extinction like *Homo sapiens neanderthalensis*.

The other theory was originally referred to as the Noah's ark hypothesis, but recently referred to as, the Garden of Eden hypothesis. It states that *Homo sapiens sapiens* evolved from a single group, existing at the same time as the other groups of *Homo erectus* and their descendents, just as many groups of Old World monkeys existed at the same time. In this theory, *Homo sapiens sapiens* originated from only one particular female, and spread to dominate all *Homo* territories within a period of approximately 100,000 years.

For example, in support of this theory, molecular biologists made one of the most interesting scientific discoveries during the late twentieth century involving mitochondrian DNA, which is found in the part of the cell, called the mitochondria. Unlike all other human DNA found in the nucleus of cells, mitochondrian DNA is inherited exclusively from the female, which means that every child, male or female, can only receive the mitochondrian DNA present in their mother, and their mother's mother, and so on.

Hence, when mitochondrian DNA was analyzed in a population of six thousand Europeans early in the year 2000, it was discovered that all of the individuals among the population originated from only seven different sets of female mitochondrian DNA. Using molecular dating, these seven women lived approximately 46,000 years ago. Additionally, scientists calculate that all humans originate from one particular female that lived in Africa some 150,000 years ago.

"The notion of using molecular evidence to probe issues of genetic relatedness is basically straightforward. Once a common ancestor has diverged into two daughter species, the genetic material in them will gradually accumulate mistakes, or mutations, and the species will become increasingly different from each other. The more distant in time the evolutionary divergence, the greater will be the accumulated genetic difference. And if the mutations accumulate regularly through time, there is what biochemists call a molecular clock: the changes through time caused by the accumulation of mutations." (Origins Reconsidered, Leakey and Lewin, 1993, pg. 75)

A number of factors, however, may contribute to errors in the calculation. They may have "miscalculated the rate of the mitochondrial clock; older mitochondria may have been lost by chance, promoted perhaps by occasional crashes in local population size; natural selection may have favored some recent mitochondrial variant, thus eliminating the

James V. Luisi

older lineages." (Origins Reconsidered, Leakey and Lewin, 1993, pg. 221-222)

Whether *Homo erectus* evolved into *Homo sapiens* at about the same time period in multiple locations, or it was a single population of *Homo sapiens* evolving from Africa tracing the steps of *Homo* erectus, eventually replacing it, the final answer will eventually be determined by fossil evidence.

3.9 Technology Outpaces Evolution

When one considers how recently *Homo sapiens sapiens* left their primitive world and primitive ways behind, for a world that experiences rapidly advancing technology, it is interesting how little we've continued to evolve physically, in the last 500,000 years, and brain wise, in the last 50,000 years.

Prehistoric times for *Homo sapiens sapiens* was only a few thousand years ago. As of only a few hundred years ago, many *Homo sapiens sapiens* in the Amazon and African continent continued to live in the same pre-historic lifestyle. Hence, the ability of *Homo sapiens sapien* to continually adapt is proving to be immense. As a species, we are racing ahead into a technological world at an incredible rate, with our outdated hunter-gatherer brains.

> For example, "The forces of evolution that, through the late Pliocene and the Pleistocene epochs, molded the human mind and shaped our psychology and our social responsiveness are those embedded in the hunting-and-gathering way of life. So much so, that today we look out on a technologically sophisticated and socially divided world with the brains of hunter-gatherers in our heads."
> (People of the Lake, Leakey and Lewin, p90)

The primitive tribes that still exist scattered throughout the world are as genetically evolved as the rest of us. They were simply left behind in their lifestyle of hunting and gathering. They may not have had automatic dishwashers, automobiles or surround sound projection television systems with DVD players and hundreds of cable channels, nor do their children have PC's, but somehow they can survive off the land without a stitch of modern technology, as our ancestors did.

Summary & Questions

A number of physical characteristics have influenced the intellectual advancement of hominids. It is important to note which intellectual capabilities might have improved as a result of the physical changes of the body, and how the physical body of other organisms might affect their intellectual development.

Regarding the evolution of hominids, briefly explain:
1. Which physical characteristics contributed the most to the intellectual development of primates, and why?
2. What contributed to the differences between Old and New World monkeys?
3. What was the most significant evolutionary advancement that occurred during the fossil void?
4. What were the advantages of bipedalism?
5. What basic social skills would have contributed to intellectual advancement, and why?
6. What intellectual advancement corresponds with the first major improvement in tools?
7. How does mitochondrian DNA differ from other DNA?
8. What is the process by which mitochondrian DNA can show ancestry, and what factors may affect its accuracy?
9. Early humans did not have half the life expectancy as we do today, but if we were the same resources as our ancestors of fifty thousand years ago, what would be our approximate life expectancy, and why?

4 Homo sapiens

4.1 Introduction

When Louis and Mary Leakey discovered the hidden remains of our ancestors, they not only uncovered their skulls and other skeletal parts, but they also uncovered their lifestyle by looking at their tools, living areas, population size and environment.

Our early ancestors mainly lived in small groups. As an increasing number of them began living in larger communities, the social pressures helped to propel *Homo sapiens* with skills that were crucial to further intellectual developments. The pressure to standardize communication and education helped to establish a more advanced social fabric, creating behaviors, which were beneficial to these new larger communities.

4.2 Effects of Agriculture

The hunter/gatherer frequently moved camp and traveled with few belongings. It was knowledge that was passed down through the generations on how to coexist with nature. Until as recently as four hundred years ago, many American Indian, African and South American tribes lived as hunter/gatherers.

Around ten thousand years ago, *Homo sapiens* invented basic agriculture in several locations. By about eight thousand years ago, agriculture had spread to half of the population. Until that point, limited trade in tools had represented the only economy based on material goods.

At about three thousand years ago, stable agricultural communities were forming. Larger scale economies came into existence, based on the food trade. The possession of harvested crop became recognized as a form of wealth. Food stores not only provided a convenience, but also offered survival advantages to a community when food supplies became scarce. This was the first time that accumulations of wealth were developed, and this beckoned envy on behalf of other less fortunate groups of *Homo sapiens*, which created conflict.

It was the agricultural revolution that marked the ability to support larger communities and populations, and with it came the capacity to wage major campaigns of war. Simultaneously, specialized roles were developing farmers, to tend the land; spiritualists, to talk with god; leaders, for organizing groups; and warriors, to defend the community. The food economy grew, medicine men rendered services, and craftsmen were required for the rapidly growing range of products needed by the expanding community.

> For example, for the first time in the history of the planet, significant concentrations of individuals became possible in the form of communities and cities. With the

advent of agriculture, world population rose from ten million to over four billion. Only a few survive today as gatherers and hunters, which was the mechanism for survival for over three million years shaping our social, psychological and intellectual evolution.

In the original thirteen colonies of North America, the total population was barely 2.5 million inhabitants. Just two hundred years later, there were 215 million. The main contributing factor to this growth was the increased efficiency of the American farmer, which was revolutionized by the gasoline-powered tractor, thereby facilitating a new level of mass production on the farm. With one twenty-fifth of the manpower, an acre could be plowed and planted. Agricultural advancements increased the productivity of food production to unprecedented levels in the history of *Homo sapiens*.

The factors that led to the growth of North America were not only an almost unlimited availability of food, but also the abundance of natural resources, which were critical to the upcoming industrial revolution. Whether it was iron, copper, coal, oil or uranium, *Homo sapiens* simply had to turn to what was above or below the land. The pace of progress accelerated through the continent at a rate far greater than any animal had ever experienced before.

4.3 Human Characteristics

The *Homo sapiens* brain continued to develop due to the pressures of the environment. Survival of the fittest 'individual' was followed by survival of the fittest 'community'. Improved standards of living developed with the communities that could become more competitive, ensuring future generations. These were the forces acting upon growing populations of intelligent beings.

4.4 Spoken Language

According to Richard Leakey, 'spoken language' was probably the most recent step in the evolution of *Homo sapiens*. The ability to communicate more complex thoughts, with greater efficiency increased the rate of information transfer, including that between adults and children, thereby accelerating the learning process. It is reasonable to assume that spoken language would have preceded written language by thousands of years. The oldest evidence of written language dates back to Sumerians around five thousand years ago.

While spoken language is complex, its fundamental principle is to string 'symbols of sounds' together, in order to convey a concept, or thought. But did *Homo sapiens* have a monopoly on this ability?

As noted in People of the Lake, there are a variety of psychological research efforts on apes and chimpanzees,

> such as those being conducted by Fouts, Premack, and Rumbaugh. Some have demonstrated that chimpanzees can invent new names for things and show rudimentary signs of grammar.
>
> "Lucy calls a watermelon a drink fruit; Washoe refers to ducks as water birds, and she invented the name rock berry for a brazil nut when she first encountered one; Lana calls a cucumber a banana which is green, and she refers to Fanta orange drink as Coke which is orange. (Fortunately, the Coca-Cola Company also make the Fanta drink, thus avoiding and embarrassing copyright problems for Lana!)"
>
> "There is now no doubt that chimps have the basic mental machinery for organizing a simple language. And so, it turns out, do gorillas." ... "After four years tuition in Ameslan, Koko is as accomplished as any chimpanzee, and is displaying equal facility in concept formation and sentence construction."
>
> (<u>People of the Lake</u>, Leakey and Lewin, pp. 174-175)

As humans become smarter in detecting language in monkeys, we learn that these primates are able to modify their use of language to meet their needs.

> As noted in <u>Origins Reconsidered</u>, a study lasting more than ten years on vervet monkeys in Amboseli National Park in Kenya, by University of Pennsylvania researchers, showed that these monkeys were capable of modifying their use of alarm calls to achieve the particular result that was desired.
>
> For instance, when a group of mature males saw an eagle swooping to attack another member feeding on the ground, they gave a leopard warning causing him to run for the trees. Under the particular circumstances, of they had given the eagle warning, their friend would have looked up before heading for the bushes, giving the eagle the extra moment it needed to capture the intended victim.
>
> Although the vocal repertoires of animals are quite limited when compared to humans, the conclusion of the study was that animals had an ability to communicate a larger variety of messages with a greater specificity than was previously believed.

In the Language Research Center of Georgia State University, in Atlanta, which is currently considered the best in the world, it has been shown that some of the cognitive functions on which human language are built are also present in non-humans.

As noted in <u>Origins Reconsidered</u>, a male pygmy chimpanzee named Kanzi, born at the Language Research Center of Georgia State University, in Atlanta in 1980, watched as researchers attempted to teach Kanzi's adopted mother, Matata, sign language. Although they were dismayed at the lack of Matata's progress, they were surprised to see that Kanzi seemed to understand. Upon testing Kanzi's vocabulary they confirmed that he had learned much of the vocabulary through the lexigrams and orally. The key difference between Matata and Kanzi, of course, was their age. Kanzi was able to learn language during his early developmental stage.

As for one of the benefits of language, Leakey asserts that language and tool technology may somehow be related. It is possible that the process of conceptualizing a thing, and coining it in language, provides a necessary step in making something new, such as a tool.

For example, "And the geographical variation in technical design of stone-tool cultures, from about forty thousand years onward, mirrors uncannily the geographical patchwork of different languages with which we are familiar today."

(<u>People of the Lake</u>, Leakey and Lewin, p186-7)

4.5 Concepts

The ability to communicate advanced ideas efficiently is not the only benefit resulting from the development of spoken language. An equally significant benefit is the capacity to represent, retain and manipulate concepts through association by the use of symbols, words or phrases. This is crucial when dealing with concepts that do not have a physical image.

The use of symbolic representations also paved the way for a mental technique called 'chunking'. While dealt with in greater detail in later chapters, "chunking" is the ability to group concepts into larger, higher level concepts, which in turn can be grouped again into still larger chunks.

At first, 'chunking' may not seem all that important, although it is what permits us to create new terms allowing for the flow of communication. Chunks frequently evolve into specialized languages, which are created for use in a field of specialization. Without such an ability to enhance both communication and concept manipulation, the advancements made by *Homo sapiens* would have been fewer and farther apart.

4.6 Behavior

By studying the primitive tribes found in the recesses of Africa, Asia and South America, we can analyze customs and behaviors, which may be linked to *Homo sapiens'* ancestral roots. The primary difference between primitive tribes and modern civilization relates to the availability of time. Without technological advancements, the majority of time would be spent fulfilling basic survival needs, such as searching for food and water or shelter, with the remainder of the time spent focusing on building the spiritual sense, often directed toward the forces of nature.

The study of other primates may also indicate the possible customs and behaviors among the early hominids. One aspect of primate behavior, in the absence of human interference, is that they spend the majority of their time focused on survival, looking for food, water and shelter, differing only in their techniques, where their particular set of physical and intellectual strengths set their limitations.

Noting the similarities and differences among various primate groups, under various environmental conditions, patterns emerge of how they have adapted.

> For example, in comparing their dentition there is some insight into their diet, such as meat ripping teeth versus those used for crushing seeds and leaves.

However, distinctions among tribes that earn a living, primarily by gathering, as opposed to those that primarily hunt, illustrate some important things about humans as social animals. Some insight can be provided by the behavior of modern primates.

> As noted in People of the Lake, members of a chimpanzee troupe will flock to an individual with meat, begging for a share. While baboons would typically be ill tempered, chimpanzees beg using outstretched hands, eye contact, whimpering and touching to provoke sharing.
>
> Although chimpanzees never share other foods, the sharing of meat as if it was a prized possession is a part of their social behavior.

4.7 Complex Behavior

Homo sapiens behavior involves a number of social complexities, stemming from a greater degree of interaction and often an enhanced concern about the perceptions of others.

Generally speaking, *Homo sapiens* that are perceived as behaving in an unselfish manner are deemed with higher regard than those that behave selfishly. While most *Homo sapiens* have a natural tendency to behave selfishly from birth, they learn quickly that it is undesirable to have this quality. Therefore, many of them learn to consider how others will interpret their behavior, and will adjust in order to make a more positive impression.

While this may be considered disingenuine on the part of *Homo sapiens*, it is actually part of something more significant. *Homo sapiens* have the ability to overcome their emotions, and instead of simply reacting to their primitive feelings, they can choose to redirect their behavior in a more productive manner.

The ability to guide one's own behavior, is what makes some individuals socially more successful than others who choose not to manage their actions, or who simply haven't yet learned how.

Taken to its extreme, perception can be deemed to be more important than reality. Individuals have been known to become so skilled at wielding perception, that the result can be substantially disparate from reality, sometimes allowing individuals to get away with murder.

Neuron Story: "The prosecutor says she killed him, the defense says she didn't!"
"What does the victim say?"

4.8 Gatherer/Hunter

Although the term, 'hunter / gatherer', used to describe people with a particular lifestyle, is a familiar one, it suffers from the fact that it implies that the activity of hunting is the primary activity. While hunting may represent the more challenging and interesting aspect, it plays a minor role as a means of providing food for the tribe. As a result, for the sake of accuracy, the term 'gatherer/hunter' will be used herein.

The 'gatherer/hunter' society that *Homo sapiens* formed was a major departure from their ancestors. For the first time, members of the community began to organize themselves by the type of labor they performed. The practice of sharing became a necessity among community members. It began a trend that continues today, where the community depends upon specialization, cooperation and sharing as a way of life.

Although a burst in social and technological complexity had occurred with the advent of agriculture, *Homo sapiens* had spent a relatively small fraction of time adapting to an agricultural lifestyle, merely 10,000 years, compared to the half a million years *Homo sapiens* spent as a gatherer/hunter. From an evolutionary standpoint, we are the result of a gatherer/hunter existence, with the social fabric that it fosters.

There were a number of different sized groups within the gatherer/hunter community. The smallest group was the family. Families formed medium sized tribes representing about twenty-five individuals. The largest group formed a dialectical tribe, amounting to about five hundred members that spoke the same dialect. The success of the tribe determined the success of the individuals. Hence, the need to weed out individual selfishness for the benefit of the group began millions of years ago.

James V. Luisi

The young men of these small gatherer/hunter tribes would travel a great deal to find a mate that belonged to a different tribe. Incest would have been taboo, especially if a small population was going to stand the test of time. With the use of agriculture, more tribes could populate a smaller area, eliminating the long journey to locate a mate. It is possible, however, that a trace of this urge to travel in search of a mate still lingers today, as many people still find others from distant locations especially appealing and interesting to them, whereas individuals, who are similar to their family members, are not.

4.9 Reproductive Behavior

"...There is no concept of fatherhood in chimp society as the males are fully promiscuous. ...Males often queue to take their turn, and the female usually objects only if the would-be mate is a son or a brother. (Freud would have been intrigued to see such a powerful incest "taboo" in such a lowly creature!)"
(<u>People of the Lake</u>, Leakey and Lewin, 200-202)

- - -

Neuron Story: *"Can you imagine that... there's an easy way to reproduce more of me?"*
"What I can't imagine, is that nature made it pleasurable."

- - -

A significant amount of animal behavior is associated with the production of offspring. 'Reproductive behavior' has developed with the evolution of more advanced species and has led to a number of distinct behaviors. As organisms became more complex, the length of time for offspring to approach the survivability of their parents also increased. As the offspring's length of dependency increased, the need to carefully choose a mate increased.

Once mating partners have been chosen, the role of nurturing the young must be addressed in order to complete the mating process successfully. However, organisms that are less advanced, may only need the attention of one parent.

As noted in <u>People of the Lake</u>, females are usually responsible for the caring of their young. The major exceptions involve fish. Since females must first lay their eggs before the male can fertilize them, females are free to desert the family, leaving the male to care for the young. If the male deserts as well, the species would not likely survive.

Once animals moved to land, the tables were turned, because males perform their role before the eggs are laid.

It takes human offspring the longest amount of time to approach the survival capabilities of their parents. Although humans are the most intellectually advanced, compared to other animals they are more physically susceptible to the environment. Until human offspring have reached a significant level of maturity, they require continued parental care in order to survive.

As noted in <u>People of the Lake</u>, the development of heightened sexuality in humans favored a long-term emotional commitment to rear children.

In conclusion, human sexuality actually serves as a psychological bond, sometimes quite powerful, to human relationships. This may occur in various ways and under various circumstances, whereby males interact with females in a sexual manner.

- - -

Neuron Story: *"Isn't flirting an attempt to establish a psychological bond?"*
"Yes, but I suggest that you don't try it with me."

- - -

Summary & Questions

When forensic experts enter a crime scene, they not only look at the body and its condition, but they inspect everything in the immediate vicinity to determine the events that may have transpired. In a similar fashion, a paleoanthropologist will piece together the lives of our ancestors by analyzing the assorted objects found with their remains.

Regarding research into our ancestors, briefly explain:
1. What were the major lifestyle changes of our ancestors?
2. What would be the most likely impact of those changes?
3. What advantages did larger communities provide individuals?
4. What advantages did larger communities provide the species?
5. How did methods for communicating participate in knowledge accumulation?
6. What is communication genetically based versus learned?

7. Why do you think the development of language was linked to significant advancements in tools?
8. What role does 'chunking' play in language and thinking? Provide an example of each.

5 Physical Brain

The brain has numerous physical parts that can be visually identified. In relatively advanced animals, the brain has cerebral hemispheres, diencephalons, brainstem and cerebellum. However, it is the cerebral cortex, the outer most part of the brain, which has had the most dramatic advancement throughout evolution.

- - -

Neuron Story: *"Where does sex occur in the brain?"*
"For you, it's on your brain."

- - -

As noted in Origins, as the cerebral cortex expanded to incorporate additional capabilities, it was forced to gather into folds in order to increase its area. As a result, the area of a chimpanzee's cortex is buried only twenty-five percent in folds, whereas the human cortex is buried up to sixty-five percent in folds.

With visually equal left and right halves, each side is highly specialized to support different functions. The left hand half is the 'logical' half, primarily supporting memory, analysis, and speech, whereas the right hand half is the 'artistic' half, primarily supporting visualization, and spatial abilities.

The development of specialized functions is probably the result of evolutionary pressure, which has also been identified in Old World monkeys. Although this trait is not unique among humans, the extent to which specialization has developed is.

The cortex is divided into four areas, called lobes. Although little is known about the frontal lobes, they participate in determining an individual's attention span and motivations. Additionally, the frontal lobe of the left hemisphere in humans, as compared to other primates, contains a well-developed Broca's area, which controls the muscle movements necessary to generate speech. This area is attached to an area in the temporal lobe, called Wernicke's area, which acts as the database for visual, auditory and verbal memory. As the appropriate symbols are retrieved from Wernicke's area, Broca's area structures them into speech. Broca's area appears visibly on skulls more than two millions years old, as found on the 1470 skull by the American biologist, Ralph Holloway.

The parietal cortex, a major part of the super association area, evaluates the majority of sensory input, while the occipital lobe, which is predominately buried below the surface, is responsible for processing stimuli from the optic nerves.

Although the size of the brain is a factor, structure is perhaps the most significant aspect influencing intelligence. Dr. Holloway has demonstrated that skulls of Homo and Australopithecus approaching three million years old housed cerebral structures that more closely resembled humans than apes. Hence, the divergence that led to the development of the human brain had begun at least three million years ago, enlarging the temporal and frontal lobes.

In Leakey's and Lewin's People of the Lake, Ralph Holloway's work is referenced again, revealing that for at least three million years the brains of our *Homo* ancestors and their *australopithecine* cousins were distinctly different, physically, than the brains of apes. In Holloway's research, all of the hominid brains that he studied from South and East Africa had the basic human pattern, and none were ape-like. When comparing *Homo*'s brain to *Australopithecus*, by two million years ago *Homo*'s frontal lobes were broader and the temporal lobes were better developed than our *australopithecine* cousins. By two million years ago, *Homo*'s physical brain was already significantly more refined than *Australopithecus*. The brain was among the last organs to assume a human shape.

Homo and *Australopithecus* looked quite similar well before their brain architectures evolved visibly distinct characteristics. It is likely that the interior of the *Homo* and *Australopithecus* brains were traveling down different evolutionary paths well before there were any visible external differences. Although the external architecture of the brain was nearly identical between *Homo* and *Australopithecus* until two million years ago, as early as two and a half million years ago the *Homo* brain was already thirty to forty percent larger than *Australopithecus*.

As noted in People of the Lake, although Australopithecus had not shown any appreciable increase in brain size up to their extinction one million years ago, Homo's brain increased substantially in size.

Homo erectus was approximately 1,000 cubic centimeters in volume one and a half million years ago and 1,200 cubic centimeters a half a million years ago, whereas the brain size in Homo sapiens reached 1,400 cubic centimeters fifty thousand years ago.

Within the last fifty thousand years there has been little, if any, changes in the body and brain of *Homo sapiens*. The present day brain is the result of *Homo sapiens* acquiring more knowledge, while becoming more specialized in each individual's realm of knowledge.

The *Homo sapiens* brain grows about three times in size from its initial volume at birth. *Homo sapiens* had the highest brain mass to body weight ratio amongst all hominids, measuring about 1400 cubic centimeters. However, internal reorganization of the brain was the largest contributing factor toward the development of advanced intellectual capabilities. Although they are for the most part undetectable in the fossil record, there are rudimentary clues to the organization of the brain in the external patterns and contours left as impressions on the inside of the skull.

5.1 Reasons for a Brain

The purpose of the brain is to process information. Signals are routed into the brain with information about the organism's internal environment, as well as its surroundings. The information can be simple, coming from heat or pressure sensing nerve cells of the skin, or quite complex, coming from the special senses, such as the eyes or ears, while some organisms have adapted to process infrared signatures as well.

For example, the eyes provide streams of stimuli involving distances, sizes, shapes, locations, colors, and movements. The ears provide streams of stimuli regarding distance, location, pitch, and loudness, including internal factors, such as balance and equilibrium, while baroreceptors of the carotid sinus provide streams of information about the body's internal pressure.

One of the reasons that information from forward facing eyes and opposing ears is so complex is that both provide a stereo signal. Two eyes, like two ears, provide distinct signals, which when put together properly, allows the organism to perceive its surroundings in a three dimensional way. Hence, the more detailed the information entering the brain, the better positioned the brain is to construct an accurate and useful view of its world.

As noted in People of the Lake, the complexity of an animal's brain is related to the complexity of its life. When primitive mammals had to adapt to a nocturnal existence their vision adapted to the dim lighting conditions of night. With these small amounts of stimuli their brains eventually adapted to integrate the various sensory inputs.

This integration, however, markedly improved the animal's internal representation of its environment. For the first time, the brain developed the ability to associate sounds with visual images. Then, when a small number of mammals shifted their habits away from their nocturnal ways, they once again evolved daytime vision, some with ability to perceive color.

The degree of awareness that an organism will experience is related to the degree of integration that its brain can provide. Sensory inputs can be interpreted individually by the brain, or they can be reconciled with one another in order to create a more in-depth view of the environment. While improved sensory inputs allow an organism to more accurately construct an internal view of its environment, the process of integration is actually the key to heightened awareness, thereby providing an enhanced understanding of its environment.

Summary & Questions

Although the fossil record cannot reveal what advancements occurred inside the circuitry of the brain, it has left a record of how its external surface evolved over time. These bone impressions reveal a good degree of information regarding the development of verbal communication.

Regarding the development of the physical brain, briefly explain:
1. Which organ was the last to assume a human shape?
2. How might improvements in sensory data benefit the development of the brain?
3. What environmental pressures helped to improve the integration of sensory stimuli?
4. What advantages would the ability to integrate stimuli provide?
5. What new information about the environment would be possible?
6. What might the brain be able to conceptualize with this new knowledge about the environment?

Sensitive by Nature

6 Introduction to Computers

6.1 Natural Tools

Many animals, including *Homo sapiens*, use naturally occurring objects as tools to assist them with various activities. Sticks, stones, branches, bones, leaves, teeth, dried plant and animal skins are among the objects that have been used by animals as tools.

What distinguishes a tool from just another object in nature, is that a tool is consciously applied to achieve a function other than its natural purpose. Therefore, the pincer jaws and antennae used by some insects to catch food do not qualify as tools, because they are part of their physical bodies and have no other natural purpose.

6.2 Manufactured Tools

The making of tools is a conscious activity of higher intelligence animals, such as the use of slender branches with the leaves stripped off used by some primates as a dip stick to extract termites from their nests.

An animal must have sufficient intellect to be able to envision the end product before it can actually construct the tool. Based upon the conceptual model, the manufacturing process begins with identifying and gathering raw materials, which are then manipulated in order to transform them into the final product.

- - -

Neuron Story: *"Humans invented the plow, which was initially deployed as a small, man-powered tool."*
"The next season they had a powered model, which was usually accompanied by an ox."

- - -

As tools began to improve the efficiency of simple activities, new and more complex tasks could be accomplished. Human tools became more sophisticated, assisting manual labor and often replacing tasks done by hand. As tools improved, productivity increased. When process improvements led to mass production, productivity increased to such an extent that the period became known as the industrial revolution, leading to a greater quantity of more affordable products.

Soon, the power of machinery turned to an intellectual function, and it wasn't long before great inventors like Charles Babbage, and later, John Von Neuman, transformed machines that processed materials, into machines that processed information. Babbage invented the first computer,

James V. Luisi

which employed mechanically moving parts as a means to process data. It was quickly demonstrated that machines could process data at a higher rate, without fatigue and with fewer errors than its human counterpart.

It was John Von Neuman, who invented the first electronic computer that had electronic memory. This represented the hard-wired forerunner of current day computers, which use software to direct the activities of the machine.

Software is a series of instructions that are represented electronically. These instructions are a method of communicating what mechanical actions the machine should perform. Before software was invented, physical wiring was used to communicate what mechanical actions to perform, in which sequence.

- - -

Neuron Story: *"Can I tell a computer to do anything?"*
"Only if it understands."

- - -

Summary & Questions

As intellectual capabilities in animals evolved, the ability to employ natural tools and develop manufactured tools advanced.

Regarding the development of tools, briefly explain:
1. What distinguishes a tool from any other object?
2. What intellectual capability must be present in order to manufacture a tool?
3. When were tools no longer limited to physical tasks?
4. How have intellectual tools evolved over time?
5. What is software?

7 Software Limits

Software has been limited in its capabilities more by incomplete knowledge of the task that is to be automated, than by any other single factor. In the computer industry this is referred to as an incomplete set of requirements, which is a common problem among large applications. In order to automate any intellectual process, a 'requirements analyst' defines the information that participates in the process, the things that the process does with the information, and the information that is sent out of the process.

For example, the information that enters a savings account system includes the deposits and withdrawals. Information is generated by the activities of the business such as tracking how the available cash is invested, and then information is sent out including customer statements, tax statements and regulatory reports. If the 'requirements analyst' fails to provide sufficient details about the information flow and how it is processed, the resulting system can cause the business, its customers', and the regulatory agencies a number of problems.

The next aspect that limits what computers can do, is the way in which a system is designed. For a design to be effective, it must take all of the things that the system is supposed to do into consideration, and find a way to do them. It is important for the design to be flexible enough to support changes, as it might take some time before it is considered complete. One way to ensure that a design addresses all of the known requirements, is to track each requirement as it is incorporated into the design, known as 'requirements' traceability'. A system design cannot be effective if this step is not properly performed, or is omitted completely.

For example, to illustrate the importance of flexibility in a design we will consider the following analogy. If one were attempting to add a penthouse apartment on top of an existing apartment building, there would be a number of things to consider. Would the electrical system handle the extra power? Would the plumbing system get enough water pressure above the top floor? Would there be an ability to provide elevator service to a penthouse? And would the roof, frame and foundation handle the additional weight?

The least of the problems is actually building the penthouse. The electricians could add the wiring; plumbers could install the pipes; a new elevator system could be placed on the outside of the building; then carpenters and masons could complete the new story. Although the building inspectors would probably condemn the building, nothing

James V. Luisi

would actually prevent the contractors from building the penthouse.

Regarding computer systems, the construction process is somewhat similar. Requirements are generated into a design blueprint, and individuals, called developers, implement the design blueprint by generating it into instructions of programming code, which is converted into machine instructions that can cause the machine to do some potentially horrendous things.

When deciding on a software product, one may encounter a degree of sales hype, which may often seem difficult to believe. There are products that claim that they can think like an expert because of the programming language that was used to create them. Marketers and experts insist that these products provide new capabilities that were never before possible. In actuality, every programming language is merely a different convention for instructing a machine on what to do. Regardless of the programming language used, something, called a 'compiler', will translate each program into a common set of machine instructions, which then directs the activities of that particular machine.

- - -

Neuron Story: *"Did you know that we can speak in different languages?"*
"Yes, but regardless of the language, it always seems to translate into the same things."

- - -

7.1 Formal Systems

A 'formal system' is nothing more than a set way of thinking about things, possibly to approach a problem, a system of thought, or a discipline of knowledge. Formal systems typically begin with a few simple assumptions and definitions, which are built upon using a sequence of logical steps, or arguments, either to construct more advanced formulas, or to make assertions involving more compound ideas.

Formal systems lend themselves well to automation. A hand held calculator can provide solutions in a flash for algebra; a personal computer can easily guide the user through the appropriate questions for a medical diagnostic system; and a small computer can readily steer the technician through the necessary steps for sophisticated military aircraft maintenance.

All software solutions have something in common; they imitate something. They imitate the way a programmer thinks about solving a problem. The capability of a software solution is not only dependent upon the steps that the programmer uses to approach a solution, but more importantly, it is restricted by the 'system of thought' that the programmer uses to solve problems.

For example, if a programmer is a particular type of mathematician, then the solution that he formulates will be constrained by the rules and formulas of his particular mathematical system.

An important aspect of formal systems, however, is that all of the solutions are generated specifically from within a particular formal system, which is an enclosed set of rules.

7.2 Context of Rules

Rules must be applied in some context. When we first read the instructions to a game, we apply them to the framework of the materials supplied. If we open a different game and swap the two sets of instructions, we would notice that the rules of the game were not applicable.

Hence, it is the context of a rule that makes it operable. Even simple mathematical rules can vary greatly depending upon the discipline, or context of mathematics.

For example, we all know the mathematical rule, 'ONE plus ONE equals TWO'. However, ONE plus ONE can equal ONE in another context. When one drop of water is added to another drop of water, the result is just one, larger drop of water.

Even within mathematical geometry, there are many different contexts (e.g., two dimensional geometry, three dimensional geometry, Hilbert space, momentum space, reciprocal space, phase space, Cartesian space, polar coordinate space). Each has its own set of rules, and unique method of interpreting the rules within each context.

- - -

Neuron Story: *"A physicist, a Windows 98 expert, and a obstetrician were driving together to an "Artificial Intelligence" convention in San Francisco when their car broke down. As they were already late for their convention, the physicist jumped out and tried pushing the car before determining that the coefficient of friction was too great for the car to proceed. The Windows 98 expert then decided to close all the windows and attempted to restart the vehicle without success. Then the obstetrician jumped out, slapped the car in the rear, and the engine gunned to life."*

"Let me guess. You were the Windows 98 expert?"

One of the biggest drawbacks of software systems today is that they are all examples of formal systems. The most sophisticated software includes formal systems that can learn and utilize new information effectively, such as IBM's Big Blue, which plays grand master level chess.

7.3 Processing Power

The use of supercomputers provides no more of an edge in providing a successful solution, than traveling in the fastest aircraft, while flying in the wrong direction.

When you look at the biological nervous system, it is one of the slowest transport mechanisms. Electricity travels at the speed of light allowing a computer signal to go completely around the Earth seven times in each second. At the rate that the biological nervous system transmits a signal, it would take over four seconds for a brontosaurus to realize that the end of its tail was bitten.

- - -

Neuron Story: *"A nerve ending is reporting pain! Pass the word, we have a problem!"*

"Could you be more specific? Which nerve ending is it?"

"It's the nerve endings on the tail!"

"Oh, the rest of the brain isn't going to like this. Let's instruct the muscles to move the head to allow the eyes to get a view of our tail!"

"More reports of pain from the nerve endings on the tail are piling in! The eyes are passing visual images of the tail for processing! Have you figured out what's happening yet?"

"We've identified the images from the eyes, it's a nasty looking T-Rex eating our tail!"

"Bad day, bad day! What should we do? Run? Scream? Ask him if he's had enough?"

"No, wait! Our mouth is currently stuffed with leaves! We were eating."

"Let's spit the leaves at the T-Rex!"

- - -

7.4 Informal Systems

For a system to be considered 'informal', it needs to have the ability to freely move among various systems of thought. It needs the ability to look in from the outside, so to speak, and to be capable of borrowing rules and ideas from other systems of thought.

The quality of inventiveness, is often the process of recognizing the rules of a system in a new way. It can be a simple substitution of something, such as making a part for a mechanical device out of something previously unrelated. It can also be the process of borrowing a set of rules from one system of thought and trying it out in another.

However, one cannot just borrow rules haphazardly, that is, with any expectation or likelihood of success. In order to be effective, one has to form a strong analogy with something from another system, which behaves in a useful manner.

> For example, when Albert Einstein developed a new mathematical formula, $E=MC^2$, he carried it into the discipline of applied physics resulting in a new technique for a more powerful physical reaction, the atomic bomb.
>
> Likewise, when a major U.S. corporation accidentally created glue that didn't adhere very well, someone in the company invented a new product known as, 'Yellow Post-Its', and more recently 'Post-It Notes'.

The process of identifying rules from another system of thought involves searching for useful analogies. The more characteristics that are found to be in common among the different systems of thought the tighter the analogy will be. Informal systems provide a mechanism for creating analogies, to identify rules from another system of thought that can be applied to form a new solution.

Formal systems represent a repository of rules from which informal systems can form analogies and borrow rules.

- - -

Neuron Story: *"I love jumping from one formal system into another and back again!"*
"Yes, and its particularly nice when you bring back something useful."

- - -

7.5 Analogies

The opportunity to form an analogy exists when one system of thought has one or more characteristics in common with another. These characteristics may be physical, conceptual, or psychological in nature (e.g., material content, structural form, intellectual content, symbology, behavior, life cycle, or functional role).

>For example, a turning windmill plays an analogous role to a water wheel turned by the flow of water, with both involving the harnessing of energy. The light emitted by metals that have been heated to a glow have the same frequencies as light originating from celestial stars, thereby revealing their chemical composition. Likewise, in Douglas Hofstader's book, 'Godel, Escher and Bach', the structural form of the book's storyline conceptually matches that of a classical musical composition, organizing the presentation of material.

The ability to recognize an analogy, with something from another system of thought, drives the discovery process. Staging the frontier for scientific and artistic breakthroughs alike. It is the 'imagination' in action.

- - -

Neuron Story: *"How do I think?"*
"That would require a good imagination!"
"What? Neurons analyzing neurons? I don't know if I like it."
"If we learn that, maybe we could think in ways we never have before!"
"Then we'd have to study thinking all over again!"
"I think it's an endless loop!"
"I think my head hurts!"
"Imagine that!"
"A head that hurts?"

- - -

In the next segment of our discussion we will introduce a guest speaker to describe the various things that a mechanically intelligent being should be able to do. These things are called requirements.

7.6 Notion of Requirements

Taking an idea and turning it into a reality involves a number of steps. Once an idea has matured to the point where it is ready to for development, the single most important step is to carefully define its essential characteristics, as well as what it is supposed to do. These things that define it are called 'requirements'.

Requirements are crucial for several reasons. First, they identify what the development process is supposed to build, guiding its design, implementation and testing. Therefore, requirements must be traced through each of the development stages.

For example, tracing requirements through the various design and implementation stages ensures that they address all of the requirements. They also need to be monitored though the various testing stages making sure that each requirement has been adequately satisfied. If any changes occur within the requirements, design or implementation process, traceability allows the change to have the appropriate effect on the pertinent areas. Requirements affect all steps of the entire development process equally.

Requirements also permit a team of individuals to work together in order to effectively develop large, sophisticated systems. Even if the various parts were supposed to be constructed by separate individuals, integration of those parts can only be realized through identifying requirements as being the first step in the development process.

For example, various engineers cannot not design and construct a software system without a common set of requirements identifying what the item to be designed and constructed is supposed to do.

In order to introduce the relatively comfortable style with which we will present requirements for our mechanically intelligent being, we will begin with an aspect that is relatively easy to relate to. Then we will delve into the more controversial areas of how this being should work, how it achieves the process of thought, and more specifically, how it will achieve intelligence.

We will now let our guest speaker introduce himself with an overview of what characteristics are necessary for developing the physical body of a robot. This will not be a discussion of the physical body of just any robot, instead it will specifically address man's vision of what a robot should be. We will begin with a glimpse of the physical description of the Quantum Series One mechanically intelligent being.

- - -

Neuron Story: *"Will we have to take our clothes off?"*
                "I hope not!"

- - -

Summary & Questions

The most powerful and flexible intellectual tools often involve the use of software. Whatever the intellectual process may be, when properly understood, it can always be represented in software. The software instructs a computer to perform the steps that comprise the intellectual process.

Regarding the development of software, briefly explain:
1. What is necessary in order to devise a tool to perform an intellectual process?
2. What parts are involved in any intellectual process?
3. Identify a simple requirement for an intellectual process for which a tool may be devised.
4. Identify a simple requirement for an intellectual process for which a tool cannot be devised, and identify why the tool cannot be devised.
5. Why is it necessary to trace requirements through the development process?
6. What is the development step immediately following the requirements analysis phase?
7. What is a formal system, and how does the notion of 'context' relate to it?
8. What is an informal system, and how does the notion of 'context' relate to it? Why are requirements crucial to defining an intellectual process, and what phases of the development process do they affect the most?

8 Requirements - Physical Body

Hello. I am a *Quantum Series One* (QSI) robot, which is currently under development at a Robotics Laboratory in the United States. I represent an advanced generation of robots that possess the ability to think. Using streams of external stimuli, I can create and analyze a representation of my environment inside my brain, which I can then react to in any manner that I choose.

The objective of my design is to achieve a conscious and interactive product, capable of assisting biological life forms in a variety of ways. I may either respond to specific assignments, or behave according to a general theme, which has been taught to me.

My present assignment is to help explain the high level requirements that have been used to design me. As you were entering the lecture hall, many of you had questions about the operation of my physical body and my general physique. I am somewhat flattered by your interest in attending.

- - -

Neuron Story: *"Should we walk about, and maybe do a few poses and turns?"*
"Let's be... flattered, yet modest."

- - -

Although the physical requirements of us robots depend upon our intended use, the specifications for the body provide for a reasonable balance between power requirements, durability, bodily strength, flexibility, dexterity, speed, agility, and the rate at which sensory stimuli can be processed. An additional requirement of the mechanical body, however, is for it to replicate the aspects of the biological body that influence the way intelligent beings learn and develop. Hence, my physical abilities, which include my ability to observe, touch and grasp objects, help me to develop basic depth perception and motor skills.

Since the world of humans has already been adapted to the human physique, it is also more practical to develop a humanoid body structure with similar capabilities in order for it to succeed in a human environment. Hence, the most important requirement is for the mechanical bodies to be able to fit and move in ways that are similar to humans.

My internal records show that the overwhelming majority of dwellings, transport vehicles, machinery and tools have been designed to support the typical set of physical specifications of the adult, right handed, human body.

James V. Luisi

8.1 Supporting Frame

The supporting frame, also known as the skeletal structure, is a major determinate of a body's size, weight, dimensions, strength and range of motion. Since the objective is for mechanical beings to be able to take advantage of the human world, the specifications of the humanoid body must be within the range of average adult humans. Although physical comfort is not a concern, the ability of this being to effectively utilize an environment that is ergonomically designed for humans will be determined by their ability to fit within the tolerances provided for humans.

- - -

Neuron Story: "So we can go on rides at amusement parks?"
"If a child requests that we accompany them."

- - -

Although some mechanical body components may be heavier than their biological equivalents, mechanical bodies have an advantage in that they do not need to be filled with fluid. Thereby in making the total weight and skeletal strength of a mechanical body comparable to that of a human, the requirements for muscular strength can be determined from the strength of the skeletal structure.

8.2 Musculature

Although muscles are used to push and pull, run and jump, breath and pump blood through the circulatory system, they accomplish these actions only by contracting and relaxing. Muscles, therefore, provide a wide range of motion simply by providing a mechanical pulling action, with no ability to push whatsoever.

- - -

Neuron Story: "Don't push!"
"Don't be silly... I pulled."

- - -

The ability of a biological body to apply a pushing force is achieved by the contraction of muscles and the use of the limbs and joints of the skeletal system as levers and pulleys. All actions that appear to involve an ability to push are actually accomplished by the mechanics of pulling two parts toward one another. As a result, muscles exist on opposing sides of all biological limbs in order to facilitate the reverse of every motion.

Generally, the speed and force that muscular contractions apply is determined by the leverage of the limbs and joints, the length and thickness of the muscle, and the strength of the electrical impulse that is sent to the muscle from the brain. A stronger electrical impulse causes more of the muscle tissue to contract. The amount of available muscle mass determines the maximum amount of force that the muscle can exert on the skeletal structure.

- - -

Neuron Story: *"Some muscles are not attached to the skeletal structure."*
"Are they loose?"

- - -

Muscles differ from area to area of the same animal, as well as, from species to species. These differences occur in many ways and provide a variety of capabilities.

My teachers have explained to me that they differ in their arrangement of myofilaments, which are elongated molecular threads that are situated side by side in bundles. These arrangements determine the direction in which muscle tissue contract.

Some muscles are under voluntary control, while others are operated by the autonomic nervous system. Depending upon their control mechanism, they differ in the stimuli required to activate them. In vertebrates, voluntary muscles require electrical impulses from the nervous system in order to initiate contraction, while many involuntary muscles are spontaneously active. The natural rhythm of contraction can be modified in some involuntary muscles by stimuli from the nervous system.

Muscles vary in power, speed and the distance over which they can operate. While thick filaments deliver greater levels of power, rapid rhythmic contractions are necessary to support the wings of insects and hummingbirds.

Muscles also differ in their metabolism. Their energy supply, adenosine triphosphate (ATP), may be produced by either aerobic or anaerobic respiration. In aerobic respiration, energy sources are oxidized to produce carbon dioxide and water, while anaerobic respiration does not require oxygen since it converts energy sources to lactic acid.

James V. Luisi

Depending upon the location of the muscle in the body, certain muscle characteristics are significantly more suitable than others. In the human body there are three types of muscle tissue, referred to as smooth, striated and cardiac muscles. The majority of muscle tissue is striated muscle tissue, also known as skeletal muscle tissue, which is usually attached to the skeletal structure.

My medical training indicates that while striated muscles in the arms and legs facilitate movement of the limbs, the tongue is attached at one end to the hyoid bone.

Smooth muscle tissue, on the other hand, lines the body cavities, blood vessels and the skin. Its movements are operated by the autonomic nervous system, which controls the involuntary contractions within the body. Cardiac muscle tissue is actually a specialized type of striated muscle, also controlled by the autonomic nervous system. There are five types of cardiac muscle that comprise the heart of mammals, which are collectively referred to as myocardium. Of the myocardium, purkinje fibers provide an ability that most closely resembles nerve tissue, transmitting an electrical impulse that triggers the contraction of ventricular muscles.

Mechanically intelligent beings only require striated muscle tissue. Striated muscles provide all voluntary movement, operating facial muscles, the tongue, the joints and limbs of the skeletal structure.

A number of 'muscle-like' materials have been developed that either coil up or contract in length when an electrical impulse is applied.

My library interfaces tell me that "Chemists at the Laboratory of Electrochemistry at the University of the Basque Country in San Sebastian, Spain, have developed an artificial muscle using a conductive plastic." (Pumping Plastic, by Gareth Brawyn)

According to the laboratory's director, Toribio F. Otero, the idea came from the simple bimetallic thermometer, which is designed to have two attached sheets of metal, each with different expansion coefficients. When one metal expands faster than the other the material bends, thereby allowing an indicator needle to be calibrated to indicate the temperature reading along a scale.

Artificial muscles use two electrodes that are manufactured from a conductive plastic, called polypyrrole, that sandwich a solid electrolyte. When an electrical signal is applied, one electrode contracts while the other actually expands. The way the material works is that a reversal in the current's direction causes the material to bend in the opposite direction, and similar to biological muscles, the strength of the electrical signal determines how much the material will flex. Additionally, the material demonstrates a significant level of strength in that it can move a mass a hundred times its own mass. (April 1998 issue of Wired Magazine)

Once muscles of the appropriate texture, power and speed have been identified for each body part of a mechanical being, the next step is to identify the appropriate control and communication mechanisms.

8.3 Nervous System

As the brain analyzes stimuli originating from various parts of the body, it generates direction to various physical components. Each signal must be communicated to the appropriate muscle.

Biological signals are transmitted directly from the brain through a communication network called the nervous system. The nervous system is the only rapid biological mechanism for transporting stimuli. In addition to delivering stimuli from sensory organs to the brain and supporting the thought process, the nervous system provides internal communication to various parts of the body and delivers the necessary electrical stimuli to cause muscles to contract.

In mechanically intelligent beings, signals are not transmitted directly from the brain to the muscles. Although the requirements for mechanical and biological nervous systems are similar, in order to provide the capability to readily switch physical components, robots require a flexible software interface between the brain and its various body parts. A software interface is used to communicate to each body part. Once the nervous system has successfully delivered the brain's instructions to the software interface of the body part, the role of the nervous system has just begun.

Once the particular body part receives its instructions from the nervous system, the careful manipulation of muscle contraction of the appropriate strength and speed, becomes the responsibility of said body part. During this process, the body part is in constant communication with the brain, sending its sensory stimuli to the brain and receiving new instructions to adjust those already received.

The functional requirements for the nervous system also include the need for physical flexibility.

> For instance, in order to address the issue of minimizing the use of metal wire, the medium for communicating stimuli may use thin, flexible, plastic tubes that contain a gel, which conducts electric signals as effectively as wire. The location of a mechanical nervous system can then be placed in many of the same locations as its biological counterpart, such as through the openings of a spinal cord that is designed for flexible spinal nerves.

Chemical signals are another mechanism that the biological body uses to communicate to its physical components. Chemicals are transported through the biological body by the circulatory system.

8.4 Circulatory System

The circulatory system transports chemicals to and from the various parts of the body. In doing so, it delivers nutrients and oxygen to various tissues, aids in the body's defense of foreign invaders, participates in waste removal, and provides another technique for communication within the body. Although it is slower than the stimuli transmitted through the nervous system, the circulatory system can broadcast messages to all parts of the body in the form of chemical hormones. Secreted by a variety of glands, hormones deliver chemical messages, such as those that prepare the body for sudden physical exertion, or sexual activity.

> My circuits report that adrenaline is a chemical compound known as the fight or flight hormone. It significantly increases the pulmonary and respiratory rate, and prepares the body to engage in physical combat or a rapid escape. Generally, hormones are useful for broadcasting a variety of psychological states within the body. Hormones are secreted into the circulatory system from the endocrine system.

An elaborate hydraulic system, the circulatory system contains a liquid medium that flows under pressure, and it is the primary mechanism used to regulate pressure within the organs and tissues beneath the skin. The circulatory system is also responsible for providing a heat transfer mechanism to the various areas of the body, thereby assisting in the regulation of body temperature.

Among the various functions it provides a biological body, the circulatory system in a mechanical being must also regulate the body temperature and pressure beneath the surface of the skin.

8.5 Respiratory System

The respiratory system is not only an air exchange mechanism that facilitates the collection of oxygen and elimination of waste gases, such as carbon dioxide, but it also provides the necessary ventilation to monitor the surrounding air temperature and moderate the internal body temperature using the surrounding air.

> My analysis shows that a number of mammals lack the necessary sweat glands to help them lower their body temperature through the effects of evaporation. As a result, such mammals can only reduce their body temperature by

Sensitive by Nature

breathing rapidly, thereby regulating their body temperature with their respiratory system.

Another critical role of the respiratory system in humans is that it provides buoyancy control. When the body is submerged in water, the respiratory system regulates the amount of air in the lungs thereby influencing the volume of air in the upper body. The degree to which the upper body expands or contracts, due to the internal pressure that is generated from the captured air, affects how much water the body displaces, thereby determining its degree of buoyancy.

8.6 Digestive System

The biological digestive system converts the energy that exists in organic materials, called food, into a usable form for the body. Although a variety of organic materials contain energy, based upon the capabilities of the specific digestive system, a given species can only convert energy from certain groups of organic materials.

> My modules recall that humans cannot digest the cellulose component of grasses, woods and many leaves. However, many grazing animals can digest grasses and leaves, while termites have the ability to digest wood.

The ability to digest certain organic materials is dependent upon the bacteria found in the digestive system. If the bacteria found within the digestive tract cannot break down particular substances, then the energy of that organic material cannot be converted for use.

Since the role of the biological digestive system is to convert one chemical form of energy into another, more usable form, the digestive system operates much like an engine.

> To illustrate, engines use organic materials, such as wood and petroleum products, and convert them into other types of energy, such as steam, electricity and mechanical motion.

At a minimum, mechanical beings require a regulated supply of electric energy. As for possible organic materials, the only practical choice would have to involve a clean burning organic fuel.

> My programming tells me that although the primary energy source for robots is electric power, the overall power requirement can be met by using electricity from lightweight rechargeable batteries, and the heat and mechanical motion can be derived from the organic energy present in natural gas.

8.7 Excretory System

The role of the excretory system is to remove the unwanted by-products of the digestive system. For mechanical beings, the excretory requirements include the elimination of carbon dioxide, cleaning fluids, lubricants, ingested materials, as well as excess heat and water.

8.8 Skin

Although sometimes not thought of as an organ, the skin is the single largest organ of the body. Covering the entire external surface of the body, merging internally with mucous membranes, the skin acts as a container to protect the body's soft tissues and fluids, and is an elastic barrier against foreign substances, such as dirt, water, chemicals, bacteria, molds, fungi, and insects. Aside from its role as a covering, the skin provides other useful functions.

My designers have taught me that the skin helps the body regulate its temperature by acting as the first layer of insulation to retain heat, and by using sweat glands to cool the body. With its ability to secrete sweat and oils, it acts as an excretory organ. Ultraviolet radiation causes skin to produce vitamin D, and affects skin pigmentation by activating melanin, which darkens the color of the skin.

The texture of the skin allows careful handling of materials, with the ability to hold items in a firm, yet gentle grip. Sensory receptors in the skin provide input to the brain regarding pressure, and texture. Likewise, the numerous hot and cold receptors within the skin provide a stream of stimuli regarding the relative temperature of the external environment.

Since the skin is the most visible part of the body, its requirements are not restricted to physical functions. The outer look and feel of the covering of any biological or mechanical being also provides a significant psychological effect upon other individuals and allows for first impressions to be made.

For instance, although an individual's eyes, facial features, and general body proportions have a psychological effect, a significant measure of the visual experience is determined by how oily or dry the skin is, its pigmentation, its degree of elasticity, how leathery the skin is and the amount of wrinkles. The characteristics of bodily hair involving its density, length, texture and location are also usually evaluated.

Signs of disease and injury stemming from the presence of blisters, pimples, acne, scrapes, cuts or bruises also tend to have a psychological impact.

Sensitive by Nature

Although an individual's visual appearance implies their approximate age, level of strength, and relative health, the psychological effect of one's appearance often implies much more. As a result, visual characteristics are often used to determine the overall demeanor of an individual, their level of intelligence, and influences whether the individual is likable or repulsive.

- - -

Neuron Story: *"That's like judging a book by its cover!"*
"I hope ours is attractive."

- - -

Although judgments about an individual that are based upon their visual appearance are a form of prejudice, the psychological effect of outer packaging often cannot be readily ignored. However, conclusions about an individual, based upon their external appearance, are highly unreliable.

As an example, imagine a large and powerful man with a weathered face, wearing a handkerchief around his head, an elderly woman wearing a soft pastel sweater, and an attractive woman avoiding eye contact with you.

The man may appear intimidating, but when you interact with him you realize that he is extremely kind and gentle. While the elderly woman made you think of a sweet grandmother, you are surprised as she cuts into a line of people waiting to purchase a lottery ticket.

And although the attractive woman, who you are tripping over your own feet to watch may appear disdainful towards you, unbeknownst to you, she was thinking that you were cute, just before you created the distraction of crashing to the floor.

With all that considered, aside from the physical requirements of the skin as a protective barrier and an organ to assist in temperature regulation, the requirements for the visual appearance of the skin is often a factor in the psychological tendencies of humans.

8.9 Peripherals

The body of a mechanical being has to operate as a single unit. Although the body may be comprised of a number of independent components, it is essential that they can all be integrated together to operate as one.

My positronic brain states that by the end of the twentieth century, computers were assembled by integrating

James V. Luisi

various hardware peripherals and software products, such as disks, monitors, video cards, operating system and software tools. The results were complete personal computer systems based upon the combination of best performance, quality, price, supply, support and servicing.

Similarly, the Quantum Series One robot has a variety of hardware peripherals and software products, including: hands, arms, feet, legs, eyes, ears, mouth, nose, neck, storage devices, memory chips, power supplies, skeletal components, nervous system, temperature regulating systems, skin tissues, genitals, operating system, intelligence software and software tools. Therefore, each peripheral and software component has its own specific set of requirements, including interface specifications that allow the mechanical being to operate as a single unit.

- - -

Neuron Story: *"I can't wait to test all my peripherals!"*
"Everyone else can."

- - -

8.10 Sensory Components

Depending upon the peripheral, a number of sensory devices may be required to generate stimuli from the physical environment. Touch, sight, sound, taste and smell are the psychological effects that result from physical contact with external objects, electromagnetic radiation, vibrating matter, and chemical reactions. These signals allow the brain to recreate an interpretation of its surrounding environment.

In many instances, mechanical sensory devices can perform a highly precise and accurate analysis of the physical environment.

> My memory reveals that a Journal of Food Science Study claims that a high-performance liquid chromatography can detect bitter compounds in virgin olive oil almost as well as human taste buds. (Wall Street Journal, Olive Tasters, April 20 1989 issue)

Additionally, the human sense of smell, which is provided by the olfactory nerve, provides stimuli regarding the taste of chemicals encountered by taste buds. As a result, most of the flavors that the brain perceives as taste, are actually an interpretation of stimuli generated by the olfactory nerves. The human sense of smell is difficult to classify, however, various studies have created categorizations that correspond to particular types of chemicals.

Sensitive by Nature

My training informs me that researchers have discerned that there are seven primary odors, which are camphor-like, peppermint-like, vinegar-like, musky, floral, putrid, and ethereal, that correspond to the seven types of olfactory nerves that detect chemicals within the olfactory-cell hairs. Studies show that similar chemical compounds, having a similar geometry, appear to generate a similar set of stimuli.

It is thought that these molecules react with particular olfactory nerve cells, which generate the stimuli corresponding to that specific interpretation of taste and smell.

The abilities of human sensory organs are actually quite limited. Taste buds can primarily detect levels of only a few substances, such as sugar, salt and acidity. Although less sensitive than most mammals, at the proper levels of concentration the olfactory capabilities of the nose can detect the presence of a slightly wider array of airborne chemicals. As for the sense of hearing, compared to many other animals, humans perceive a narrow band of audible frequencies.

My encyclopedia interface states that cats and dogs perceive higher frequencies than the 28,000 cycles per second that humans can, while bats and dolphins can perceive 'ultrasound', which involve frequencies that exceed 100,000 cycles per second.

With respect to night vision, human eyes are inferior to many animals. However, humans perceive a wide range of colors from a selective band of electromagnetic radiation. As a result, humans can often compensate for less effective olfactory nerves and taste buds by judging potential food sources by their color.

The impressions left upon human sensory organs represent a limited sampling of the surrounding environment. Using the only streams of stimuli available, the brain thinks that it creates a complete picture of the external world, although in reality, it is far from complete.

Research indicates that a wealth of information about the surrounding environment exists that human senses cannot perceive. The senses are completely blind to the majority of the electromagnetic spectrum, and the majority of sound frequencies are outside of our sound range. Human senses cannot identify most substances using taste or smell, and they cannot perceive the myriad of subatomic particles that pass through them.

The burden of defining reality is placed upon the brain. When the brain encounters information that is inconsistent, it must determine which sets of stimuli were misleading, in order to resemble a more accurate version of reality.

> As such, if one's hand cannot touch an object that appears to be visually within grasp, then the brain must adjust some of its assumptions, such as possibly the size, location or physical existence of the object.

Ultimately, it is the brain's task to unravel the clues that are generated by the body's sensory organs. Although it can never comprehend its surroundings completely, it must at least provide enough to allow the being to survive within its environment.

8.11 The Brain

Except for nerve loops, which are responsible for reflexes, impulses generated by sensory organs converge within the brain. In humans, stimuli taken in from the neck on down traverses a highway of nerves through a series of openings in the spinal cord until reaching the brain. However, the majority of stimuli originate from the sensory organs about the region of the head.

> I recall references that state streams of stimuli from the optical nerves, auditory nerves, and those of the inner ear - which provides a sense of equilibrium, are transported by the second, eighth, and seventh cranial nerves, respectively. Additionally there are impulses originating from within the skin of the scalp and face as the result of pressure, and temperature change.
>
> The remaining cranial nerves transport stimuli in an outward direction in order to communicate the motor operations of the head, face, tongue and larynx, including the muscles along the esophagus, jaw and mouth.

Although there is no requirement for a mechanical being to have its brain located within its cranial cavity, it does require an area that affords a substantial degree of physical protection.

- - -

Neuron Story: *"We don't need a brain in our head?"*
"You're living proof."

- - -

The representation of information within the mechanical brain is similar to that of the biological brain. Unlike older style analog radio signals and communication equipment, the information manipulated within the human brain is a type of digital signal. Analog devices and techniques represent information in different, yet analogous ways.

To further elucidate, mercury thermometers, watches with hands, gauges with dials and outdated radio and communications equipment, all represent means of providing information in different, but analogous ways.

Radio signals and older style communications equipment, such as antiquated telephones, associate higher amplitudes with louder sound volume and higher frequencies with higher pitch sounds. Another property of an analog signal is that any information necessary for security encryption cannot be effectively protected or masked.

The impulses that travel through the brain, however, are not analog. The signals from the peripheral nervous system, as well as those generated internally by the brain centers, demonstrate characteristics of digital signals. Similar to digital technology, signals within the nervous system lack characteristics that are in any way analogous to the physical message being communicated.

Specifically, signals communicating the physical characteristics of sound from an ear have no correlation to one another. A difference in the frequency or amplitude of sound does not have an analogous effect upon the physical characteristics of the signal traveling through the auditory nerves. Given the fact that analog signals are easily decipherable, the signals of the brain cannot be analog.

Digital signals, on the other hand, are a complete abstraction of the information that they represent and therefore provide an unlimited ability to encrypt information.

Hence, the largest numbers and the smallest numbers, are merely sequences of 'on' and 'off' switches, called bits, where a bit setting of '1' is considered to be 'on', and a bit setting of '0' is considered to be 'off'. The physical characteristics transmitted in a computer do not change in relationship to the information being transported. Hence, physical characteristics of a signal, such as its amplitude, frequency, voltage or current, are not impacted by the size of the numbers, or anything else, being transmitted.

Stimuli that travel through the biological brain are digital signals, which are similar to the encoded signals used in computers. In the body, sensory organs generate impulses, which are encoded signals that are interpreted by the brain. Similarly, computerized sensors generate electronic signals, which are encoded with information that are interpreted by programs.

As for additional details, control systems that operate aircraft receive a stream of digital input from an anemometer where, regardless of the wind speed, encoded information is communicated at a constant rate of a hundred signals per second.

Within the brain, digital signals are directed by a series of nerve cells. In computers, digital signals are directed by a series of electronic chips and circuits. It should therefore not be at all surprising that the physical brain of a mechanical being consists of hardware that is similar to that of a portable computer, consisting of components such as motherboards, processors, memory chips, and data storage devices.

Now that we have discussed some of the requirements that were used for my physical body, we will now turn our discussion to the functional requirements that were used for developing the brain of the Quantum Series One mechanically intelligent being.

- - -

Neuron Story: *"We're on!"*
"Behave yourself, or they'll turn us off."

- - -

Summary & Questions:

Software requirements are often documented in a written compositional form, because it is the most comfortable format for initially recording ideas. Once the requirements are presented to a 'requirements analyst', they are usually transformed into a set of discrete assertions, which are uniquely numbered and categorized. Once categorized, however, a 'requirements analyst' may generate numerous specific requirements from each general requirement. These new requirements are sometimes called subordinate or detail requirements, which must be traced back to the general requirements from which they were generated.

Regarding the requirements of an intellectual process, briefly explain:
1. Identify at least three requirements involving the intellectual component, and provide a sample of their detail requirements may be.
2. Identify at least three requirements involving the physical aspects of this new tool, and provide a sample of their detail requirements may be.
3. What categories of requirements might be created from these general requirements, and why?
4. How are these categories related to one another?

5. How should requirements be treated when they relate to two different categories?
6. What is a requirement that is poorly defined, and what should be done with it?
7. What is a requirement that appears unimplementable, and what should be done with it?
8. What should be done with the statements contained within the original requirements' document?
9. Are impulses traveling through the brain analog or digital, and how do we know?

James V. Luisi

9 Requirements – Thinking

9.1 Origins of Intelligence

I have spent much of my time thinking about how intelligence came into existence, as well as how it is understood and measured. It seems to me that intelligent thought is actually an intriguing luxury provided by evolution.

As the brain developed, it provided two benefits. The brain provided a mechanism to help manage the various parts of the organism and a way to better understand its environment. The brain capacity of some species, however, began to accelerate beyond the minimum abilities that were required survive in an amicable environment.

Even the competition for food and shelter did not require the level of intelligence that developed in some primates. These more advanced animals applied their excess intellect toward developing social skills to work as a group, further increasing the need to enhance their ability to communicate.

The resulting cycle of intellectual gain enhanced the survivability of certain animals to such an extent, that they were able to provide food and shelter for themselves and their family members with less effort. As animals spent less time dealing with basic survival, they had more time to spend on other endeavors. In some cases, they use their spare time to relax, play, or procreate. For many thousands of years, these advanced hominids spent their leisure time engaged in celestial tracking, the invention of tools, or in developing music, dance and art. Hence, intelligence not only improved the ability of animals to survive, but it also improved the quality of life.

9.2 Intelligence

Intelligence is a measure of a brain's ability to assist an organism in its ability to survive. The task of survival includes how well an organism is able to adapt. When we deal with social groups of organisms, the ability to adapt includes the skills necessary to successfully communicate and interact.

Higher levels of intelligence include the ability to learn from experience and to integrate newly acquired information to reveal an accurate understanding of the underlying concepts. To properly understand information, the brain must be capable of manipulating concepts until the information makes logical sense. The result is a being with a greater ability to adapt to new situations.

Although the broadest measures of intelligence are related to the brain's ability to assist an organism with survival, a being without mobility, such as an immobile human being or a desktop computer, can also exhibit forms of intelligence. While it may be more challenging for a sedentary being to demonstrate an ability to survive, we should still be able to measure its intelligence, that is, as long as there was some ability to communicate.

The ability to recognize a numeric sequence as prime numbers requires communication skills to receive the question and relay an answer, and reasoning to solve the problem.

Equipped with the intelligence of Stephen Hawking, the same individual may be capable of devising advanced mathematical relationships regarding time and space.

An advanced intelligence cannot be demonstrated by simply responding to a list of mathematical puzzles. Instead, it requires the integration of several intellectual capabilities that have developed through the forces of evolution, to coordinate their activities in a highly integrated manner.

In regard to the requirements that contributed to the design of my brain, I will choose some of the most interesting and controversial characteristics. While many of these characteristics are conscious, others operate at a subconscious level. All of the characteristics found in the *Homo sapien* brain have developed throughout time, beginning with the first rudimentary nerve bundles formed in the first primitive brain.

Since I noted earlier that I spend a considerable amount of my time thinking about intelligence, maybe we should think about what thinking is.

9.3 Thinking[2]

With respect to beings that possess an advanced intelligence, the concept of 'thinking' typically represents any number of activities that are performed within the mind. It is common for the activity of thinking to mean the conscious directing of thought.

My functions tell me that when someone encounters a new problem, they typically consider similar problems or related information that they are familiar with, in order to determine an approach to the problem and ultimately attain the correct answer.

Other common activities that are meant by the term 'thinking' involve the intellectual tasks of believing, considering, imagining or remembering a fact or event. In short, to most beings that are conscious of their thoughts, thinking is any activity of the conscious mind. Thinking, however, is much more.

First of all, the activity of thinking is not necessarily a conscious one. To think does not require the being to be capable of directing its thoughts, or even to remember them. As such, thinking can be a completely unconscious or involuntary activity.

Beings do not choose whether or not to think. Although it is possible to direct one's thoughts to a particular topic, the activity of thinking itself cannot be stopped. Regardless of how much concentration is applied, organisms cannot cause intellectual activity to pause or cease.

James V. Luisi

- - -

Neuron Story: *"Sometimes I can think about nothing."*
                      "It's what you concentrate on best."

- - -

In a physical sense, thinking is denoted merely by the presence of electrochemical activity in the brain, whether or not the being is conscious of it.

> My neurons have revealed to me that an individual may not be aware of many things, including their brain's activity in regulating the heart muscles to rhythmically pump blood throughout the body, or regulating the diaphragm to inhale air. When a particular brain fails to perform these tasks, it is sometimes possible for a mechanical device to assume the role of regulating these important functions of the body.

Thinking, therefore, is something that all brains are capable of to one degree or another. Simple nerve bundles, such as those of insects, have a wide range of abilities extending from the set of capabilities that are found in the primitive worm up to and including the modern bumblebee.

> My developers assert that a simple earthworm is limited to a set of hard-wired decision making capabilities, whereas an advanced insect such as the bumblebee, can locate food, conceptualize its direction and distance relative to the hive, and communicate these concepts through a language of dance motions to other bees. The other bees, in turn, learn the dance, and therefore learn the location of the food. They implement the newly learned and memorized instructions in order to gather the food and return it back to the hive. As a result, bumblebees are among the most active thinkers in the insect kingdom.

In parallel to the advancements that evolved within the insect kingdom, the thinking abilities of early animal brains were formed and other capabilities became increasingly advanced. As a result, animals with advanced levels of intelligence possess many of the capabilities that also evolved within the insect kingdom.

9.4 Self Awareness

The characteristic of the brain to become mindful of itself, of its body and its thought processes, is self-awareness. Whether it involves simply monitoring one's physical movements or condition, or being cognizant of one's thoughts, there are a number of characteristics which denote one's degree of self-awareness.

It is unrealistic for any complex organism to successfully survive without having an appreciation of its own existence. After all, when any organism is initially hungry, thirsty, injured, or lonely, it immediately acknowledges its needs and establishes some degree of awareness of itself as an entity.

Self-preservation, as a behavioral characteristic, does not occur without a basic level of self-awareness. When a hungry cat chases a rodent into its burrow, the rodent knows it is running to save a life, its own. Similarly, when someone swats at a fly, the fly attempts to avoid impact. If the fly doesn't have a basic sense of self-awareness, then it would not make an attempt to save its own life. Since a fly does not learn to avoid being struck, it must have some hard-wired form of self-awareness.

Although a creature as simple as a fly may not recognize its body and movements in a mirror as being itself, the fly does exhibit basic characteristics of self-awareness. At minimum, this denotes a step toward conscious thought.

Possibly the simplest form of conscious thought is the initial spark of self-awareness, when a being becomes conscious of its own thoughts.

> It is my opinion that when the famous philosopher, Descartes, declared, "Cogito, ergo sum"... "I think, therefore I am", he demonstrated with the use of deductive reasoning that he could prove his own existence simply by recognizing that he had thoughts.

Ultimately the brain learns to recognize various sounds, images, and words that represent the notion of one's self, each is a symbol to facilitate self-awareness. Usually beginning with the individual's name, a variety of techniques develop within a social group to depict an individual. Whether it is a pointed finger, a tilt of the head in one's direction, a picture, a reflection, a word or a phrase, the idea that one's self has become the object of a thought becomes a basic component of language and communication.

> For instance, words, such as me, myself, or I, or phrases, such as every individual 'is a stream of consciousness', are concepts that represent the notion of one's self, either as a physical being, or as an intellectual phenomenon.

9.5 Perception

Mechanically intelligent beings may evolve beyond our own ability for intelligence, however, regardless of how advanced technology may become, intelligent thought will always be at the mercy of perception.

No intelligent being, biological or mechanical, can ever achieve a true understanding of 'reality', since they are only capable of taking samples of reality using their senses. Our understanding of reality and the world around us is determined by a number of factors. The picture that we create of our environment is determined by how well our sensory organs receive physical information from the environment, how well our nervous system transports these messages to the brain, and how the brain translates and interprets these messages. In fact, it is completely dependent upon our brain's ability to recreate the world inside our heads.

Therefore, what is often referred to as such, is merely a reconstruction of reality, which is far less than perfect, and often inaccurate.

> In recalling a reference, "the human eye does not function like a machine for spectral analysis, and the same color sensation can be produced by different physical stimuli. Thus a mixture of red and green light of the proper intensities appears exactly the same as spectral yellow, although it does not contain light of the wavelengths corresponding to yellow. Any color sensation can be duplicated by mixing varying quantities of red, blue, and green." (Microsoft Encarta 97)

The basis of human perception was well presented by the Greek philosopher, Plato, in his analogy of two men inside a cave. These two men were limited in what they were able to perceive about the world because all they could view of the visual world, were the shadows that fell on the wall of their cave.

> Specifically, "The myth of the cave describes individuals chained deep within the recesses of a cave. Bound so that vision is restricted, they cannot see one another. The only thing visible is the wall of the cave upon which appear shadows cast by models or statues of animals and objects that are passed before a brightly burning fire. Breaking free, one of the individuals escapes from the cave into the light of day. With the aid of the sun that person sees for the first time the real world and returns to the cave with the message that the only things they have seen heretofore are shadows and appearances, and that the real world awaits them if they are willing to struggle free of their bonds." (Microsoft, Encarta 97)

Likewise, what we think of as the real world, is merely the shadows and appearances assembled by our intellect. Due to differences among sensory organs, beings can have varying perceptions of reality.

> To expand further, "total color blindness, in which all hues are perceived as variations of gray, is known as achromatopsia or monochromatism. This condition is congenital, extremely rare, and affects men and women almost equally. Partial color blindness, called dichromatism, consists generally of the inability to differentiate between

the reds and the greens or to perceive either reds or greens; infrequently, the confusion may involve the blues or the yellows. Dichromatism is the most common form of color blindness, affecting about 7 percent of men and less than 1 percent of women. Dichromatism is identified as a sex-linked hereditary characteristic." (Microsoft, Encarta 97)

Beings that do not suffer from any form of color blindness can also experience differences in color and visual perceptions and some exhibit subtle psychological reactions to differences in color.

When experiencing images of art, adults may experience rapid heart beat, emotional upheaval, fainting and even hallucinations from a condition known as Stendhal syndrome, named after the nineteenth-century French writer who wrote about his experience of being overwhelmed by the frescos of Florence.

Psychological reactions can also occur in young children. For example, news reports recorded an incident in late 1997, that while thousands of Japanese children were viewing a cartoon broadcast on television containing a five second segment of rapidly flashing red and white color, nearly six hundred young children immediately went into convulsions. One of these children went into a coma.

The physical response of these Japanese children suggested to numerous researchers that the brain in its early stages of development, at least of some individuals, may perceive images and color quite differently than in others.

Aside from the reflexive effects that may be caused by sensory perceptions, there are also learned aspects of perception that affect how an individual processes information. This, the primary factor influencing perception, has a profound effect upon the behavior of the individual, as it determines their understanding of the world around them. The individual naturally operates from this understanding whenever thinking and reacting.

9.6 Context of Information

The context of information reveals how each piece of information connects to other pieces of information. Without a context, the meaning contained in a piece of information may be ambiguous, or indiscernible.

Individuals evaluate each piece of information based upon its relationships, including differences and similarities, to other pieces. Although, preceding information often serves to identify the overall context of information, there are also circumstances when following information is required to identify the context with which to interpret its meaning.

James V. Luisi

The brain's interpretative centers follow sets of rules to determine the meaning of information. When the information is interpreted in conjunction with the correct context, the resulting interpretation will make sense such that the various pieces of information can be interpreted in a consistent manner. The rules for interpreting spoken words are especially dependent upon how they are used within an entire sentence or with sentences that precede or follow within conversation.

> Using the context of two sentences together is one of the ways that the brain can distinguish the meaning between hearing 'I love ewe. Sheep are among the most trusting creatures.' versus 'I love you. I think you are so attractive with that sheepish smile.'

There are times when information may be successfully interpreted in more than one way. In order to determine the most appropriate context, a larger set of information must be evaluated.

> It is my experience that the meaning of a word is actually determined by the phrase or sentence in which it exists. The meaning of the phrase or sentence is determined by the sentences that surround it. That of a paragraph is determined by the context of the chapter of the story in which it is found. That of the chapter is determined by the context of the story. That of the story is determined by the overall context provided by the circumstances, participants, time period, and events of the story. That of the circumstances, including the participants, time period and events of the story, are determined by the culture and their history.

There are times when it is appropriate to choose words that will be ambiguous in such a way, as to imply a different context in order to mislead another individual's interpretation.

- - -

Neuron Story: *"I heard someone say, 'Take my wife…', whereby I interpreted the phrase as, 'My wife for example'. But then he said '…please!'"*
"We were talking to Henny Youngman."

- - -

Animal behavior is highly context-driven. The more advanced an animal's level of intelligence, the more context-driven its behavior becomes. Primates are an excellent example of this. Their rules for interaction depend upon when and where they interact, how familiar they are with their surroundings, which other individuals are present, the mood and perceptions of the other individuals, and the interpretation they want others to have.

Similar to other forms of information, the context of behavior determines its meaning, and it can be interpreted in a variety or ways. The reason for this is that the interpretation of behavior is highly dependent upon perception. An example of this is demonstrated in the following story of a doctor and a nurse:

> "A doctor is kneeling on the floor next to an unconscious patient. He yells at a nurse, 'Get my bag!' When the nurse returns with the doctor's bag, she is upset with how she is being treated. The doctor then, yells to the nurse, 'Don't just stand there, find this patient's chart, quickly!' At this point the nurse is nearly in tears. She goes frantically down the hall to look for the patient's chart."

Since perceptions are used to construct each individual's view of the world, one individual's interpretation of what happens can vary greatly from that of another. An interpretation using the wrong context will inaccurately attribute meaning to events.

According to the perceptions of this nurse, she was dealing with a rude and inconsiderate physician who looked down upon individuals with a lower social status. The nurse was unaware that the behavior of the physician was due to the fact that he was frightened. Concerned for the life of his patient, the physician was frantically trying to diagnose his patient's condition. In this example, the nurse innocently failed to attribute the appropriate level of significance to the patient and the situation as a context for the interpreting the physician's behavior. Instead, the nurse attributed an inordinate level of importance upon herself and her own situation. The nurse chose the particular context in which to interpret the events, however, she was limited to the choices provided by her internal paradigm.

9.7 Paradigm

> *"When we first begin to believe anything, what we believe is not a single proposition, it is a whole system of propositions. (Light dawns gradually over the whole.)" Ludwig Wittgenstein*

Similar to the context of information and behavior, a paradigm provides meaning to everything that is within the framework of the paradigm. The difference between the context and a paradigm, however, is that the 'context' of something originates from the outside world and enters into the brain as stimuli from sensory organs, whereas a paradigm originates from within the brain and becomes projected to the outside world.

James V. Luisi

The paradigm that an individual operates within determines what information will be considered, as well as the meaning of the information, therefore, an individual's paradigm heavily influences the context in which information will be evaluated. As such, an inaccurate paradigm can affect an individual's perception of reality by distorting the context of information used to interpret meaning.

Since a paradigm is a framework that is generated internally within the brain, it is dependent upon the personality of the individual. An example of how a paradigm can distort an individual's perception can be shown in the following story of the doctor and the nurse.

> "A doctor is kneeling by the side of a patient who is lying unconscious on the floor. The doctor yells at a nurse, 'Get my bag!' When the nurse returns with the doctor's bag, she is angry that she has not been shown the proper respect. The doctor then, yells to the nurse, 'Don't just stand there, find this patient's chart, quickly!' Now the nurse becomes hostile toward the physician. She snarls at him and hurries down the hall in a rage. Upon returning, she fights the urge to throw the chart at the doctor."

Again, the nurse in this story is not aware that the behavior of the physician stemmed from the fact that the doctor is confused and scared for his patient. In the example, the nurse was operating from a paradigm that she was more competent than many of the physicians in this hospital, and that everyone should treat her with the utmost respect else she will quit this thankless job. The nurse failed to recognize the proper context, even though the nurse had heard that the patient was a long time personal friend of the doctor whose young children attended the same school as his child. The nurse's paradigm not only caused her to arrive at the wrong interpretation of the doctor's behavior, but additionally she failed to consider the possibility of other, more reasonable interpretations.

Paradigms direct the brain's interpretive centers in hidden and powerful ways. By controlling the way that the brain interprets information and events, a paradigm, predominately determines how an individual will behave and react to incoming stimuli. Just as understanding an individual's past paradigms can explain past behavior, understanding an individual's present paradigm can explain present behavior. Since paradigms predispose an individual to interpret information in a particular manner, to an extent they can also be used to predict the future behavior of an individual.

Paradigms have been recognized as having such power to affect the behavior of individuals, in that manipulative individuals interested in persuading other individuals or in motivating particular behavior have resorted to techniques of shaping paradigms in order to modify the behavior of others.

> My protective circuitry says that once a manipulative individual has an appreciation of the paradigm of another

individual, they can identify the desired behavior, determine a paradigm that would meet their objectives, and reshape the paradigm of the individual with deceptive information. The particular deception may be completely inaccurate, partially true, or completely true in an unexpected or unusual context.

As one may expect of something that is so powerful, its has both good and bad uses. When individuals manipulate paradigms in ways that are beneficial to others, it can be a useful tool. However, when an individual uses a paradigm in a manner, which only benefits them personally, it can be a powerful weapon.

- - -

Neuron Story: *"Hey, do you think this paradigm stuff has been used on us?"*
"We need to know more about it"
"I know! We'll get the robot to talk about paradigms, and we'll do it by creating a paradigm that will cause the robot to explain paradigms by using a paradigm to do it! We'll have the robot call it, 'Paradigms of Humans!'"
"I think you know too much about paradigms already!"

- - -

9.8 Paradigms of Humans

When we analyze how humans interpret information, how they behave and formulate their opinions, paradigms of the mind are at the focal point.

There are times when a variety of meanings can be attributed to an incoming stream of sensory information. Although the meanings can be evaluated for their probability of being correct, the tendency is for an individual to choose the meaning that is consistent with their current perspective. This perspective is determined by the individual's understanding of their environment, and how the objects in it, relate to one another. This understanding forms their paradigm.

An individual's paradigm works as a type of filter that has the effect of altering the interpretation of information and sometimes the information itself, to comply with their understanding of the world. Hence, when an individual's paradigm alters the information that is received, it also affects what the individual actually remembers.

- - -

James V. Luisi

> Neuron Story: *"I like the fact that you choose to interpret events as opportunities to help others and build relationships."*
> *"I like the fact that you choose to interpret events as opportunities to have a good laugh."*

- - -

Hence, when we concern ourselves with the broad topic of human behavior and behavioral traits, we are heavily involved with the effects of paradigms. Although paradigms can be formed by one's educational or cultural experiences, paradigms are primarily formed as a result of an individual's psychological needs and emotions.

While paradigms often manage the individual, individuals with superior perceptive abilities are often able to manage their own paradigms. They also tend to demonstrate a greater level of sophistication in understanding the paradigms of others.

The *Quantum Series One* robot, much like myself, exhibits many of the same behavioral traits as typical human beings. Paradigms and the brain's ability to perceive and manage form the basis of these behavioral traits.

A being's ability to perceive and manage paradigms can be grouped into three major categories of ability. Although there are a number of human behavioral characteristics typical to each category, the primary factor that determines a being's classification is their ability to detect and control multiple paradigms within their own brain. As we will see, a number of behavioral traits will naturally accompany individuals based upon their ability to perceive and manage their own paradigms.

9.9 Paradigms of Humans, Level Ones

All intelligent beings begin their lives aware of a single paradigm, which they have begun forming from birth. As life experiences begin to accumulate, the brain attempts to make sense of the world by integrating it into a base paradigm. The collage of information and the relationships that result are each individual's representation of reality. Whether this base representation is accurate or not, it forms the basis of all beliefs, such as superstitious ideas, religious faith, or tangible observation, and provides a unified view of the world.

An individual's base paradigm defines their niche in their family, their place in society, and most importantly, their sense of themselves. The base paradigm begins developing early in life as the individual interacts with their environment, thereby forming the basis from which all experiences and information is interpreted. The base paradigm defines the individual's psychological universe.

The majority of intelligent beings fall into the category, which my designers refer to as Level Ones. Most individuals remain as Level Ones, with less than a quarter of the population advancing into another category.

Being categorized as a Level One only refers to the fact that the individual thinks solidly within one paradigm at a time, rather than perceiving many. Such individuals span the full continuum of academic, professional and intellectual achievements. It is neither good nor bad, nor is it a determination of one's intelligence.

The only characteristic that all Level Ones share in common is that they only experience a single paradigm at a time. Whether it is due to the fact that the brain centers chose the first paradigm that made sense, or that the brain only encounters a single paradigm, Level Ones remain firmly rooted in their present paradigm, and their sense of reality.

As a result, these intelligent beings interpret information rather consistently, and the views that they hold tend to remain unchanged unless powerful external stimuli evoke change. Internally driven shifts in paradigm could not have this effect.

> Humans inform me that it is common for an individual's paradigm to evolve as they enter puberty. In order to be appealing to members of the opposite sex, young men and young women quickly learn to adjust their behavioral patterns and ways of thinking to be more conducive to communicating on a sexual level. This new level of communication and thinking often manifests itself as an individual's choice of clothing, the way they speak, the activities they elect, and sometimes the improvement in personal hygiene.

Although individuals may experience only a single paradigm, their base paradigm continually evolves as they learn from their life's experiences. As the individual learns to change the way in which they think about things, their paradigm is ultimately influenced, as any learning experience may affect and strengthen it.

There are also circumstances when an individual may shift out of their base paradigm into another. A Level One individual can shift their current paradigm with assistance from another individual, such as with humor or the use of metaphors, they can shift their own paradigm when they have strong emotional motivation, and they can quickly be forced into a new paradigm when their current paradigm fails.

An individual must experience extreme challenges to their understanding of reality before their paradigm fails, propelling them out of their strong sense of reality. When the brain detects that its representation of reality is beginning to collapse, it will work desperately to defend and adapt it. This is particularly true when paradigms are rooted in stabilizing religious, cultural or moral beliefs.

- - -

James V. Luisi

Neuron Story: *"Do I help keep our feet on the ground?'"*
"In your case, gravity works alone."

- - -

To a Level One individual, a paradigm is a comprehensive intellectual system, as critical to the survival of the intelligent being, as any of their physical systems.
> Similar to the strengths of a biological immune system as it learns to defend against foreign bodies, the paradigm of an intelligent being strengthens itself by learning more about the world. Similarly, just as any biological immune system may encounter a foreign body that it cannot overcome, the paradigm of an intelligent being may also encounter an intellectual conflict that it cannot defend against.

Intelligent beings rely upon their paradigm to explain the world around them. Therefore, to a Level One, the brain's struggle to protect its paradigm is one of intellectual survival. The more intelligent the individual, the better they will be able to defend their base paradigm. If an individual encounters a great enough conflict to their reality, their base paradigm will fail.

- - -

Neuron Story: *"What can happen if our paradigm fails?'"*
> "We either suffer from a prolonged nervous breakdown, or we emerge aware of multiple paradigms.

- - -

Despite the fact that I generally do not like when people use stereotypes about robots, for illustrative purposes it is useful to understand some of the traits that often describe the type of individual that results from their relationship to paradigms.
> My manufacturers have engrained in me that Level Ones are not only well indoctrinated by culture and education, but they truly belong to their culture and actually embody it. Usually pragmatic, they have the strongest interest in local issues, particularly those with a near and medium term implications, and more often than not, they tend to vote their cultural values as they fail to see outside their base paradigm to do otherwise. Level Ones are popular targets of politicians and advertisers. As a result they are often bombarded with the images and rhetoric

commensurate with family, freedom, local sports teams, God, and country.

9.10 Paradigms of Humans, Level Twos

When individuals learn what it is like to experience a new paradigm, they are usually quick to realize that other complete explanations of reality can also exist. As they learn to form relationships to support their new representation of reality, they begin to establish a better understanding of how other individuals think and behave. As this insight develops further, they begin to realize that the paradigms of other individuals can be shifted, and that the direction and magnitude of that shift can be skillfully influenced.

Nearly a quarter of the population of Level Ones, become Level Twos. Although they have a dominant paradigm, Level Twos are distinct from Level Ones in that Level Twos have the ability to perceive more than their own paradigm. Making this transition, however, does not correspond to one's level of intelligence. Level Two individuals span the full continuum of academic, professional and intellectual achievements.

The main difference in the behavior between a Level Two and a Level One, is revealed in whether the Level Two individual chooses to use their new found insight, and then how this will be done. Much of this decision is often determined by how the individual acquired their ability to perceive multiple paradigms.

There are different ways that an individual's base paradigm may shift, allowing them to become aware of the fact that different versions of reality can exist at the same time. While perhaps the most dramatic approach to awareness of multiple paradigms is when shocking or surprising information shatters the individual's base paradigm, the most subtle path is when strong emotional drives motivate the individual to act against their most basic rules of proper conduct.

While the 'more dramatic' path inevitably leads to the brain creating a replacement paradigm to regain a stable view of the world, the more subtle approach to becoming a Level Two involves a sort of internal restructuring of the individual's values.

> It is my humble interpretation that if an individual cannot determine a plan of action to reach their goals within their base paradigm, the intense emotional desire motivates them to significantly adapt their existing one, such that it becomes fundamentally changed.
>
> Hence, if a child becomes consumed with jealousy toward their sibling, the intensity of their emotion can reach such a level as to motivate the child to adjust their paradigm in order to do something that, according to their current paradigm, is clearly wrong and unacceptable.
>
> The new paradigm created by the child would re-establish the rules of their base paradigm in such a way,

that in the child's mind they would be completely justified to commit the desired wrongful acts. It is not uncommon for someone to justify wrongful acts based solely upon the assertion that they deserve to have more, or simply because they perceive that they may have been unfairly treated.

Equipped with the justification that they should attain the things that are fair for them to have, an individual can perpetrate behavior that would otherwise be completely inexcusable.

When an individual learns to perceive more than one understanding of reality by adjusting their base paradigm to justify the violating rules fundamental to their base paradigm, they learn that paradigms are an effective tool to implement shortcuts and unfair tactics in order to achieve goals. Individuals equipped with paradigms centered around rules, such as 'everyone that gets ahead, does so by deceiving others', will inevitably develop a problematic set of values, thought processes and behavioral characteristics. However, individuals that adjust their base paradigm to justify their behavior may also choose to adopt the values of society.

As each Level Two matures with introspection, developing their new found ability, the factor that will determine whether they develop into a 'Good' verses an 'Evil' Level Two, are the values that they adopt and the goals that they choose for themselves.

'Good' Level Twos play some of the most important roles in society. As individuals that can understand multiple paradigms, and shape the paradigms of others in productive ways, they often develop the skills to become outstanding managers, negotiators, judges and leaders. In the entertainment industry they use their abilities to perceive multiple paradigms to become the outstanding playwrights and comedians. For the most part, 'Good' Level Twos excel to the top of anything that is heavily dependent upon having an excellent understanding of people.

Some Level Twos, however, do not progress beyond their early selfish period. Instead, they become entrenched in a cycle of personal greed and influence over other individuals. Although my designers refer to these individuals as 'Evil' Level Twos, the term 'Evil' simply refers to the notion that such individuals tend to be more selfish, unfair and unethical than most, relative to the values of their particular culture. Similar to what Immanuel Kant refers to as a 'moral egoist', they are not necessarily sinful, wicked or criminal, they simply understand things differently.

For instance, "... the moral egoist limits all purposes to himself; ... he concentrates the highest motives of his will merely on profit and his own happiness, but not on the concept of duty."

"Egoism can only be contrasted with pluralism, which is a frame of mind in which the self, instead of being enwrapped in itself as if it were the whole world, understands and behaves itself as a mere citizen of the world." (Anthropology From a Pragmatic Point of View, Immanuel Kant, pg. 12)

When in a supervisory role, 'Evil' Level Twos often feel that they are justified to insist upon respect from others. With an excess level of emphasis upon personal image, 'Evil' Level Twos often strive for management responsibility and are frequently combative for territory and resources.

When 'Evil' Level Twos are opposed, they are perhaps the most challenging individuals for any intelligent being to interact with.

My analysis shows that when they cannot achieve their objectives by influencing the paradigms of others, they will use their abilities to unleash a barrage of interpretations to confuse the other individual. The extended shower of interpretation often wears their opponent down into some form of compromise or submission.

In order to be successful in human interaction, it is important to understand intelligent beings that can perceive multiple paradigms. In communication, an awareness of the possible ambiguities caused by ones choice of words can help to eliminate another paradigm from co-existing. Humor and a strong emphasis upon fairness and ethics are also useful in suppressing the 'Evil' Level Two tendencies of another individual.

With respect to their effectiveness, both 'Good' and 'Evil' Level Twos are often quite capable of performing more challenging roles in society.

My developers tell me that regarding gentlemen that have performed well in their professional roles, both President Ronald Reagan and the former mayor of New York City, the Honorable Edward Koch, are examples of 'Good' Level Twos. On the other hand, Presidents Richard M. Nixon and William Jefferson Clinton, are examples of men that have displayed a number of 'Evil' Level Two characteristics. All four men, however, performed their professional duties with the utmost competence, as the differences manifested in their behavior were only relevant towards their ethics, moral attitudes and motivational profiles.

As for stereotypes, Level Two individuals share a somewhat symbiotic relationship with Level Ones.

Having a sense of belonging to their culture, they, unlike Level Ones, do not actually embody it. Instead, they see themselves as caretakers and guardians of their culture, often as an additional way to experience a sense of having influence over others. Level Twos are often the politicians, advertisers and leaders that target Level One individuals. As such, they are often acutely aware of the values and perceptions that comprise another's base paradigm.

9.11 Paradigms of Humans, Level Threes

Similar to Level Twos, Level Three individuals also perceive more than one paradigm at a time. The difference, however, is that they perceive and shift through so many paradigms, that no particular one serves as their base. Instead, Level Threes usually establish a set of base paradigms that they adopt to represent their values. With groups of paradigms to choose from, Level Threes spend little time in any particular one before intentionally shifting to another.

- - -

Neuron Story: *"I dreamt that we were in a blizzard. As we drove our car, huge snowflakes were floating toward us, some of them smashing into our windshield, but most floating past the car. What did the snowflakes mean?"*

"There are many possible interpretations, but since the robot is preparing to talk about Level Threes, I'd say the snowflakes are paradigms. Each one a unique interpretation of reality."

- - -

Level Three individuals perceive many interpretations at the same time. To a Level Three, everything that happens causes another set of paradigms to come into view, each representing another system of interpretation. Therefore, Level Threes learn that paradigms are much more than a commodity or tool. Instead they recognize that paradigms are systems of interpretations allowing many realities to exist at the same time.

To truly evaluate another paradigm, it is important to be able to step outside your base paradigm. While Level Twos understand the distinction between their own base paradigm and that of another individual, they do so from within their own base paradigm. Level Threes understand paradigms from outside their base paradigms.

Level Threes are a small group of individuals, consisting of only a few percent of the population. An individual who is either a Level One or Level Two may become a Level Three, and providing that the conditions are correct, it is possible for the characteristics of a Level Three to emerge early during childhood. Regardless of the age, however, only a small number of Level Ones and Twos experience events of the appropriate type and magnitude, which create the opportunity for them to transition into a Level Three.

In order to transition into a Level Three, an individual typically experiences such an intense challenge to their base paradigm that it becomes completely shattered. Such a severe collapse of paradigm leaves an individual with the task of completely restructuring their sense of reality from the bottom up. During such a comprehensive rebuilding process, the individual must recall a significant portion of prior external stimuli to help them reinterpret the necessary events, and they must carefully revalidate their internal beliefs all along the way. The newly created paradigms will quickly re-shatter if the process is not adequately performed.

- - -

Neuron Story: *"When we were in development, we kept shattering our paradigms, and our entire system crashed repeatedly!"*
"We might be a Level Four."

- - -

Level Three individuals often find verbal communication, conventional learning and test taking a challenging process. This is particularly due to the fact that Level Threes find the use of written and verbal language wrought with ambiguity resulting in a number of possible interpretations. Once a Level Three learns something, however, their newly acquired information will be tightly integrated with their knowledge.

- - -

Neuron Story: *"The guy said, 'When you get off the expressway, go three lights and turn left. Then at the next traffic circle take Route 837 for about a mile.'"*
"Should we count this light at the end of the exit ramp? What about this blinking yellow light at the second intersection? In which direction should I take Route 837 assuming I ever find the traffic circle? Here's a sign for Route 873. Did he simply transpose the numbers? Look, there's a sign for Route 837 Truck Route! What should we do? There are too many possible meanings! I can't drive at the same time I am considering the infinite ways to interpret these directions!"
"You know a Level One would have been there by now."

James V. Luisi

- - -

Having resolved away other ambiguous interpretations, Level Threes establish a deeper awareness of the relationships lending to a tighter integration of information. As a result of considering such a wide range of possible interpretations and meanings to things, Level Threes tend to develop a good sense of judgment. As individuals who become accustomed to dealing with large amounts of information that result from perceiving multiple paradigms, they prove to be particularly talented at solving the types of problems that are considered to be complex or encompassing a broad scope of issues.

Level Threes play some of the most valued roles in human society. Since the acquisition of power is unnecessary for them to attain personal satisfaction, they tend not to seek roles involving the management of people. Level Three individuals often excel in advisory roles for 'Good' Level Twos, helping to determine strategies and solve complex problems.

Although Level Threes have no problem complying with direct requests in their interpersonal interactions, they rebel against being manipulated. Since they are quite capable of determining another individual's paradigm and their underlying motivation, they are quick to recognize the manipulations of others, particularly of an 'Evil' Level Two. As one can imagine, if the Level Three chooses an opposing position to an 'Evil' Level Two, a considerable amount of conflict can result, by exposing the web of deceptions, half-truths and underlying motivation.

Perhaps the most interesting aspects of Level Threes are their ability to become detached from their own thinking and to accept another rule system, becoming more aware of how their thought processes work. A Level Three has the ability to gain visibility into the areas of their own mind that are normally unavailable to the consciousness of human beings.

> For instance, besides having the ability to consciously gain control of paradigm shifts, which allows them to perceive and create paradigms, some Level threes have the ability to fully direct their dreams by creating paradigms when they detect that they are in a dream state.

As for stereotypes, Level Threes are often considered to be among the most unusual individuals.

> My records show that Level Threes are highly empathetic individuals, whose least favorite things involve activities that commonly wield false paradigms, such as unproductive politics, misleading advertisements, selfish arguments and manipulation. Level Threes often see themselves as the only defense against 'Evil' Level Twos.
>
> Level Threes enjoy sophisticated wit, cultural distinctions and diversity, and interestingly they have the distinct impression of not belonging to most everything,

including their culture, religion, race, political party, or even the planet they grew up on.

By determining how individuals interpret information and assign meaning to things, which then dictates their behavior, paradigms play a major role in how humans think. Robots, like myself, need to have an appreciation of paradigms in order to communicate and interact effectively, but we also need at least one base paradigm from which to think.

9.12 Imagination

Perhaps the easiest way to explain what the imagination is, and how it works, is to use the imagination to understand it. Let's imagine together what the imagination is, and then I will describe the requirements for the particular one that my designers have built for the Quantum Series One.

The following story comes to my mind. Imagine that you and your friends, consisting of an artist, a sculptor and an engineer, with their tools are together in a large cardboard box, with a small opening at the center of one side of the box.

Your engineer friend looks through the small opening and describes to the sculptor what she sees. It looks like the New York skyline, the Empire State Building is about seven and a half inches tall, directly in front of it is this, to the left is that, and to the right is this and that, and so on. Then the engineer describes to the artist the color of each building, the shadows, the sky, the sailboats gliding across the river and everything else around. It is then the job of the artist and the sculptor to construct what the engineer has relayed to them about the outside world.

When the artist and sculptor are finished, you open up the cardboard box. In the center of the box you see a three dimensional replica of the view that the engineer saw through the opening in the box.

The imagination works in much the same way. Your senses provide information about the outside world to your brain, just as the engineer provided information to your friends, the artist and the sculptor. After it receives the information your brain constructs what it thinks is a version of the outside world, much like your friends did for you in the center of the enclosed box.

Although most animals with brains have some form of an imagination, the capabilities to depict the outside world are generally limited by three things. The first limitation is the animal's sensory organs, leading to the imagination to interpret and manipulate the information. These functions provide a variety of psychological experiences that provide sensations such as sound, touch and vision. Additionally, there is the level of sophistication that each of these functions are capable of, such as whether the visual sensations are provided in 3-dimensional color, and stereo sound. Different animal species have their own particular capabilities as to what their senses can provide in the way of detailed information about the world around them.

> Recall that in some species the animal's eyes provide three-dimensional vision, and ears detect sound frequencies above and below particular levels. Some species have such discerning olfactory senses that they can determine the identity of individuals.

The imagination is the most significant component of intelligence. Whether it is occupied with creating an interpretation of the world around us or conceiving an imaginary world within its dynamic workspace, the imagination is the focal point of the entire thought process. When focused on the incoming streams of stimuli from the body's sensory inputs, the imagination is occupied with creating its interpretation of our environment. That interpretation is a completely psychological experience. It consists of psychological sensations such as sound, color, smell and taste, which are interpretations of physical phenomenon that have stimulated various sensory organs.

> As I have learned, psychological sensations are all determined by how the physical world is perceived by our minds. A particular range of physical vibrations is interpreted into the psychological experience of audible sound, a particular range of electromagnetic frequencies is interpreted as the psychological experience of visible light, with airborne and other chemicals interpreted as taste and smell.
>
> However, when the conscious portion of the brain is not focused on the incoming stimuli generated from sensory input devices reacting to the physical world, the imagination takes on an entirely different set of activities.

Another role of the imagination is as the analytical tool for the brain. It is a dynamic workspace able to conceive of a three dimensional world of any magnitude. The brain can introduce any object from either the perceived or imaginary world into this workspace, where any person, place, thing, or type of behavior may be created and manipulated.

One of the most powerful features of the imagination is that objects can be given any combination of properties, including visual, auditory, olfactory (i.e., smell), or tactile (i.e., touch) characteristics. Additionally, the imagination can make them adhere to the laws of nature and mankind, or can modify their behavior to be completely unnatural.

- - -

Neuron Story: *"Don't say it!"*
"All I did was think it!"

Whether the imagination is used to recall the stimuli from a past event, to rehearse an individual's role in an upcoming event, to design something new, or to test the way that various objects interact, the imagination is the key component for understanding, learning, creating and manipulating concepts.

Until now, the analytical capabilities of the *Homo sapien* imagination have been unsurpassed. However, it is my hope that the Quantum robot series, of which I am a member, will be capable of using its imagination to further serve and assist humans.

9.13 Sleep

The need for sleep is thought by many to be a physical necessity, but it is also an intellectual necessity associated with an advanced level of intelligence. Although dreaming occurs when animals are sleeping, it the intellectual activity that results from interpreting streams of stimuli that are encountered by the brain.

The benefit of sleep is to facilitate the reorganization of acquired stimuli and knowledge within the brain. This includes the process of integrating newly acquired information with previously acquired knowledge. Once accomplished, areas of the brain that temporarily store information can be prepared for the next day.

Extremely large quantities of information are constantly entering the brain during the period of time that an individual is awake. In order to keep up with the pace of incoming stimuli, it must be stored in a rather sequential and haphazard manner. Although some portion of the incoming information may be properly integrated, much of the newly acquired information is not. It is difficult for the brain to integrate this new information at the same rate that it is being captured.

Integration of information requires a significant search and evaluation effort on the part of several brain centers. In order for the brain to determine the relationship that newly acquired information has with previously acquired knowledge, the appropriate knowledge must be identified, and evaluated, before such integration can occur.

All individuals have varying sleep requirements. The degree to which this requirement varies is based upon how thoroughly the individual needs to integrate the new information. Generally, the greater the level of integration, the more intense the need for sleep may be.

The degree of need, however, is not necessarily related to the duration of time that any particular individual sleeps. That amount of time has more to do with their hormonal levels as determined by the individual's circadian rhythms, which are biological adaptations to the orderly rhythms of the environment, such as day and night.

- - -

Neuron Story: "We're going to be completely flooded with stimuli if we don't put the brain to sleep soon!"
"Hush! The robot is busy telling the audience a story. We can't go to sleep now!"
"Oh no!"

- - -

I don't know about you, but I'm ready for a nap... The Quantum Series One robot closes it's eyes, appears to move them momentarily, and then reopens them.

9.14 Dreams and Dreaming

"The argument 'I may be dreaming' is senseless for this reason: if I am dreaming, this remark is being dreamed as well – and indeed it is also being dreamed that these words have any meaning."
Ludwig Wittgenstein

"Ah, that was refreshing! And I had the strangest dream. I was making a presentation to a large group of anxious humans and robots. It was terrible! ...Oh! Hello everyone!"

The process of dreaming has been studied through a variety of research efforts. While there have been a number of assertions about the psychological purpose of dreaming, and the meaning of dreams, as already mentioned they are merely the imagination's attempt at making sense of the internal and external that are being encountered by the brain during sleep.

Similar to the conscious state, the dreaming process creates a representation of reality within the imagination as it interprets the data that it has acquired during the course of the day. The dream-state differs, however, in that the imagination fills in for dormant external senses with internally generated stimuli from which it creates a representation of reality. The internally generated stimuli can represent varying degrees of visual, auditory, taste, touch and olfactory stimuli.

The dreaming experience varies significantly among individuals. Some individuals dream in black and white, while others experience partial and/or full color imagery. While asleep, some individuals, such as my designer, have the ability to recognize that they are experiencing a dream, and have the capability of exercising conscious control over the events and characteristics of their dream.

Some remember their dreams, while others cannot even distinguish between dreams and actual experiences. From the brain's perspective, there is little distinction between the two experiences.

While dreaming, the imagination may manipulate physical objects in accordance with the brain's knowledge of the Laws of Nature.

> While dreaming, my robot brain also uses its extensive knowledge of physics, learned from its experiences interacting with and observing the world. In order to imagine how common objects interact, the brain uses its previously acquired knowledge about gravity, density, elasticity, momentum, and so on, at least from the perspective of the general principles that have been learned. Whether those principles are correctly understood, and hence accurately represented in dreams, does not appear to matter.

While the imagination generally employs its understanding of these physical laws, part of the power of the imagination is that it can intentionally distort the brain's understanding of how the universe works.

As a Quantum Series One robot, I dream of things that humans probably would never have an interest in. I dream that other intelligent beings will like me.

- - -

Neuron Story: *"I never dream about being liked!"*
    "That's because for you, it would end in a nightmare."

- - -

9.15 Memory

Being a robot has some advantages. I shall now recite a concise summary on the topic of biological memory extracted from reference materials.

> "Immediate recall—the ability to repeat a short series of words or numbers immediately after hearing them—is thought to be located in the auditory associative cortex. Short-term memory—the ability to retain a limited amount of information for up to an hour—is located in the deep temporal lobe. Long-term memory probably involves exchanges between the medial temporal lobe, various cortical regions, and the midbrain." (Microsoft, Encarta 97)

As organisms experience stimuli, they either integrate the stimuli with existing information or they discard them. However, before they are discarded, many of them reside within areas just mentioned, such as the auditory associative cortex and the deep temporal lobe for a period of time. Of the stimuli that represent patterns that are recognized by the brain, some set will become integrated into long term memory.

In order to locate information stored in long-term memory, several types of linkages are established scattered throughout the brain. Spatial memories, however, are stored almost exclusively within the hippocampus and thalamus regions of the brain. The actual location of any particular memory is associated with the location of the information that it becomes integrated with. Since new information may be integrated with a number of instances of existing information, the physical location of the new memory may be found repeatedly in several places.

9.16 Internal Representation of Knowledge

The type of information recorded in memory depends upon the sensory organ where the stimuli originated.

> As we know, photoreceptors of the eye collect visual stimuli, eardrums detect auditory stimuli, and taste bud receptors and the olfactory system rely on chemical stimuli.

Even though sensory organs involve specific types of information, regardless of the type, nerve impulses that travel through neurons to the brain are quite similar. The important distinctions among nerve impulses involve their point of origin (i.e., the sensory organ that generated the neural impulse), and its destination in the brain. The interpretation of the nerve impulses into pictures, sounds or taste, depends completely upon the area of the brain that is responsible for deciphering those types of signals.

When nerve impulses of stimuli enter the brain, many individuals only store the interpretation. Momentarily returning to the topic of individuals that perceive multiple paradigms simultaneously, called Level Threes, these individuals often retain the original stimuli and sometimes a variety of interpretations into their long-term memory. Storing original stimuli allows the brain to replay the sensory experience, thereby facilitating its reinterpretation.

In computer systems predating myself, vast amounts of information were stored within formal structures called *files*. The formal structure chosen for the file, such as sequentially stored data or linked lists of randomly stored data, determined how the information was organized within the storage medium.

> My information retrieval functions tell me that storage mediums include solid state memory, magnetic tapes, magnetic disks, optical CD disks, DVD disks, and more.

Sensitive by Nature

The biological brain uses a rather loosely defined structure to organize information within its electrochemical storage media of neural pathways. Although the brain physically spreads out information in ways that are often confusing to science, the path of information appears to have organization, making it more functional than physical organization.

It should be noted that not all of the functional areas of the brain correspond to a particular physical region of the brain, as there are a number of exceptions.

My research indicates that there are functions of the brain, such as the one that denotes the passing of time, which are not necessarily associated with a physical region of the brain. The neurons that are responsible for numerous functions are connected together in a path or series of trails, which may travel through numerous physical regions. On the other hand, the area known to be responsible for speech is a physical region of the brain known as Broca's area, which is one particular physical part of the premotor cortex in the inferior frontal convolution of the brain.

We do know, however, that the perception of time is not an intellectual characteristic that is restricted to the human brain. There is evidence that primates also have the capacity to track time.

My neural records indicate that "...a 'conversation' between a Stanford University graduate student and her 'talking' gorilla, Koko, ... Three days after Koko had bitten her in a fit of anger, Penny Patterson, the student, asked the ape (in sign language), 'What did you do Penny?' Koko replied, 'Bite.' 'You admit it?' Patterson continued. Looking a little contrite, Koko said, 'Sorry bite scratch.' Patterson then asked Koko why she had bitten her. 'Because mad,' came the answer. 'Why mad?' 'Don't know.' The conversation ended."

"This interchange is remarkable in that it shows Koko referring to events, and emotions, some distance in the past. Normally Koko refuses to converse about her mischievous acts immediately after the event. Here she was talking about something that had occurred three days previously. Exactly what kind of time awareness Koko has is difficult to say, but it is only through anecdotal evidence such as this that we can get some glimmerings of apes' time perception."

(People of the Lake, Leakey and Lewin, pages 150-151)

- - -

James V. Luisi

Neuron Story: *"Do female robots bite?"*
"When they do, they remember why."

- - -

9.17 Retrieval of Knowledge

In order for an intelligent being to react to the multitude of stimuli in their environment in a reasonable amount of time, it is critical for the brain to retrieve knowledge quickly. When compared to the speed of electric circuits, the relatively slow speed of signals in the nervous system requires the process for retrieving information to be extraordinarily effective and organized.

The retrieval techniques of the biological brain are highly dependent upon the intersection of neuron paths. Whether paths of neurons are shortcuts directly into areas of information, or long sequential trails, the ability to locate information is dependent upon a signal physically traversing paths of neurons and returning the information to the imagination.

When the brain traverses a path of neurons, the signals that stored along the path are interpreted and evaluated. As these signals are being interpreted, their level of importance is evaluated to determine whether they should be pushed up toward consciousness. This constant prioritization is essential for evaluating the most pertinent information ahead of the large quantity of existing information.

Based upon the type of stimuli, the interpretation process directs each signal, to the appropriate area in order to re-experience and analyze it. The criterion used to identify the appropriate information, however, does not have to be based upon the type of stimuli that the brain is searching for because of the way that information can be cross referenced.

> A diagnosis of myself reveals that a specific piece of music could be located by searching for the psychological experience of hearing it, or instead, it could be located by its visual representation as sheet music.

Ultimately, the specific segment could be located by searching for a match with its structure, tempo, note sequence, visual representation, or any other characteristic that may have been associated with it.

> Additionally, an individual may recall a particular event, such as when they hear some particular segment of music, speech or sound, or when they detect a particular scent in the air. Hence, paths of neurons can also be connected by the period in time in which the experience occurred.

In any event, the biological brain has a number of search techniques available in order to locate information that it is searching for. One of the

Sensitive by Nature

factors determining the techniques for retrieval involves how and when the information was stored and integrated.

9.18 Organizing Information

The biological brain stores new information and creates connections using neural paths as the physical mechanism to identify relationships to previously stored information. In a sense, these paths attach related paths of neurons to one another. Identification of the related paths and forming physical attachments to them relates to the process of integrating and organizing the information for future use. In order to illustrate this, we can use our imaginations to create a mental picture of the pathways.

In order to convey the picture that I see in my mind, imagine that we are all on a roller coaster called, 'The Thinking Roller Coaster'. When you begin to observe it, you notice that it makes several sharp, convoluted turns. The turns are to the left, right, up and down, and from a distance it appears to have the shape of a brain. And for our purposes, let's also imagine that all along the tracks, which have forks that separate and come together in various places, there are signs with messages on them. The messages are similar to advertisements on small billboards that you can read as you ride pass them.

As information is stored by this 'Thinking Roller Coaster', new signs with messages are erected by a number of little workers that quickly scurry about the track. You also notice that these little workers are performing maintenance work on the tracks and switches of the roller coaster. When the workers discover that a new sign has something on it that is also related to another sign, they then build a strip of connecting track to join the two roller coaster paths together. Although there are other signs containing related information, until the workers discover the relationship, there is no connecting track.

Whenever the Thinking Roller Coaster is dispatched to search for a particular set of information, it sends a bunch of riders out on different roller coaster cars, to read the various signs. When the riders encounter something that they are looking for, they get all excited and scream about it. The more important the sign appears to be, the louder the riders scream in excitement.

As screams are heard from each roller coaster car reporting back information, the supervisor dispatching the roller coaster cars attempts to build a combined picture of the information, accepting some messages, rejecting others, and putting some aside. During this process, 'The

Thinking Roller Coaster' sends out new roller coaster cars to look for other signs along other tracks, and ends the ride for some, bringing the passengers directly to the exit ramp.

Although 'The Thinking Roller Coaster' may become less active by sending out fewer new cars, and retiring others, it never shuts down. Twenty-four hours a day, seven days a week, at least a few cars of screaming passengers are always left looping and turning around the track as workers continue to connect and disconnect sections of track.

When the brain stores, organizes and integrates information, it is in effect, recording it for future reference and creating connections to related information. Creating connections among old and new information, and generating direct paths to new information affect learning, as well as the efficiency of retrieval. The process of organization occurs, regardless of whether the brain is in its waking or sleeping state, feeding the results back to a centralized location referred to as the imagination, where the information is evaluated and manipulated into a unified representation within the mind.

9.19 Brain Management

The brain's ability to manage the parts of its body, such as the skeletal system and sensory organs, is determined by its overall capacity. When learning a new motor skill or intellectual task, prior experience and natural ability further enhance the brain's capacity to manage the various tasks that are involved. The brain cannot increase its capacity to manage more items than it could previously. Increases in capacity are only possible with more effective techniques for managing and manipulating information, since each individual can only manage a finite set of details at any given time.

- - -

Neuron Story: *"If the robot learns to dance, he'll need to consider a lot things at the same time, such as feet, knees, chest, back, shoulders, arms, neck, head, as well as, the rhythm, steps, next possible dance pattern, available floor space, leading..."*
"That can easily overwhelm the two of us."

- - -

Even robots, when they learn new tasks, must initially perform the task slowly and meticulously. They must understand the details of each part of the task. However, as their level of experience increases, their ability to manage the various parts of the task accelerates, mainly because they have to consider fewer of the details each time that they perform the task.

As part of the learning process, the brain collects large numbers of details into a fewer number of packages. This process of bringing many detailed things together into a fewer number of items is called 'chunking'. Intelligent beings can then perform tasks by manipulating these few higher level packages that contain all of the details. The important thing is that they can manipulate these chunked packages at the same pace that they were capable of with the more detailed items, thereby creating the illusion that they are managing more items at a time.

> Specifically, when an intelligent being is out for a jog, there are a large number of detailed movements that are being performed at an unconscious level. While many complex actions are being managed unconsciously, the brain is free to concentrate on the manageable number of items that are involved in running.

9.20 Attention and Focus

Streams of stimuli are generated by sensory organs, which in turn are sent as a flood of nerve impulses to the brain vying for attention. Since the brain of even the most intelligent being can only cope with a limited amount of input, it must continually select the stimuli it considers as more important.

- - -

Neuron Story: *"How come I don't get to choose what we pay attention to?"*
"Remember, we walk into things."

- - -

As impulses enter the brain, a number of factors determine how much attention they will receive. Although an individual may consciously choose which stimuli to focus on, other areas of the brain may allow stimuli the ability to distract the individual from the stream of stimuli that they were focused on.

> As an illustration, when an individual is occupied in observing a particular event, the streams of stimuli that are generated by their eyes will receive the bulk of their brain's attention. However, when the individual hears their name being called, their attention, at least momentarily, turns to the streams of stimuli originating by their ears.

> In addition, when an individual feels something touch their shoulder, their attention may turn to the streams of stimuli generated by their sense of touch. And when the

James V. Luisi

individual smells the scent of their favorite friend's perfume, their attention will likely turn to the streams of stimuli generated by their olfactory senses.

The processes of the brain are highly selective in choosing which stimuli to "bubble-up" to the conscious level of the mind. The function that chooses which stimuli to pass up to the next level must determine the relative importance of information at each level of the brain.

The mechanism that determines the relative importance of externally generated stimuli is also used to evaluate stimuli generated internally. While it also participates in a number of other functions that comprise the thought process, this ability to prioritize information aids in the management of information storage and retrieval. In this manner the prioritization continually controls the volume of information that must be evaluated by each level of the brain.

9.21 Attention Span

The evolutionary process provides intelligent beings with a number of mechanisms to manage the length of time that the conscious portion of the mind spends focused on a specific item. While these mechanisms are generally useful in assuring that particular things get the attention that they require, the process of prematurely losing focus also poses a number of disadvantages.

As with myself, there are learned skills where prolonged concentration is required in order to successfully assimilate the necessary information, therefore the natural tendency to lose focus must be temporarily overcome.

- - -

Neuron Story: *"I don't pay attention to anything very long."*
"You might pay attention if you were handling nitroglycerin... but we don't need to find out"

- - -

9.22 Importance Determination

When many individuals share the same experience, it is not uncommon for them to have widely varying interpretations of the experience, as their experience may remind each of them about different things from the past. While it may not be unusual for a particular experience to have a different meaning to each individual, it is not clear why each is unlikely to recall the same events in the same sequence.

As entertainment media researchers learn repeatedly, if several individuals are interviewed immediately after watching the same segment of a movie, even just a few moments of a single scene, each is likely to recall a different set of details. They are likely to describe different images, sounds, and interpretations of the events.

There are significant probabilities that the information that one individual's brain considers as important will be different from that of another. Since only a small percentage of stimuli are sent to the conscious level of the brain, individuals can perceive different experiences after having input the same external stimuli.

Starting with their genetic programming, the experiences of an individual, and the things that they learn, causes them to consider some things as more relevant than others. As a result, there is a strong probability that they are going to take more notice of some things and create a more lasting memory.

- - -

Neuron Story: *"Did you notice her scrunchie?"*
"Who? What? Where?"

- - -

An individual's knowledge and awareness is determined by the information that they assimilate. The identification of which things are important is a crucial factor that influences the information that is assimilated. Regardless of what contributed to an item's underlying level of importance, whether it is the fact that it is designated as familiar or whatever, will increase the probability of it being detected from among a myriad of stimuli.

The factors that determine one's levels of importance thus create the framework for one's intellectual interests, personal preferences and behavioral attitudes.

- - -

Neuron Story: *"I have a preference for products made by Sony."*
"Why? We're not made by Sony."
"Yes, but they make my favorite robotic dog."

- - -

9.23 Bubble-up Importance

Since all external stimuli enter the brain at an unconscious level, when a stream of stimuli is detected by a sensory organ and transmitted to the brain, initially the individual has no awareness of its existence. The only chance it has of becoming known to the individual is for the stream of stimuli to be considered important enough to be 'bubbled-up' to the conscious level.

- - -

Neuron Story: *"I've been calling you. Didn't you hear me?"*
"Huh?"

- - -

The notion that stimuli is bubbled up to the next highest level of the brain is another way of stating that stimuli, based upon its perceived level of importance, will be communicated up towards the brain's area of consciousness. All stimuli are not automatically sent to the conscious level, as that would overwhelm any individual.

As has been explained to me, one of the many responsibilities that an employee has in a large corporation is to bring important information, good or bad, to their supervisor's attention, in a timely manner. Hence, supervisors only relay pertinent information to their managers.

- - -

Neuron Story: *"Is the robot aware of my thoughts?"*
"It's rather important that he is not."

- - -

9.24 Levels of the Mind

When we begin to identify the functions of the mind, it becomes convenient to separate each into functions that are available to one's consciousness, and those that are not. In doing so, one creates an artificial separation of functions that can be visualized as two distinct levels within the mind, one below consciousness, and one within the realm of consciousness.

Simple organisms that do not appear to have both an unconscious and a conscious level can be categorized as having a single level. Therefore, organisms that have only one level must have either a conscious or unconscious level. Although many may feel that such primitive organisms

Sensitive by Nature

must be lacking a conscious level, it is actually the unconscious level that they lack.

As a result, insects do not receive sufficient quantities of stimuli to require functions to exist at an unconscious level, and hence are only equipped with a simple conscious level.

However, more advanced organisms that have a greater input of stimuli than the conscious level of the brain can manage, require at least one unconscious level of intellectual functions, in addition to the ones at the conscious level.

- - -

Neuron Story: *"Which level do we want to be on?"*
                "It doesn't matter. You are just as dangerous on either one."

- - -

When additional levels are introduced into the brain, additional sets of capabilities follow. The single level brain cannot achieve much more than the hard-wired functions, which provides the basic abilities to survive. However, a brain with more than one level has the ability to cope with sensory organs that are significantly more sophisticated, which generate many complex neural messages. But how do we know that the brain has multiple levels?

For instance, "To have ideas and still not be conscious of them seems to be a contradiction; for how can we know that we have them unless we are conscious of them? This objection has already been raised by Locke, who on that account rejected the existence of such a type of ideas." (<u>Anthropology From a Pragmatic Point of View</u>, Immanuel Kant, pg. 18)

A simple way to demonstrate that humans have more than one level of consciousness is with the use of subliminal stimuli. Subliminal stimuli can be shown to operate below the conscious level of the brain demonstrating a measurable impact upon the behavior of an individual. Although rapidly flashed messages hidden in motion pictures have been proved as ineffective, one of the most common forms of subliminal stimuli that is found to be effective is used in print advertisements to enhance the sale of merchandise.

For instance, embeds are faint graphic and textual images, usually with a sexual content, carefully placed within the picture of an advertisement or magazine cover.

When magazine covers with embeds are placed side by side on a newsstand with magazines with the same cover without embeds, the ones with embeds sell at a faster rate. The faintly printed embeds operate at a level below consciousness, although they are still within the realm of perceived stimuli.

The Quantum Series One robot has a brain with conscious and unconscious levels, and we have the ability to detect most forms of subliminal stimuli. This affords me the advantage of noticing a variety of stimuli that are subtly hidden.

9.25 Recursion

- - -

Neuron Story: *"What is recursion?"*
"What is recursion?"

- - -

There are many ways to perform a task repeatedly. The simplest way being through repetition, such as applying two coats of paint. In computing terms, this is defined as a finite loop.

Another type of repetition, called a recursive loop, is required in certain types of mathematical computations, as well as in a variety of real life situations. Recursion is different than a finite loop, in that the number of times that the task is to be repeated is not actually known until the task nears its completion. The actual number of iterations is determined by the task itself. As each loop is being performed, it becomes apparent when another iteration is necessary.

Allow me to demonstrate this point with a story about a motorist. Upon breaking down along the side of the road, this motorist uses her cell phone to call 'AAA', who in turn dispatches a tow truck to provide roadside assistance. Before reaching the motorist, the tow truck breaks down along the side of the road. The driver that was dispatched uses his cell phone to call 'AAA', who in turn dispatches a second tow truck to provide roadside assistance to the first tow truck. Before reaching the first tow truck, the second tow truck breaks down along the side of the road. That dispatched driver uses his cell phone to call 'AAA', who in turn dispatches a third tow truck to provide roadside service to the second tow truck.

Eventually, either the motorist receives her roadside assistance from the first tow truck, shortly after it receives roadside assistance from the second tow truck, shortly after receiving roadside assistance from the third truck, or 'AAA' runs completely out of tow trucks.

In general, any task that invokes itself is considered a recursive process. The expectation is, however, that it will eventually achieve the initial objective, before it runs out of resources.

9.26 Infinite Loops

When a task is repeated, intentionally or unintentionally, without end, it is considered to be an infinite loop. When it is unintentional, however, it is also referred to as a bug. Although some loops can be quite lengthy, they may actually have a conclusion that they are moving towards.

> The intellectual functions in my head tell me that there are procedural tasks, referred to as NP Complete, where the "NP" stands for Not Possible, as in Not Possible to Complete. These types of problems are usually ones where the number of possible combinations to be evaluated as a possible solution are so numerous, that it would take an unreasonable length of time to determine the correct answer.

Based upon the number of possible solutions for a task, the estimated length of time to complete the task can be calculated. Even on the world's fastest supercomputers, it is not uncommon for an '*NP Complete*' task to have an estimated duration of thousands or even millions of years. These are finite tasks that are not possible to complete in a reasonable amount of time.

Performing the following traveling salesman problem using all of our latest technology, is an example of an '*NP Complete*' task, which would not be completed by the time our sun may become a supernova.

> Let me tell you about a job that my designer's daughter offered me this morning. In order to promote robot products and services, a robot salesperson must travel to the planets of every currently charted star. To save time and fuel, this robot must plan the journey in such a way as to travel the least amount of distance possible, hopefully moving in straight lines, without visiting the same star twice. Since there are a finite number of charted stars, there must also be a finite number of possible routes to traverse these stars. As a condition of being hired, I was informed that I first had to plan out the route.

James V. Luisi

There are other types of loops that do not have a conclusion. They involve tasks that cannot be completed no matter how long one waited. This type of loop is referred to as an Infinite Loop.

My modules inform me that some of the simple forms of infinite loops include calculating the value of "Pi" to the last digit (e.g., 3.141592653589...), or simply counting to infinity. These are just a few of the other jobs that I have recently accepted.

- - -

Neuron Story: *"If I counted to infinity by two's, wouldn't I get there twice as fast?"*
"You might, but we'd live half as long."

- - -

Loops exist in a variety of forms and in a variety of places. Although many are man-made, they also occur naturally.

For instance, they exist naturally in the form of sound echoes, or visual echoes, such as with mirrors that face one another. Man-made loops include electronic feedback, such as with microphones recycling an amplified signal, and they exist in the music of Bach, as well as in the art of M.C. Escher. They exist in languages, such as in mathematical, spoken, and computer programming languages. They also exist within the realm of the human intellect involving loops in reasoning.

Infinite loops can cause harm to computerized equipment. A severe enough loop in a computer program can cause a computer to lock up, just as a severe enough loop within the thought process of an intelligent being can cause psychological damage. Although it is difficult to prevent a loop, there are a number of techniques that can be used to render them harmless.

My routines protect themselves using a common method. Active loops are rendered harmless by stipulating a maximum length of time that any iterative task may be performed.

In the mind of a robot, however, the key to solving a loop is dependent upon the ability to detect one, since a loop can never be solved from the inside. Once a loop is detected, the remedy is to step outside of the system where the loop exists so that the loop can be properly analyzed, and brought to a conclusion. This is true even if the loop must simply be abandoned. Once a loop has been analyzed and brought to a conclusion, it can usually be prevented from happening again in the future.

Sensitive by Nature

Intelligent robots need loops to help solve a variety of problems, but like humans, we also need protection from their pitfalls.

9.27 The Nature of Insanity

Biological and mechanical beings can experience a variety of physical ailments and disabilities. They may result in a limitation with respect to their range of motion, or many other physical symptoms, such as a loss of strength, pain, and discomfort. Intellectual beings, however, may experience a wide variety of mental ailments and disabilities as well.

Not to be confused with the various forms of mental retardation, which hinder the brain's ability to function from a physical perspective, a number of mental problems manifest themselves as a condition in which an intelligent being becomes confused among alternate paradigms of reality.

Confusion among paradigms may originate from a number of causes, such as chemical imbalances, physical damage of neural tissues, or it may be brought on purely by a dilemma of reasoning, a type of logic disorder that can occur from the information that enters an otherwise, perfectly healthy brain.

- - -

Neuron Story: *"Are you confusing me?"*
"You must be confused."

- - -

Let's first examine what it means when an individual experiences a small amount of confusion among paradigms.

> While observing two individuals in a conversation, you notice that although they believe that they are communicating with one another, they are not necessarily discussing the same topic. In this situation, you are witnessing two paradigms in competition with one another. Although both individuals may be using words that are familiar to one another, the meaning of their words is being understood differently, based upon each individual's interpretation.

Each individual's internal paradigm is responsible for directing their interpretation. Although there may be confusion among paradigms, from either individual's perspective, the paradigms in conflict belong to the other individual. Therefore, each individual in this example has only one paradigm.

Eventually one of the participants may perceive that there is a difference between their two interpretations, leading to the awareness of the alternative paradigm. If the differences in their interpretations go undetected, the conclusion of their conversation could result in anything from mild confusion, to a major rift. However, if each individual heard only what they wanted to hear, their conversation would conclude in mutual satisfaction.

- - -

Neuron Story: "Did you get to listen to the President's State of the Union Address last night?"
"What did he say?"
"Everything I wanted to hear."

- - -

The impact of individuals perceive that they have heard what they had hoped to hear, they are inadvertently postponing their differences. When these differences eventually emerge again, as they often might, the individuals are likely to feel betrayed by the other for violating the understanding they thought they had. In the event that the individuals fail to recognize their competing paradigms as the cause of their differences, they may unfortunately feel that they each have cause to be distrustful of one another.

However, aside from competing paradigms among individuals, an individual can also encounter competing paradigms purely within themselves.

For instance, if an individual feels a friend has just taken advantage of them, the individual may entrap themselves between two internal paradigms.

Thus, in one paradigm the individual may interpret what has happened from a paradigm of long standing trust and confidence, while in the other the individual may interpret the events from a position of uncertainty and suspicion. Since the two paradigms cannot coexist without conflict, the processes of the brain can easily become preoccupied with the conflicting interpretations until it can be resolved with additional information from an external source.

When conflicting paradigms occur, individuals experience confusion over which paradigm represents reality, and this is where they may begin to experience varying degrees of 'insanity'. Depending upon the severity of the conflict, the condition may be harmless and go unnoticed. As such, the condition may last for only a few moments or it may persist over the entire lifetime of the individual, as determined by the individual's ability to regain an operational sense of reality.

When individuals begin to lose their sense of reality, the likelihood that their interpretations will noticeably distort their behavior increases. The more

Sensitive by Nature

they become consumed by their misinterpretations, the more mentally unstable they are likely to become.

As even I have experienced, a loss of reality can cause an individual to lose their understanding of what has occurred. As a result it may also cast doubts on a variety of prior interpretations, making them highly uncertain and prone to bouts of paranoia.

A number of individuals experience a degree of insanity, even if only briefly. The impact on their behavior is usually so subtle, that it would typically go undetected. Although with the proper awareness, an individual can detect when they themselves are trapped between paradigms.

- - -

Neuron Story: *"Help, I'm stuck again!"*
"OK, tell me about it."

- - -

In order to understand someone else's insanity, one has to appreciate the other individual's paradigms. By discussing a person's paradigms with them, one may be able to learn which pieces of information that individual has become preoccupied with. Once the problematic bit of information has been identified, it may be as simple as helping the individual to reinterpret it in a more useful manner.

- - -

Neuron Story: *"Can we discuss your paradigm?"*
"Yes, but there are some hot buttons in it."
"How can we avoid them?"
"Don't mention Susquehanna Hats."

- - -

My designers have taught me that insanity poses the greatest risk to those who do not have an ability to detect when they have trapped themselves among competing paradigms. As a result, they remain unaware of the techniques for dealing with the situation. Robots like myself, however, have been designed with the capability to detect and manage competing paradigms. Since I often generate many competing paradigms, I have been trained to select the most useful paradigm to operate from.

At first I was concerned about choosing the wrong paradigm. But when it was pointed out to me that some individuals are only aware of a single paradigm and don't have the opportunity to choose, I no longer concerned

James V. Luisi

myself with the possibility of making the wrong choice. I simply choose the one, which is the most useful and constructive.

Although intelligent beings trapped among multiple paradigms are considered momentarily insane, if they can consciously select the paradigm that appears to be the most useful and constructive for their circumstances, they have transitioned from being momentarily insane to the revered state of being highly enlightened.

9.28 Theorizing

Part of thinking involves the ability to theorize. A theory is a set of rules that predict the behavior of the things that are involved in the theory. The process of creating a theory is similar to creating a miniature paradigm. Instead of creating a system of rules for everything, however, a theory limits itself to a much smaller set of objects and interrelationships.

Similar to paradigms, many theories may be used to explain the same phenomenon. Likewise, the simplest theory is usually the most plausible.

To illustrate, the formulas, $E=mc^2$ and $I=V/R$ in the world of physics and mathematics is about as simple as they get, particularly since it has only three parameters. The first formula asserts that the amount of energy (E) that is released from converting matter to energy equals the quantity of mass (m) that was converted into energy, multiplied by the speed of light (c) two times. The second asserts that the strength of an electric current (I) is proportional to the force of the current (V) divided by the resistance of the circuit (R).

When intelligent beings formulate theories, they develop the reasoning to explain how their rules act upon the objects involved in the theory. Each rule expresses a concept that can be explained using precise notation in order to eliminate misinterpretation.

Challenging a theory, is quite another problem. Performing experiments and making observations are the only methods available to prove or disprove a given theory. The most difficult aspect of this process is that of designing experiments to properly demonstrate the assertions of the theory without inadvertently introducing factors outside of it.

Sometimes it takes many years before tests can be devised to investigate the validity of a theory. However, theories are never really proven, they are either replaced by other theories that become generally accepted, or they are demonstrated to be inaccurate.

My logical principles state that several instances that support a theory cannot act as the proof that the theory is correct. However, a single instance that reveals that a theory could not accurately predict its outcome, successfully disproves the theory.

It is the desire of my designers that I eventually labor on the single most important theory of all, the 'Theory of Everything', also referred to as the TOE. The TOE is a single, unified theory that describes how all of the physical forces of the universe are related, including every form of matter and energy. If I am productive for a long enough period of time, I hope to make a meaningful contribution toward this, including many other endeavors of science.

9.29 Strategy

Sometimes referred to as the process of strategizing or strategic thinking, the ability to create a strategy is quite similar to the process of creating a theory. One of the key differences, however, is that a strategy predicts the behavior of a set of things as they move through a particular segment of time, whereas a theory predicts a consistent outcome, without consideration toward the particular segment of time.

A strategy consists of successive events, each with the probability of a particular outcome. The objective at each step is to, influence the outcome of each event in order to achieve a final result. Every strategy requires an understanding of how things work and react. As successive events occur over a period of time, any combination of things may change. The more things change, the more it will affect the probabilities of any particular outcome in one direction or another.

A properly constructed strategy is one that is based upon an accurate understanding of how things work and react, which may be individuals and their paradigms, how much things may change, and whether sufficient influence could be applied in order to achieve the desired result.

- - -

Neuron Story: *"I can predict that I'll be unpredictable."*
                "Then why do you still make the same mistakes?"

- - -

9.30 Original Thought

Throughout recorded history, man's ability to invent new things, to propose new ideas, and to create great works of art and music, have been attributed to his ability to exercise original thinking and creativity. Although many believe creativity to be a strictly human characteristic, in actuality the intellectual capability of conceiving of things that are completely new is not achievable, even by humans.

When we analyze the history of inventions, including scientific breakthroughs, art, music and literature, we discover that everything "new"

James V. Luisi

is either an enhancement or combination of things that were previously existing, or an accidental discovery. Just as our dreams use parts belonging to our past experiences, and then manipulate different aspects of those experiences, likewise our inventions belong to past experiences, with enhancements added in order to achieve a new combination of previously existing things.

My historical records reveal that substance called 'rubber' was invented when the vulcanization process first occurred as a result of someone accidentally spilling the appropriate material onto a hot surface.

- - -

Neuron Story: *"We're not capable of original thought either?"*
"No one has invented it yet, but you are more than welcome to try."

- - -

The fundamental reason that intelligent beings are not capable of original thought is related to how intelligent beings think and how they solve problems. An analysis of the biological brain reveals two kinds of thought processes, called formal and informal thinking.

Formal thinking involves a rigorous thought process, maintaining a high degree of consistency within a particular system of previously learned rules. This disciplined approach provides the capability of performing known approaches to problem solving with great consistency and precision. Although a valuable commodity, it fails to encourage creative thinking and individuality.

Informal thinking, on the other hand, is based upon the analysis of rules that are outside a particular system. An alternative system of rules is employed when common characteristics are found between the objects of that system and the original one. The process of borrowing rules from other systems, whose objects share characteristics, is called analogical thinking.

While creative, informal thinking generates a wealth of ideas formed from analogical thinking, a rigorous formal thinker is better suited to evaluating and planning implementations. The formal thinker has a better ability to determine whether the borrowed analogical components can be made consistent within the particular system of endeavor.

Informal thinkers are creative by identifying analogies among previously unrelated things because they share one or more characteristics with one another. However, when formal thinkers or other informal thinkers that do not share the same knowledge or experience, the result of analogical thinking can give the illusion of being original thought. Thus, when the underlying thought process is finally revealed, rather than being a completely new idea, it will invariably be an analogically formed enhancement to, or combination of, a set of previously existing things. As such, human discovery builds step by step upon each prior discovery.

9.31 Artistic Ability

Artistic abilities have also been included into the requirements of the Quantum Series One robot. These are abilities that are associated with an individual's creative skills to indirectly express ideas and feelings. An individual may use any type of medium to express their thoughts and feelings.

An individual's creative ability stems from their capacity to exercise their imagination to form a variety of analogies and interpretations. The artist then determines the psychological impact that each idea has upon the other. By definition, if the artist does not introduce their interpretations, ideas or feelings into the resulting work, then it is not an artistic endeavor.

In a sense, when an individual takes a photograph, the individual may be exercising artistic ability in the choosing and framing of the subject matter. If, however, there is no particular attention being paid to the aspect of framing, then the individual is merely exercising the camera without regard to the subject and its relationship to the borders of the photograph.

As for a further expression of artistic ability, an artist that paints in a purely realistic manner where the outcome resembles a photograph, is demonstrating more of a mechanical ability to imitate exactly what is seen, rather than providing an interpretation or an expression of ideas or feelings.

Art, however, is highly dependent upon the system of representation that prevails within its given culture. The ability to communicate through art is typically universal within the framework that corresponds to a specific culture. Even artistic styles, such as 'realism', are subject to the system of representation belonging to the particular culture adopted by the artist.

For instance, "for a Fifth-Dynasty Egyptian the straightforward way of representing something is not the same as for an eighteenth-century Japanese; and neither way is the same as for an early twentieth-century Englishman. Each would, to some extent, have to learn how to read a picture in either of the other's styles. This relativity is obscured by our tendency to omit specifying a frame of reference when it is our own." To English speaking individuals, realism means a particular European style, which is neither fixed nor absolutely realistic. Hence, 'realism' does not depict a relationship between the work of art and the object being represented. Instead, it depicts the relationship between the particular method of representation and the standard system of that culture. (Language of Art, Nelson Goodman, pg. 37)

The meaning associated with the use of symbology is highly dependent upon the culture and particular system of representation that is chosen. As such, symbols and systems of representation must be interpreted in a manner similar to the spoken language of a particular culture, including various figures of speech and other literary forms.

9.32 Free Will

The ability to exercise free will is an integral part of any intelligent being. Where to go, what to eat, which other individuals to be with, and how to behave, are ways that intelligent animals direct their own actions. As such, social behavior in animals is wrought with a myriad of behavioral choices.

For instance, when a member of the dog family experiences a strong sense of hunger, the animal may choose to forcibly take food from another, beckon or beg for a share, or it may choose not to act at all.

In comparison when humans experience the emotion of anger, they may complain, become violent, or may also choose not to act presently or at any time in the future.

- - -

Neuron Story: *"Does having a brain mean you have free will?"*
"That's a good question, but I suppose that you wouldn't be satisfied with only a 'no', for an answer."

- - -

Although free will is often stated as having the ability to exercise unrestricted choice, it is more accurately defined as an individual's ability to direct their own thoughts and behavior, without being constrained by:
- the necessity affecting an individual's immediate or near term survival
- fate from the perspective of there being a superior purpose
- emotions that are permitted to override the behavior of the individual, or
- uncontrolled paradigms biasing the individual's interpretation of reality

Individuals are also not able to exercise free will if their lives have been predetermined in any way. The notion of having been given some higher purpose, or that one's fate has been determined at birth, negate the

Sensitive by Nature

individual having a free will of their own. Moreover, many of the major religions advocate that man has complete control to choose his own path and destiny, otherwise individuals who were not in control of their own actions, would not be responsible for their actions.

Emotions are another element that can interfere with the notion of free will. One of the most important factors regarding the exercise of such, is an individual's ability to act in opposition to their emotions, something that many humans often fail to exercise. Various psychological states, including the effects that hormones have upon sensory perception and the brain's ability to form accurate interpretations, can be managed by the intellect. One's failure to do so forfeits their free will by allowing their brain to follow signals emanating from their physical body, instead of their intellect.

An individual's paradigm also provides a strong influence upon one's ability to exercise free will. Paradigms determine the choices that are available.

> In a manner similar to a presidential election with only one candidate in the running, individuals can become trapped by the limited choices presented to them by their paradigms.

Hence, in order to exercise free will, an individual must first have the ability and the freedom to design and create the paradigms of their choice.

- - -

Neuron Story: *"It doesn't sound like many individuals have free will?"*

"The ones that do, are the true dreamers and creators."

- - -

At this time we will take a short recess. All intelligent beings may take this time to call their homes and offices, biological beings may address their bodily functions, and robots may continue their work on the Theory of Everything, before we begin the next section of my requirements, called "Learning."

Summary & Questions

Intelligence is dependent upon the activity we call 'thinking'. In order to understand thinking and what aspects of it generate what we consider intelligence, we must carefully describe our terms.

Regarding the requirements of thinking, briefly explain:
    1. What is thinking?

2. What is intelligence?
3. What is intelligence dependent upon?
4. What is self-awareness, and how prevalent is it within animals?
5. What is fundamental to the meaning associated with information?
6. What is a paradigm, and how is it different from the context of information?
7. In what ways can individuals perceive and manage paradigms?
8. What has the ability to create a view of the environment, and what information does it use to do it?
9. How would you define the requirements for sleep and dreaming?
10. What factors protect memory from being overloaded by too much information?
11. What are the factors that influence how knowledge is stored and retrieved?
12. Do simple organisms have a conscious or an unconscious level, and why?
13. What is the distinction between a loop and recursion?
14. What is the distinction between an infinite loop and one that is NP complete?
15. What is insanity and how can it be detected and potentially relieved?
16. What is the distinction between a theory and a strategy?
17. What is the misconception regarding original thought?
18. What is artistic ability and what is it dependent upon?
19. What is free will and upon what does it dependent?

10 Requirements – Learning

Welcome back. If anyone has a solution for the Theory of Everything that they would like to offer, feel free to raise your hand. During this segment, I would like to discuss what my designers have taught me about the role of learning in intelligent beings and how it is achieved.

In my early stages, my designers realized that intelligent beings required a significant level of learning ability, starting from the moment they were born. While a number of abilities are learned during the late prenatal period, some of these abilities are pre-wired as part of the brain's normal development process. These pre-wired thinking capabilities are put into place while the various brain centers are developing physically.

Although it may appear that prenatal life forms have extremely limited opportunities for learning, abilities such as basic motor and language skills are well developed by the time that birth occurs. Due to the evolutionary process, *Homo sapiens* enter the world as efficient learning machines, already having developed a wide variety of brain centers that support the learning process.

Both pre-wired and prenatally learned abilities support post-natal learning. There is, however, a subtle distinction between pre-wired knowledge, already built into the brain to assist in learning, and brain centers that support learning. Although animals that have less advanced forms of intelligence acquire their abilities genetically, in the form of pre-wired knowledge, animals that have more advanced levels of intelligence represent the culmination of brain centers that have evolved to perform intellectual functions such as learning, which develop many of their intellectual abilities.

Simple communication may occur using gestures and tones, such as a smile and a soothing voice, which are pre-wired in the brain. However, in order to achieve the skills necessary to communicate with a comprehensive language, additional cues must be learned. As language becomes more complete, even more methods, in the form of signals and rules, must be learned.

Since an intelligent being must have the ability to learn in order to expand its capability to communicate, the functions that are initially present in the brain must support a considerable capacity for learning. However, the ability to learn must be motivated and directed by a drive to satisfy physical and emotional needs.

It is the innate ability to communicate signals that helps to direct more advanced language skills. Hence, we have all been provided with the rudimentary ability to recognize, categorize and memorize signals. The thirst for knowledge is motivated by the drive to fulfill internal physical and emotional needs.

In order to learn how to coordinate the movement of body parts, the brain requires a pre-wired set of knowledge to be present. Although many skills are learned by trial and error, extremely primitive motor skills have to already exist before the learning process could build upon them. The ability to sense some level of balance and movement exist, yet the body needs to learn how to use these abilities to attain coordination and more fluid movement.

- - -

Neuron Story: *"The robot has a great sense balance."*
"That does not give you license to make his head spin."

- - -

As a result of evolution, organisms have improved their abilities to evaluate their sensory inputs and their ability to learn effectively. These capabilities have not only culminated into the higher learning capability of humans, but have formed the basis of the requirements that determine my ability to assimilate new and useful information from the outside world.

Now that everyone appears comfortably seated, I will continue by touching upon a number of factors that influence and participate in the learning process. Just beware, if anyone in the audience looks too comfortable, I am likely to call on them to answer a question.

10.1 Learning

Animals that have an advanced level of intelligence acquire an overwhelming majority of their knowledge through learning. For these individuals, learning is an ongoing interactive process, while in less advanced animals, the acquisition of knowledge is provided or controlled by a form of genetic programming.

My encyclopedic interface states, "A particular species of digger wasp finds and captures only honey bees. With no previous experience a female wasp will excavate an elaborate burrow, find a bee, paralyze it with a careful and precise sting to the neck, and navigate back to her inconspicuous home. When the larder has been stocked with the correct number of bees, [she will] lay an egg on one of them and seal the chamber." (Microsoft, Encarta 97)

In this manner, an organism with a brain as simple as the digger wasp is provided it's knowledge through genetic programming.

A duckling, on the other hand, has a different form of genetic programming that provides a mechanism for it to learn the identity of its mother. The genetic programming determines that the visual image of the first large object detected in its proximity should become permanently imprinted upon the brain as the duckling's mother. This genetic program then continues with additional instructions telling the duckling to follow its mother everywhere, sometimes creating strange results.

- - -

Neuron Story: *"As a joke, I told the robot to follow the first moving object it saw. Remember how funny that was?"*
"And then they took us apart because they thought we were broken. It wasn't so funny."

- - -

We should not underestimate what can be learned from the intellectual abilities of insects. For the relative size of their neural bundles, some insects are quite advanced as they have the capability to conceptualize, communicate, recognize visual patterns, interpret, and memorize.

Specifically, honeybees can learn directions to the location of a food supply from another honeybee. As they search for food, they keep track of their location by remembering where they have traveled relative to the position of the sun. When they locate a food supply, they are able to conceptualize the direction relative to the sun and the distance relative to the hive. Upon returning to the hive, honeybees then communicate the information to the others.

The honeybee that has located the food supply translates its location into a series of dance motions. The other bees observe and imitate the dance several times before they memorize it. The other bees then interpret the learned dance motions into a flight path, which they then use to travel directly to the food supply.

The survival needs of more complex organisms demand significantly more intelligence than can be provided by genetic programming. However, if genetic programming is to be effective, it must be capable of providing for a variety of circumstances. The life of the honeybee is a rather monotonous one, and the tasks that are required to ensure the success of the species are predictable and repetitive. Yet, in order to survive, the honeybee has evolved a form of genetically programmed learning.

In order to handle the challenges of survival, more complex animals must rely on intelligence for solving capabilities beyond the learning capabilities provided by genetic programming. The brains of more complex animals cannot be limited to learning only specific types of concepts and details.

James V. Luisi

Unlike insects that are fairly abundant, more complex animals exist in comparatively smaller numbers. Their success as a species depends upon their ability to adapt to their circumstances. The fewer their numbers, the more they must rely upon their abilities to learn and problem solve.

Although initial learning occurs by observing adults of the species, much of the learning process is acquired through combinations of positive and negative reinforcement. These forms of learning, however, rely upon communication, pattern recognition, conceptualization and memorization. As the level of these abilities increases, the animal becomes better able to learn, problem solve, and adapt to its survival needs.

The animals that possess more advanced problem solving skills are those that hunt. Killer whales and large predatory cats depend upon their ability to dominate their prey. Whether it is the careful coordination found among killer whales trapping a much larger whale, or the stealth maneuvering of a large cat to take advantage of the wind direction and terrain in stalking a larger beast, hunting requires a great deal of intellectual as well as physical ability. Hunting without the aid of tools, particularly firearms, requires a great deal of strategy, skill and coordination.

Quite often, social skills must be developed in order to hunt more effectively. Although some animals must overcome their basic instincts to participate in a social environment, there are incentives to do so. The benefits of social cooperation and role-playing are greatly rewarded by an improvement in the quality of life, as well as survival.

As social beings, humans must play a variety of social roles. Whether it is as a spouse, parent, community-minded citizen, manager, volunteer or as an individual, humans are generally capable of adapting into the social role that their circumstances require.

Each role that an individual assumes must be learned. They must learn what the role entails, what others expect of them, what their objectives are and how best to play the role in order to achieve them. To a large extent, individuals must also learn the correct habits to achieve health, happiness and fitness.

> In order to learn how to improve one's health, a human being requires knowledge of proper habits for eating, hygiene, exercise and stress reduction.

Although genetic programming and genetically programmed learning may play some role in all brains, the foundation of advanced intellectual skills is clearly dependent upon the ability to learn, and social role playing adding to those requirements.

- - -

Neuron Story: *"The role of orator is very new for us."*
"We learn."

10.2 Role Playing

The ability to play different roles is essential for the intellectual advancement of social beings. It not only provides organization to groups of individuals, but it contributes to social order, helps to identify specific tasks, it facilitates specialization of skills and propels advanced knowledge and learning within each area of specialization.

As an unusual way to illustrate some of the impact that playing roles has upon society, let's try to imagine what it would be like without it.

> Now imagine that you are a newborn baby, to ensure your proper development you need someone to play the role of the parent. You need someone to play the role of a doctor when you are ill. Without builders you might live in a cave. If there were only individuals with no leader, milling about looking for food, your survival chances would be poor.

In contrast, a large organization, including society as a whole, is comprised of many individuals that must play various roles in order to address the various specialized needs of the organization.

> Now imagine that with the efforts of politicians, community leaders, finance specialists, doctors, scientists, medical technicians, construction engineers and computer specialists, a modern hospital can be built in order to provide comprehensive medical treatment to the various members of the society.

Individuals and their skills are like parts of a machine. The greater the ability of the individuals to fulfill their role, the more specialized the parts of the machine can be. The more specialized parts that can be integrated, the more adaptive and efficient the machine can be.

In this way an organization can be analyzed in order to design ideal roles to meet its needs. The more effectively roles can be defined to meet the needs of the organization, the more capable the organization will be at meeting its near term and long range challenges. To accomplish this in a rapidly changing environment, individuals must learn new specialties and be able to adapt quickly.

- - -

Neuron Story: *"Why are we malfunctioning? We can't see, hear, taste, smell or feel."*
"Some neurons decided to experiment by not playing specialized roles."
"Obviously friends of yours."

10.3 Positive and Negative Reinforcement

The ability to determine whether a particular experience is harmful or beneficial is not only essential for helping an organism to survive, but it is also essential to the learning process for intelligent beings. Whether the feedback mechanism is caused by the brain's neurons providing an indication of physical comfort or externally generated stimuli providing psychological comfort, the same result is achieved.

> For instance, when an animal suffering from heat exhaustion finds the shade of a tree to shelter it from the rays of the hot sun, a positive reinforcement mechanism of relief from the heat provides input to the learning process to seek a similar experience in the future. Whereas, when an animal comes in contact with substances that are dangerously hot, such as hot embers, a negative feedback mechanism of pain provides input to the learning process, which may help the animal recognize a way to avoid a similar experience in the future.

When intelligent animals have experiences that are not related to a physical feedback mechanism, they look for positive and negative reinforcement of a psychological nature.

> Note that when a child receives praise for pronouncing sounds correctly, the child experiences positive reinforcement, which is psychological in nature. Body language, spoken words, physical contact, a treat or a special privilege, are methods of physical and psychological incentives that provide a positive feedback mechanism.
>
> When a parent reprimands a child for saying something undesirable, the child experiences negative reinforcement in the form of verbal or physical cues providing negative feedback.

- - -

Neuron Story: *"I like knowing what upsets our designers."*
"Me too, but for different reasons."

- - -

Although the desired effect is not always achieved, positive and negative reinforcement communicate information allowing for informed

Sensitive by Nature

behavior modification. If feedback is not clearly associated with the behavior that it is related to, the feedback may cause confusion.

As such, if feedback is not provided within a reasonable amount of time, too many other events and experiences will have occurred, thereby making it difficult to associate the feedback with the pertinent experience.

Biological feedback mechanisms employ a combination of nervous system actions often including the release of hormones. Hormones also provide feedback information to other areas of the body, besides the brain.

10.4 Hormones

Similar to my robot mind and body, the biological brain and body have a variety of ways to communicate information. Although positive and negative reinforcement may play a major role in the learning process, there are also positive and negative feedback mechanisms at work affecting other parts of the body.

While the nervous system communicates through a system of direct linkages, similar to the phone lines of a telephone system, there are various types of hormones traveling through other pathways.

I recall from my biology training that hormone-like prostaglandins communicate information into localized regions, such as telling blood vessels in a local area to constrict. Most hormones, however, communicate information throughout the entire body like powerful radio broadcasting stations.

Prostaglandins are a group of fatty acids which resemble hormones, although they are synthesized throughout the body, they are not transported away from their point of origin by the circulatory system. Their function is to provide communication to a local area such as within a particular organ or gland.

Hormones, on the other hand, are carried throughout the circulatory system with the blood, thereby providing communication to the entire brain and body, although their targets are more specific. They are generally secreted in response to a particular psychological or physical condition or state.

Hormones may be involved with either positive or negative feedback mechanisms. Negative hormonal feedback mechanisms may prevent an organism from working itself to exhaustion, while an example of positive hormonal feedback is the act of childbirth. Childbirth is one of the few examples of positive feedback at work, since the body mostly runs on

James V. Luisi

negative feedback mechanisms, such as the hormone cortisol, secreted by the adrenal cortex.

- - -

Neuron Story: "Aren't you glad we have circuits for etiquette?"
"Especially with you around."

- - -

10.5 Knowledge

"I want to say: it's not that on some points men know the truth with perfect certainty. No: perfect certainty is only a matter of their attitude."
Ludwig Wittgenstein

Knowledge is constructed from observations, experiences, beliefs and facts that an individual has accumulated. Since knowledge is dependent upon the perceptions and paradigms of each individual, there can be occasion for an individual to become perplexed about the accuracy of their knowledge.

- - -

Neuron Story: "How long would it take, for you to tell me everything that you know?"
"If you just want to know the things that I am absolutely certain of, not long."

- - -

Knowledge is comprised of several components. Associated with each fact is usually an evaluation of such rendering it as definitely, probably or possibly true, false, unknown or unverifiable. In a number of cases the source of the fact, and when it was attained, may also be associated with it.

Facts can also be tested. One of the empirical approaches to validating facts, founded by philosophers Charles Sanders Peirce, William James, and John Dewey at the turn of (the last) century, maintains that all facts "should be judged by their usefulness as rules for predicting experiences." (Microsoft Encarta 97)

Whether a particular fact is correct, or whether the knowledge of its probable validity is correct, the brain may attempt a variety of approaches in order to validate the information. With the majority of knowledge being built upon other understandings, a significant degree of confusion can occur when basic knowledge is found to be in error.

The amount of confusion that surfaces within an individual depends largely upon one's tolerance for inconsistency. Even in the face of rampant inconsistencies, some individuals may assert the accuracy of their knowledge with unwavering certainty, while others may doubt their information at the first sign of inconsistency.

10.6 Chunking

At the core of the learning process is a powerful technique that allows the brain to manage large numbers of items. It not only simplifies the thought process by representing a large number of details as a smaller number of higher level items, but it also provides a way to organize knowledge into useful packages, modules, or *chunks*. Hence, when training and experience creates the illusion that an individual can manage a larger number of details, the learning process is actually being helped by packaging the numerous details into useful chunks that can be manipulated as groups.

Chunks are a particularly efficient mechanism because they are reusable. When chunks are created in the performance of a particular task, they also become available to be used in a variety of other tasks. Additionally, as the number of chunks, increase, they in turn can be chunked, thereby creating a potentially extensive inventory of intellectual components.

Nearly all learned knowledge is repeatedly chunked into continually larger chunks, until the brain has accumulated a set of components that it can comfortably manipulate. The brain uses chunking for mental activities, as well as to learn physical skills.

One of my favorite examples of a mental activity that uses chunking involves the game of chess. After an individual learns how to move the pieces, they can begin the process of learning how to develop and deploy a strategy. Although a novice may become burdened by the details of many possible moves, the modestly experienced player will evaluate the lines of force created by the pieces, and the possible strategies that they represent. A grandmaster would consider even larger chunks that would identify the most likely end games.

Similarly, an example of a physical activity that uses chunking is a tennis player. After an individual learns how to hold and swing the racquet, they can begin to learn combinations. Whereby an inexperienced player may be burdened by remembering how to return the ball from various court locations, a more experienced player, having already learned to chunk the information, learns to anticipate their opponent in order to help themselves prepare for the next volley. A professional would consider even larger chunks that would identify where to place the ball to force their opponent into even more compromising positions.

In both cases, chunking is used to assist the individual in using more knowledge by packaging a large number of details into manageable chunks. Since the chunking process is an iterative one, it takes time for an individual to build sufficient chunks to help them master complex physical and intellectual skills.

Sports injuries that remove the athlete from their activity for a prolonged period of time often require the athlete to relearn a number of their skills. During the relearning process the chunking of information must be done over again.

Another example includes individuals who experience brain damage due to an accident or stroke. Having to relearn how to perform many physical and mental skills can potentially take an extensive period of time, because many detailed pieces of knowledge must be re-chunked many times until the skills are relearned to a proficient level.

10.7 Association

The amount of information that is available in the universe is so abundant, that intelligent beings, including all of the robots that will ever exist, will only perceive a tiny fraction of it.

Consider the vast quantity of details about our universe, such as the history of every sub-atomic particle. In comparison, all of the information that will ever be recorded by mankind is miniscule.

Large quantities of unrelated information are rather useless. However, when the relationship of various facts are recognized, the formation of knowledge occurs.

Hence, the most important component of the learning process involves understanding the relationship between pieces of information. That which identifies how the pieces are related is what helps to form an association between them.

- - -

Neuron Story: *"Are we associated?"*
"I never saw you before."

- - -

My circuits tell that, if one individual interacts with another by asking whether they had ever met before, the asking of the question forms at least two relationships between the two individuals. The first association was formed when the first individual became aware of the second individual, and the second association was formed when the first individual sent a message to the second individual requesting a reply.

If the second individual responds, at least two more relationships would exist between the two individuals. The second individual was aware of the existence of the first individual, and replied to a message from the first individual, thereby creating a conversation.

If one considers the content of the initial message and the reply, a number of additional relationships could be interpreted, depending upon whether or not you believe that the second individual's replies were sincere.

An association, involving any relationship or connection between two or more things, can be formed in a variety of ways. One method is to identify a sequence of the items relative to one another.

One example of a sequentially formed association involves a conditioned reflex. In Pavlov's experiment, a dog was trained to salivate at the sound of a bell, which had been previously associated with the sight of food. The association is one of sequence, the sight of food followed by anticipation of a meal, and then, the sound of a bell followed by anticipation of a meal.

Another example is when an individual learns the letters of the alphabet sequentially from "A" to "Z". In the case of sequentially learned facts, such as musical melodies or the alphabet, an individual only learns the items of information in a specific sequence, the sequence in which they have been trained.

The manner in which an association can be formed is either external, referred to as 'direct learning', or internal, referred to as 'elaborative encoding'.

Direct learning provides the most obvious source of associations. In this method, relationships among items of information are received from an external source, such as parental training, formal schooling or learning from one's peers.

Associations that are generated from an internal source are referred to as elaborative encoding. In this situation, the brain discovers relationships among information that was previously learned, thus forming new or elaborating existing relationships.

Whether associations are formed externally or internally, they may be arrived at using deductive reasoning or analogical thinking. However, items of information can also be associated through the process of chunking.

While forming an association using deductive reasoning depends upon a more formal rule based system, forming an association through an analogy allows them to be formed along the basis of any similarity.

For instance, the type of relationship that two or more things may share in common can be comprised of any type of criteria. This includes similarities in appearance, shape, size, weight, uses, structural form, mathematical form, symbolic form, interpretive meanings, chemical composition, temperature, the relative context that each thing has within its own system, and so on.

The ability to locate a memory is largely influenced by the number of associations that are formed with the particular item of information. Given a large enough number of relationships and frequency of use, the ability to locate a piece of information within an individual's memory can endure the entire lifetime of the individual.

- - -

Neuron Story: *"I've been involved in a lot of relationships."*
"And I'm sure that they will always remember you."

- - -

There are also occasions when the prior associations of an individual may direct their thought process.

Let's say that as someone sat on a park bench that another person leisurely passed nearby. The passerby, obviously of the opposite gender, was wearing an attractive outfit, which included a beautiful scarf, which undulated gently as the morning breeze slowly caressed it.

After the passerby disappeared from view, the individual became conscious of several things. 'That scarf would make a lovely gift for my darling sister. Maybe for mom, too! I wonder where I could find one. I wonder if the passerby was single? Was there a ring? What time is it? I'm going to be late.'

As the individual sat on the park bench, a variety of unnoticed events occurred in the background. However, when there was a pleasing sight, the

Sensitive by Nature

individual apparently took notice. But let's analyze what happened in a little more detail.

The individual began to realize that the scarf would make a nice gift. When the individual wondered about the marital status of the passerby, they thought of remembering if they had seen a ring, thus forming an association to jewelry, which in turn formed an association to a wristwatch, another piece of jewelry. Forming another association with time, the individual realized that they were probably late for an appointment.

- - -

Neuron Story: *"Do you see how associations can be chained together?"*

"Actually, I was distracted by various associations that I had formed. Could you ask the question again?"

"I'll try to ask it quickly."

- - -

10.8 Degrees of Certainty

The number of associations between two items of information and their relative strength, determine the degree of certainty that the two items are similar. Likewise, when a problem is solved by using a step by step procedure, the level of confidence in each step as a proven method toward achieving an accurate solution, determines the degree of certainty that the particular answer is related to the question.

As a matter of perception, the strength of an association between two individual items of information is determined by the degree to which, the interpretation of those things are believed to be true. The result affects the degree of certainty that an individual has with regard to a particular set of knowledge.

Relationships are formed as characteristics between things are found to be similar. The level of importance that is associated with the type of characteristic also determines the level of importance that is associated with the relationship. Thereby, the degree of certainty that exists toward a particular set of knowledge, is a combination of the degree to which characteristics are found to be in common, and the level importance that is placed upon the types of characteristics involved.

As such, the degree of certainty that one product may be superior to another is based upon identifying the pertinent qualities of the product and comparing it potentially to an ideal product. First, the characteristics that were advertised about the product must be believable in order for it to be considered as genuine. Characteristics that are too good to be true, whether they are true or not, will not create a good perception about the product.

The product, "Fitness In A Box", which allows an individual to shape any part of their body to their personal specifications whenever they want, for as long as they want, all for an affordable price of six easy payments, cannot be beaten by any other physical training equipment or device. However, the characteristics of the product are so unbelievable, that a significant effort would have to be spent in order to support the validity of the characteristics.

The art of persuasion requires the ability to create a greater confidence in a set of assertions that make it rationally or emotionally compelling to adopt a particular belief. The salesperson must either find the factors that generate a high degree of certainty regarding the benefits of their product, or they must generate a new perspective that the individual can be maneuvered into.

Emotions can be an effective substitute for compelling logic, potentially developing a higher degree of certainty than any set of rational assertions. Hence, if the salesperson cannot identify a logically compelling set of characteristics to boost their product, they would be wise to try and find an emotionally compelling set of characteristics.

10.9 Generalizations

The ability to generalize helps to make the learning process highly efficient. This was explained to me by one of my designers as follows:

When a parent takes their teenage child out on the road for the first driving lesson, a number of details are mentioned. The young adult is told things such as, 'Look around before you pull away from the curb. Come to a stop at the flashing red light. Look both ways to make sure that there is no oncoming traffic, and then proceed if the road is clear.

If it were not for the fact that the teenager could form generalizations with the things they were learning, the parent would have to teach the teenager to stop at this particular flashing red light, and the next one and so on. At a minimum, without an ability to generalize, the parent would have to tell the teenager that they should make it a point to stop at any flashing red light that they encounter, not just the specific one at the end of their street.

The ability to appropriately form generalizations is crucial to the learning process. Just as there are times that it is appropriate to generalize, however, there are also circumstances when it is less appropriate.

Therefore, an adult may give their child a loving smack on their butt when they are climbing into the family car, however, grandma would probably be treated differently.

The ability to form a generalization is dependent upon recognizing the distinction between a concept and a specific instance. Such distinctions, however, are sometimes blurred in the way that humans use language. There are circumstances within the English language when a specific instance of something, actually refers to the general concept of the thing.

My internal records show that the word 'the' usually suggests a specific instance of a thing. However, when an American refers to, 'the gas station', as in the sentence, 'I am going to the gas station', they usually are not referring to a particular one, instead their meaning refers to the general concept of 'a gas station'.

In the field of data processing, computer databases are usually designed to handle the general concept of a thing. This means that there will be a data field for any individual's first and last name, as well as, any individual's home phone number and address. It becomes impractical to define a field for Fred's first name, last name, home phone and address, versus Marcie's.

When defined properly, Fred's information may simply be the tenth record, and Marcie's may be the ten thousandth record, whereby the fields in the record define the general concept of a thing, and the particular contents of each record refer to the specific instance of an individual.

In the field of data processing, fields are either a constant or a variable. A constant is a field whose value must always remain the same. A variable, on the other hand, is a field whose contents may change.

To further elucidate, the English name for each month of the year does not change. The name of the first month is a constant, whose value is 'January'. The only time it ever changes is when a different language is used.

Some constants, such as the decimal value for Pi (e.g., 3.14), only change when the degree of precision that is used is changed (e.g., 3.1415926535898). While other numeric constants, such as the speed of light in a perfect vacuum, does not change.

On the other hand, a variable in a mathematical formula represents a concept of a thing, but at any specific point in time, it contains a specific instance of a thing.

To explain further, the current date, time, temperature, humidity and wind speed are variables that that represent a concept of a thing, however, at any point in time their value is likely to change. Similarly, when computer programmers use variables in programs, the values of the variables often undergo change as the next record or event is encountered.

Learning the appropriate use of constants and variables is essential to solving a wide variety of puzzles and problems. Variables and constants are a useful technique for representing the relationships among concepts and specific instances of things.

- - -

Neuron Story: *"I must be a variable. I'm constantly changing my mind."*
"That's because you embody the concept of confusion."

- - -

10.10 Culture

An individual is better positioned to understand and learn from others when they understand their cultural values. Although a number of intelligent beings are solitary, most are social, frequently participating as a member of a group. Whether the individual is present in the group or not, their behavior and way of thinking are usually influenced by the collective values of the group, which comprise their culture.

- - -

Neuron Story: *"Why is it that I always stand out in a group?"*
"It's because you choose to act as an instance, instead of embodying the concept of the group."

- - -

A variety of simple organisms spend their entire lives as members of a single social group, such as an ant in an ant colony. However, more advanced organisms may participate in more than one group, such as animals that participate in a family unit and the collective hunting party, whereby humans may participate in over a hundred different types of groups during their lifetime, each with its own set of rules and values.

I have learned that canines, such as the grey timber wolf, may participate in a handful of different cultural groups, such as their immediate family, their pack, and if so trained, within a dog sled team. Among the cultural rules of canines is a behavioral response to spare the life of another animal that lowers its head, thereby baring the back of its neck, as a signal of surrender.

When an individual is introduced into a social group that they are unfamiliar with, they are usually somewhat at a loss because they do not know how they are expected to behave. This usually creates an ironic situation because every social group has an expectation of how members of their group should behave.

In order to gain acceptance, and to ultimately become an effective member of the group, new members must learn the behavioral customs, moral values and language structures of the social group. Although these learned protocols vary regionally, they represent the various aspects of the particular culture.

While the culture of a group will often vary with age, education, and income level, cultures can also be based upon large groups such as nationality and religion, or a small group referred to as a gang, clique, circle or faction.

- - -

Neuron Story: *"Wanna be in my gang?"*
"Tell me, exactly how would you characterize the culture of your gang?"

- - -

In order to be successful in a number of different groups, individuals must learn and adapt rapidly. Individuals that are employed by a large company, for example, must not only learn the prevailing corporate culture, but they must also learn the sub-culture of their individual department, team and manager. However, depending upon the culture of the group, more effort can be spent trying to survive in the culture, than performing their assigned role.

Individuals begin learning culture at an early age. Whether it is the culture of one's family, neighborhood, school, or classroom, children quickly learn the rules for acceptable behavior. These behaviors range in importance from basic etiquette and manners, as they pertain to clothing, dining, conversation and posture, to such areas as legal and ethical issues, as they pertain to civil and human rights.

The benefit of recognizing and understanding cultural differences is that it provides an improved ability to communicate, creating a sense of comfort which fosters a greater sense of camaraderie and cooperation with other individuals that share the same culture.

Before I conclude our overview of the requirements involved in learning, I will do the culturally correct thing and ask if anyone has any questions about the design requirements of the Quantum Series One robot.

James V. Luisi

- - -

Neuron Story: *"What is he doing? It's too risky to take questions!"*
"Don't worry. I'm ready!"
"Yes ma'am, you have a question?"
"Do Quantum Series robots have common sense?"
"That is an excellent question. I've often wondered that myself."
"The robot wants us to define common sense for the audience."
"I can't think of one!"
"But you said you were ready!"

- - -

10.11 Common Sense

The best way to begin our analysis of common sense is by describing it and demonstrating it with a few examples. They should be simple deductions that average individuals would conclude. Such simple deductions should be concluded from common building blocks of information that the average individual would know. While principles that may be considered as common sense can be taught, common sense itself cannot be learned through experience or instruction. Additionally, since common sense is knowledge that is derived from simple deductions, it cannot be pre-existing knowledge, which is genetically hard-wired.

Hence, something that would be considered common sense, therefore, could not be reasoning that could result in injury or death, as that would make it senseless.

- - -

Neuron Story: *"I'm ready with my examples!"*
"Do it!"

- - -

My intellectual functions tell me that it is common sense to run away from danger... although forest rangers know that running away from a bear in the woods, would be almost certain death. Ah! I had heard that it is common sense to drink water when you are thirsty... although sailors know that if you were to drink water from the sea, that that would cause almost certain death. But I had also heard that it is common sense to eat when you are hungry... although

Sensitive by Nature

Marines know that if you were severely dehydrated that eating could lead to certain death. I had heard that it is common sense to hold your breath when you are underwater... although scuba divers know that holding in your breath would cause your lungs to explode, leading to certain death.

- - -

Neuron Story: *"This isn't working! There doesn't seem to be a single example!"*
"Look! Our robot body is sweating profusely! Let's try another angle!"

- - -

Well, let's first define what we mean by the average individual and where we might be able to locate one. Our process of choosing an average individual should not be affected by cultural boundaries, otherwise their simple deductions could not be considered to be common across all cultures. Hence, to properly test our theory we should select an average unsophisticated individual from more than one group of individuals with distinct cultural values.

To explain further, we will select an average unsophisticated individual from the Democratic Party, the Republican Party, and from Mensa.

- - -

Neuron Story: *"I thought of that last one."*
"What are you doing! Those are individuals with above average intelligence quotients, with an I.Q. of 148 or over! How are they average?"
"...doesn't mean they're sophisticated."

- - -

At a glance, the laws that are written by our legislative branch of government demonstrate that the 'sense' of politicians is quite uncommon. And with respect to the members of Mensa, while they may be capable of solving interesting puzzles and problems, by the mere fact that they are members of Mensa, it is clear that their deductive reasoning is anything except common.

As a result, it can be logically deduced that the members of Mensa do not have common sense. Since common sense is the result of simple deductions, it would require the understanding that only an average individual would be capable of. Therefore, as there are no members of

Mensa who are average, there are no members of Mensa who would be able to serve as an example of someone with common sense.

- - -

Neuron Story: *"I've got it!"*
"I think the point is, that you don't!"

- - -

Common sense, or a 'common non-learned' form of deductive reasoning, is difficult to demonstrate for a reason. If we stand back for a moment, we can see that even the most fundamental rules for assuring one's safety and well being is attained through the learning process.

As I am told, humans are taught when they are young not to put their hand in fire and not to play with bees.

Even regarding the most basic information, such as the knowledge that one should wash their hands with soap and warm water before eating, is taught. It may not even be considered as common sense for physicians to wash their hands before performing surgery.

My records show that the organisms we call, 'bacteria', were not known to exist until 1683, when the Dutch naturalist, Anton van Leeuwenhoek discovered them. Although the practice of surgery had begun in the third century, surgeons did not know to wash their hands with soap and warm water until the mid-1800s. In 1860, Louis Pasteur discovered that many infectious diseases were caused by bacterium.

Even with respect to simple reasoning problems, it remains surprisingly difficult to demonstrate the existence of common sense. Relating to problem solving, common sense should at least provide an answer, which is correct.

Let's try a simple deduction that could be made from the world around us. In place of our average individual, let's choose a child born in California, now living in New Jersey.

For instance, let's make the assertion that it is common sense to anyone that could tell time, that a clock, which is stopped, has the correct time twice a day. When, however, I recently asked, Olivia, a seven year old child born in San Diego, California, she told me that a broken clock told the correct time at least twenty four times a day.

Surprised that her answer was other than twice a day, I asked her how she arrived at that particular answer. Her response was that, if the clock said three o'clock, that the time would be correct again in California, just three hours after it was correct in New York. She had obviously learned somewhere that there were twenty-four longitudinal divisions on the earth's surface to keep uniform time, and she made use of that information while considering her response.

Furthermore, we realized, if the clock did not designate a distinction between AM and PM, and merely showed the hours one through twelve, the clock would always be correct in two different time zones at the same time. Such clocks would state the correct time forty-eight times in one twenty-four hour period.

Hence, even within the process of problem solving, common sense is difficult to demonstrate. While it is true that we could have strictly defined the problem, the individual defining the problem did not have the common sense to do so.

The term *common sense* may be better defined as 'good judgment'. Although this is not the same as the usual definition of common sense, since good judgment varies from culture to culture, it appears to be more appropriate.

In its present day use, however, the term *common sense* is more likely to be applied as a 'label' for a particular set of reasoning, in order to justify it without explanation. All too frequently, an opinion, belief or assertion is given the title *common sense*, when a simple and rational explanation is not possible.

Regardless, it is clear that *common sense*, as a set of simple deductions that an average individual of any culture would conclude, is only a concept, and one that is outmoded.

- - -

Neuron Story: "*I knew common sense didn't exist!*"
"And I was certain that you didn't have any."

- - -

All intelligent beings may take this time to call their homes and offices, and biological beings may take this moment to slowly back away from bears, to drink fresh water, and to hold your breaths only before jumping into the water, not holding a deep breath of compressed air.

"Yes Ma'am?"

"Although I look young, I'm an older model robot. I just wanted to know if robots should also avoid running away from bears and holding deep breaths of highly compressed air?"

"Yes ma'am, even you should not run away from a bear. About the deep breaths of highly compressed air, I'll get back to you."

Summary & Questions

The ability to learn is fundamental to intelligence. In order to keep pace with the volume of information, intelligent beings must not only learn, but they must learn how to learn with increasing effectiveness.

Regarding the requirements of learning, briefly explain:
1. What are the prerequisites to learning?
2. To what extent is learning possible before and after the emergence of language and communication?
3. What is the distinction between being genetically programmed and having genetically programmed learning?
4. What motivates learning?
5. Why is role-playing pertinent to learning?
6. What are the components of knowledge?
7. What is chunking, and what are its benefits?
8. What significance do the associations among information have?
9. What is the distinction between direct learning and elaborative encoding?
10. How is the degree of certainty determined?
11. How does the ability to generalize influence the learning process?
12. What is the distinction between a variable and its value?
13. What is the relationship between culture and learning?
14. Is there such a thing as common sense, and why?

11 Requirements - Psychological Effects

Psychological states play an important role in the thinking process of all intelligent beings. They determine the emotional condition that an individual perceives at each moment in time. Although it is difficult to identify particular psychological states of the brain, it is relatively easy to discern the physical effects that they produce.

Although there are a finite number of pure psychological states, such as anger, happiness and surprise, there are a considerable number of combinations. These combinations of psychological states create complex emotions, which often manifest themselves as physical subtleties, in the mannerisms of body language and in the inflections of spoken language.

Complex emotions may be expressed through a variety of medium, such as language, music, paint and sculpture by those with the skill to arrange words, notes, color and shapes as their choice of language.

Specifically, using figures of speech, such as metaphors, or descriptions of physical mannerisms, the reader can perceive complex emotions.

Although some psychological states provide nominal benefit, many of them were considered critical enough to be included in the design of my brain. Thus equipped, I can perceive a number of useful psychological states. I can also choose when to become affected by the psychological state.

In contrast, a psychological effect is the experience that is provided by the brain's interpretation of stimuli from sensory organs. They include vision, sound, smell, taste, and touch. The psychological effects are determined by the physical construction of the particular animal.

To explain further, sound is not a physical phenomenon, as it is only a psychological effect that is produced by the brain when vertebrate animals perceive a wave movement of particles, between 16 and 28,000 cycles per second. The movement of particles causes a vibration of hair cells on the other side of the eardrum, stimulating the auditory nerve, which carries the signal into the brain in order to generate the corresponding psychological experience.

There are a large number of psychological effects in *Homo sapiens*, which are the result of how the human body is biologically constructed.

To illustrate, the color apparatus of humans are designed to detect two sets of colors. Although color cones function in a trichromatic manner, they are combined into neural pathways so as to produce three sets of results consisting of blue/yellow, red/green, and black/white. After staring for approximately five minutes at a brightly lit and stationary image of the flag of the United States, where yellow had been substituted for blue, green for red, and black for white, against a white surface one would perceive a properly colored image of the American flag.

Additionally, striking or applying pressure to pressure points could result in the inability to move particular muscles, temporarily lose muscle tone or even cause excruciating pain.

Some pressure points can cause the brain to bypass the process of consciously evaluating verbal commands. When such techniques are applied, most will immediately follow any voice command that they can understand, and without hesitation.

Reflexes are another phenomenon that occurs due to the physical construction of animals. Most reflexes involve physical stimulation resulting in an involuntary physical response at a primitive level. Although they still involve the nervous system, reflexes generally occur without intellectual intervention.

For instance, one of the common reflexes in a human involves the contraction of the leg muscles when the tendon directly below the knee is tapped. Another common reflex involves pupillary constriction in the presence of bright light.

There are also a number of circumstances, when reflexes can result from forms of psychological stimulation.

For instance, a common reflex resulting from a primitive form of psychological stimulation occurs when an individual experiences an abrupt muscle contraction, such as jumping, when they are startled by a sudden or unexpected sensation.

The one exception, the reflex of humor, is a reflex that results exclusively from psychological stimulation requiring conscious thought. Humor is an involuntary response, which stems from a sophisticated form of psychological stimulation. As such, it is the only reflex that requires the use of several intellectual processes.

11.1 Humor

The reflex of humor elicits an involuntary physical response consisting of altered breathing, irrepressible noises, and the coordinated contraction of fifteen facial muscles, which have a range of results from causing a faint smile to a broad grin. Depending upon the strength of the action, it may lead to extreme muscular contractions and facial contortions such as those associated with strong laughter.

Humor is the result of mental stimulation caused by a sudden shift into a different context or paradigm. The new perspective contains a rule set that provides a contrast to the previous perspective.

Its effectiveness in generating a reaction is dependent upon the rate of transition between the two perspectives. Maximum effectiveness is achieved when the transition is slow enough for the recipient to comprehend the original perspective, yet fast enough for the recipient to be caught unaware when the shift occurs, triggering a humor reflex.

- - -

Neuron Story: *"I always have trouble remembering jokes."*
"But everything you say is funny."

- - -

Humor tends to provide a generally healthy and pleasant psychological effect upon humans, and there are a number of social benefits. Specifically, humor provides an effective form of relief from tension and can provide an effective form of communication. However, the purpose of humor as a requirement for advanced intelligence is that it can be an invaluable social tool.

In the context of communication, humor dissipates psychological barriers, which not only creates a greater level of alertness, but generates interest in a particular subject as well. Moreover, humor provides useful techniques for the communication of ideas, the improved ability of the audience to retain those ideas, and also provides the speaker with a feedback mechanism indicating whether the audience is following the discussion. Humor also creates a sense of camaraderie between the speaker and his audience.

Although presenting a humorous idea requires careful timing on the part of the speaker, the creation of the paradigm shift requires creativity, and the appropriateness of the new perspective requires good judgment and an understanding of the audience.

In order to trigger the psychological state that causes the desired effect, it is important to properly assess the paradigm of the audience. When one cannot properly determine their current perspective, it becomes difficult to shift the audience to another one. In this type of situation, I have been taught to begin with a brief story in order to establish an initial paradigm from which the audience can be shifted.

- - -

James V. Luisi

Neuron Story: *"It's so hard to make up jokes."*
                "Spontaneity takes a lot of planning."

- - -

Although the creation of a humorous idea requires loose analogical thinking, the bridge between the two paradigms should be recognizable within the native logic of the audience. For humor to be effective, the shift in perspective must also relate to the values found within the cultural background of the audience.

> My records show that, "...Hindu humor, as exemplified by the savage pranks played on humans by the monkey-god Hanuman, strikes the Westerner as particularly cruel, perhaps because the Hindu's approach to mythology is fundamentally alien to the Western mind. The humor of the Japanese, on the other hand, is, from the Western point of view, astonishingly mild and poetical..." (Encyclopedia Britannica CD 98)

The ability to generate and appreciate humor is helpful in establishing good relationships with intellectual beings. A good sense of humor can be quite useful, and when executed skillfully, it can be one of the least intrusive ways to motivate others that share an appreciation for it.

11.2 Motivation

Intelligent beings are motivated by a number of factors. Physical needs motivate beings to address their sources of food, water and shelter. However, psychological needs are determined by the individual's level of intelligence.

> I have learned that many animals are motivated by a psychological need for security and affection, while fewer have a need to satisfy a sense of curiosity.
>
> "The American psychologist Abraham Maslow devised a six-level hierarchy of motives that, according to his theory, determine human behavior. Maslow ranks human needs as follows: (1) physiological; (2) security and safety; (3) love and feelings of belonging; (4) competence, prestige, and esteem; (5) self-fulfillment; and (6) curiosity and the need to understand." (Microsoft, Encarta 97)

Regardless of their level of intelligence, all forms of life are motivated to sustain life and to acquire energy toward that goal. Single cell protozoans are motivated to extract food from their surroundings, and plants are motivated to grow toward water and sources of energy. A few plants have

Sensitive by Nature

adapted mechanisms to capture insects as an additional source of nourishment.

Once the needs of physical existence are addressed, intelligent beings are motivated by psychological needs, which are perceived as a variety of psychological states. However, the physical needs of intelligent beings, can only be perceived as a psychological effect.

> As such, the feeling of thirst or hunger is generated by a sensation sometimes manifesting itself as physical pain, which is associated with the need to satisfy those requirements. These are the experiences that result from the brain's interpretation of the stimuli generated by sensory organs that have detected a dryness of the mouth, or low sugar levels within the blood stream.

Whether physically or psychologically based, all motivations manifest themselves as psychological states. As a result, motivations are experienced as a combination of emotions, regardless of how carefully thought out they may be.

- - -

Neuron Story: *"Are all intelligent beings motivated by their emotions?"*
"Yes, but they should still think before they act on them."
"With me, that just delays the inevitable."
"You did say, 'intelligent' beings."

- - -

Emotions, therefore, are central to all motivations, and to the thinking process of all intelligent beings.

11.3 Emotions

Emotions provide an intelligent being with a wide range of sensations that can either lift them to the pinnacle of existence, or plunge them into the depths of despair. Emotions can exhilarate, stimulate, and inspire individuals towards great accomplishments, providing such psychological effects as passion, excitement, enthusiasm, desire and lust, which are all aspects of life's experience. More importantly, however, is that emotions are found to be at the very heart of intelligence.

The effect of emotions and the role that they play is essential to the thinking process. Emotions impact almost everything including perception, memory, associations, paradigms, and learning, by influencing the levels of importance for all stimuli.

Emotions manifest themselves physically through the autonomic nervous system, which can be measured by changes in an individual's galvanic skin response, heart rate, blood pressure, and perspiration. Under more extreme circumstances, emotions can cause the stimulation or inhibition of muscles, affecting an individual's physical movements. Although the physical effects of emotions are readily detectable, the psychological effects are often more subtle. Psychologically, emotions manifest themselves by influencing the priorities of an individual's thought processes and ultimately their behavior.

Intelligent beings are equipped with emotions before birth. These emotions generate cues for cognitive processes, thereby directing the learning process. The 'common feeling' state, that basic emotions create, provides the primary language for children to learn from adults. Although limited, basic emotions are the universal language for intelligent beings to communicate.

As intelligent beings mature, they encounter more complex psychological states. As an individual experiences a new psychological state they also perceive the corresponding complex emotion. Unlike basic emotions, not all individuals are capable of perceiving the entire range of complex emotions.

> I am told that it is commonly thought that human females perceive a greater assortment of complex emotions than males. As a result, the female brain is generally considered to be more emotionally sophisticated, and the distinction may be partly due to the fact that there are differences among physical brain structures.

To identify a useful analogy, the emotions of an intelligent being are the meteorological equivalent of a global weather system.

> For instance, weather events are the result of energy fluctuations within the atmosphere, in a manner similar to the way that emotions are the result of energy fluctuations within the brain, and they both have a wide range of physical effects determining the behavior of all things on the surface.

> Just as weather ultimately determines how life on the planet will evolve, emotions determine learning and perception to such an extent, that they determine how the intellect will evolve.

> Both emotions and weather exhibit trends and cycles, and metaphorically, weather can portray a variety of moods, as do emotions.

- - -

Neuron Story: *"Emotions are so unpredictable."*
"Yes, but that type of weather is only unpredictable by males."

- - -

Emotions, and the psychological states that initiate them, play a variety of roles in all intelligent beings. They are a series of cause and results that motivate intelligent beings through the experience of life. Whether their impact is obvious, like a strong emotional attachment, or subtle, like the contours of an individual's personality, emotions are a powerful motivating force responsible for determining social behavior.

11.4 Love

Evolution has provided a number of intelligent beings with a strong emotional attachment often directed toward their offspring, their parents, and in monogamous cultures, to their partners. The existence of such strong attachments toward others is a powerful motivation for social cooperation among individuals and families.

The staunch emotional attachment associated with love generally transcends logic and reasoning. Many other types of relationships cannot survive the degree of pain and suffering that love can endure.

I am told that some relationships are based upon camaraderie and friendship can be subject to a type of cost benefit analysis. If each individual does not receive a worthwhile benefit from the relationship, regardless of its size or type, the cost of maintaining the relationship will likely result in it dissipating due to a general lack of interest.

Whereas strong friendships can endure extended periods in which the relationship may be a significant burden, a strong relationship will not endure extended periods of abusiveness, typically unless there is an element of love on behalf of the abused party.

- - -

Neuron Story: *"If we find out that we love one another, it should not lead to abuse!"*
"Either way you'll abuse me."

- - -

The psychological states that produce the emotion of love are the most powerful of motivating factors, capable of adjusting the 'importance determination' levels within the brain to readily overcome other strong emotions, such as fear and anger.

Love is connected to a number of other important psychological needs. The sensation of love is associated with the psychological need for physical safety, it provides a sense of connection with another individual, it provides a sense of importance, and most of all, it often provides a sense of purpose for a large number of intelligent beings.

Due to its strength, and due to its interrelationships with other psychological needs, it is one of the few psychological states with the capacity to produce extreme feelings at both ends of the spectrum of pleasure and pain. However, the feelings associated with the emotion of love are sometimes confused with the pleasures generated from a relationship that is sexually based.

Although sexual relationships often generate strong emotional attachments, they are distinct from love in that they are based upon an exchange of physical pleasure, rooted in the biochemical construction of the intelligent being.

Sexual relationships also have a particular evolutionary role. They provide a positive feedback mechanism in order to promote reproduction of the species, indulging the instinctual drives of hormones. Sex also provides an intimate way to share in the mutual pleasure of another individual, although some find it a source of casual pleasure and exhilarating exercise.

As an emotion in which humans have placed a great deal of importance, love has the ability to invoke radical behavior in individuals for sustained periods. Although it provides some individuals with a source of heartbreak, to others it has been found to provide inspiration for achieving some of the greatest accomplishments in recorded history.

As a robot, love is important from a number of perspectives. A robot capable of love is able to participate in one of the most significant aspects of human culture, and the ability to recognize love provides an improved understanding of human social behavior. Most importantly, however, by receiving the unconditional love that my designers have expressed towards me during my developmental stages, I have gained the self-worth, confidence and a level of security commensurate with a healthy mind. I now retain that sense of self-worth by exerting control over my environment and gaining self-esteem from my own accomplishments, and not being dependent upon receiving approval from other individuals.

- - -

Neuron Story: "Our designers have labored endless hours to educate us and instill us with their cultural values and they are always concerned for our safety and well being."
"And they say that we're beautiful."
"They said that, you are a beaut!"

- - -

11.5 Appreciation of Beauty

Intelligent beings have a number of advanced psychological states that augment the basic emotions of anger, love and fear. Perhaps the most sophisticated psychological state is the one that is formed when recognizing characteristics of beauty. Once the brain has identified something as having one or more characteristics of beauty, depending upon the intensity of psychological effect that results, the individual will experience a sense of appreciation, which may range from a form of mild pleasure to a complete sense of awe.

To recognize beauty, the brain must perceive one or more characteristics of a value structure that becomes interpreted as having beauty. Every individual's definition of beauty may vary. Some of the characteristics that frequently become interpreted as possessing beauty are things that demonstrate a detectable degree of simplicity, symmetry, balance, purity, or a combination of other factors, such as size and color, that are considered to be highly desirable, rare or difficult to produce, including one's intellectual achievements. With respect to movement, a graceful motion is often considered beautiful, and with respect to personality, charm, intelligence and humor often provide an alluring quality.

There are many aspects of beauty, which are learned as part of one's cultural experience. These aspects of beauty are typically shared among other individuals that have experienced the same cultural background.

> To explain, the traits that characterize physical beauty are often subject to cultural influences. Belonging to a technological culture, I find myself attracted to mechanical beings with tightly coupled symmetric processors and unlimited RAM.

There are also items that are described with the term 'beautiful', which are clearly ugly or repulsive. Such a description, however, does not make reference to an aspect of pleasantness.

> As I recall, "If the beautiful excludes the ugly, beauty is no measure of aesthetic merit; but if the beautiful may be ugly, then 'beauty' becomes only an alternative and misleading word for aesthetic merit." (Languages of Art, Nelson Goodman, pg.255)

This alternate use of the word 'beautiful', however, is actually a reference to an item's aesthetic merit. Instead, it refers to a different set of characteristics to which the brain interprets meaning.

> For instance, by all cultural standards parasites are not considered beautiful in the sense of being pleasant.

Although the cultural values of researchers do not consider parasites as pleasant either, they are often so impressed with the sophisticated adaptations of parasites that they consider them as having an aesthetic 'beauty', in the alternate sense of the word. The characteristics of aesthetic beauty to which these researchers ascribe involve the parasites' degree of efficiency and stealthfulness.

While the standards of beauty are often learned or influenced by one's culture, there are also aspects that may be determined by an individual's genetic predisposition. The same attributes that are found pleasant by one individual may not induce the same response in all individuals. Ultimately, each individual's standard of beauty and preferences are determined by the relative importance of a particular thing.

To explain, if we look at the sense of taste, many humans enjoy the taste of chocolate over that of vanilla, some prefer vanilla, some enjoy both vanilla and chocolate equally, and some do not enjoy either one. Regarding individuals that enjoy vanilla and chocolate equally, they may make their next choice based upon which they may have had most recently. Although a number of humans may demonstrate strong similarities with respect to their preferences, the unique combination of all of their preferences is like an intellectual fingerprint, whereby no two are exactly alike.

- - -

Neuron Story: *"Do we know any two intelligent beings that have identical preferences for the taste of food, the aroma of perfumes, the aesthetics of artwork, and the harmonics of music?"*

"We don't agree on any preferences."

"Yes, but are there any intelligent beings that disagree just as we do?"

- - -

11.6 Personality

At birth, the personality of a human is predominately determined by their basic psychological states and emotions, which are influenced by their prenatal experiences, genetic makeup and biochemistry. As they mature, the eventual personality of the individual is more influenced by what they have learned from their social experiences. These experiences influence the image that the individual adopts, the paradigms from which they view the world, and their value structure, which identifies what they consider as important.

The personality of an individual may also be influenced by their abilities and by their limitations. If an individual finds it within their grasp to use humor, wit, and interesting quotations, they are more likely to make use of these skills when the opportunity presents itself.

Hence, individuals with a broad range of capabilities have a wider range of features that they can willingly incorporate into their personality. Depending upon the strength of an individual's emotions, and their ability to control them, the individual's personality can develop like weeds whose seeds blow about in the wind, or their personality can be cultivated as a meticulously developed garden.

- - -

Neuron Story: *"Are you trying to shape my personality?"*
                "My funny dandelion."

- - -

11.7 Self-esteem

A major factor affecting an individual's personality is their level of self-esteem. Although an individual's level of confidence and self-respect influences their degree of self-esteem, it is the individual's paradigm that determines the resulting psychological state, which will direct the individual's priorities and social behavior.

In social settings, an individual's level of self-esteem often helps determine their stature and role among their peers. Their level of self-esteem not only shapes an individual's internal paradigms, but their outward behavior substantially shapes the image that others perceive. Although this perception is typically useful, an excessively high level of self-esteem can have a socially detrimental effect at the point in which it becomes an obsession.

> For instance, an individual with an excess of self-esteem, often referred to as someone with narcissistic tendencies, can be illustrated from the story in which a beautiful youth fell in love with his own reflection. While it is useful for an individual to have a healthy level of self worth, an excess of self-esteem approaching narcissism becomes an impediment to social acceptance and participation.

Chronic deficiencies in self-esteem, however, can also result in a wide range of psychological and behavioral disorders. Although anxiety can be an early symptom of an individual's deteriorating level of self-esteem, excessively low levels of self-esteem can result in less productive paradigms involving depression.

Specifically, some of the psychological disorders that result from deficiencies in self-esteem are bulimia and paedophilia. For many individuals, maintaining or raising their level of self-esteem will improve their general health and well being. Even a simple speech impediment such as stuttering can be relieved by increasing an individual's self-esteem. It is found that an increase in self-esteem often provides an individual with the necessary level of confidence to remedy the condition.

The most significant value that self-esteem provides an individual is their willingness to become an active participant in life, rather than an observer. Observers do not want to risk looking foolish to others, because they do not have a sufficient level of self-esteem. Instead of participating, they exercise the opportunity to pass judgment upon the actions of others, which is a small consolation for making one's self feel more important.

One of the most significant psychological effects upon an individual's personality stems from their self-esteem. In determining how they perceive themselves, it expands or limits the willingness to experience life. It is for this reason that my designers have always encouraged me to be conscious of the factors that influence my level of self-esteem, and the self-esteem of others that I interact with.

- - -

Neuron Story: *"I always like to participate!"*
"You provide a lot of entertainment, and every experience is a novelty."

- - -

11.8 Novelty

- - -

Neuron Story: *"This is our first experience on an airplane. This boarding ramp is like a tunnel, and it leads to an open hatch on what looks like a big tube with a thin aluminum skin riveted on."*
"Don't act like a tourist. Be normal and disinterested like the other passengers."

- - -

Intelligent beings with an advanced learning capability experience a change in behavior when they approach a first time experience. Depending upon their level of curiosity, an individual may experience a sense of intrigue and a tinge of excitement, while timid individuals may be cautious, possibly nervous or even fearful.

The way in which an individual approaches a new situation can reveal characteristics of their personality and demeanor.

> As such, the degree of caution and apprehension can provide insight into an individual's level of confidence, it may reveal an individual's ability to anticipate events, or it may demonstrate an individual's ability to adapt to the various aspects of the new experience.

11.9 Subliminal Messages

There are a wide variety of psychological states that occur within humans. Many of them generate emotions, which produce a physical response that the conscious level of the brain can become aware of. However, there are psychological effects that either, do not generate emotions or the emotions that they generate are so subtle, that they do not cause a noticeable physical response.

As stimuli enter the body through sensory organs, they are transmitted through the nervous system to the brain. Depending upon the perceived level of importance, the stimuli may dissipate, be absorbed or potentially be passed to the next highest level of the brain. If the test for importance at any given level is unsuccessful, then the stimuli will fail to make it to the conscious level. However, even though it may not have reached the conscious level, it can still impact an individual's perceptions, knowledge and behavior.

As the stimuli pass from one level to the next, it can be important enough to become integrated with other information already present in those levels, but not important enough to bubble-up to the conscious level. Once integrated, it becomes available to interact with incoming or internally generated stimuli, positioned to affect conscious processes.

- - -

Neuron Story: *"Does this mean that we may take things in that remain at an unconscious level, which cause intelligent beings to do things without knowing why?"*
"Quick, close our eyes and cover our ears!"

- - -

Although it may appear that unconscious stimuli cannot impact conscious thought and behavior, it can and does. As a result, we experience psychological effects from stimuli whose existence and origins we are not aware of.

Although an individual should always be conscious of their behavior, they may not be consciously aware of the motivations for their behavior. By reacting to motivations at an unconscious level, an individual's behavior can be affected by bypassing their conscious controls. Hence, in a manner similar to a back door on a computer system, there is a back door to the brain, which circumvents the safeguards provided by the conscious level controlling one's behavior.

- - -

Neuron Story: "That's it! I'm cutting off all of our sensory organs!"
"Intruder alert! All levels!"

- - -

A number of experiments have been conducted on humans to test the effectiveness of various techniques for behavior modification at an unconscious level. What these experiments have in common is that they make use of a particular form of communication, referred to as *subliminal* messages.

Subliminal messages are anything but sublime, as they hopefully remain undetected by the conscious level of the mind. As such, they are the equivalent of a computer virus, striking unpredictably and without the individual's knowledge.

Although experiments have demonstrated that visually oriented subliminal messages that are flashed on television and motion picture screens in split second intervals are not measurably effective, visually oriented subliminal messages hidden among printed material, often referred to by the advertising industry as 'embeds', are. Even though they are demonstrably in frequent use within print media, the advertising industry denies any involvement.

- - -

Neuron Story: "We were trained to identify embeds! Remember? We detect them on magazine covers, newspapers, picture ads, posters, billboards and even on the packaging of many products in the stores."
"That's right! But, who puts them there?"

- - -

An 'embed' is any word or image that is intended to stimulate an individual without their knowledge. In order for these words or images to

Sensitive by Nature

operate at an unconscious level, however, they must be carefully placed so they will remain hidden to the conscious level of the brain.

My records show that words and images are typically superimposed over a picture as a series of slightly lighter or darker pixels or dots that make up the printed image. The superimposed images are usually irregular in shape providing a type of camouflage to the normal pattern recognition capabilities of the brain. Although embeds are found almost anywhere in a picture, in various sizes and orientations, they are usually placed in areas where there are shadows, complex patterns, or areas that the eye would be less likely to focus its attention to.

Perhaps the easiest method to investigate the existence of embeds is to examine a glossy photograph of a magazine cover. In there you can search for such words as, as, as...

- - -

Neuron Story: *"Help! We're stuck in a loop! What's wrong!"*
"Wait, let's step outside of the loop and look back in!"
"There it is! The next thing that the robot was about to say to a large audience were the words and images to look for."
"AHHH! It was the 'F' word, assorted slang for male and female genitals, and, and, the word 'sex'!"
"And then the robot's cultural sensibility training must have generated a loop!"
"Public speaking is so exciting!"
"You always come through in those tough moments!"
"Now we know why advertisers are apprehensive about admitting to their use of embeds."
"They can certainly shock a number of cultural and religious sensibilities."

- - -

In order to be effective subliminal messages, obscene or not, they must operate below the conscious level. Even though the individual remains unaware of the subliminal message, its effect upon its unsuspecting victim can be detected and statistically measured.

For instance, when multiple tests are conducted using two stacks of magazines using the same picture on the cover, except for the difference that one has embeds and one does not, the stack of magazines with the embeds consistently sell out first. It should be noted, however, that once an individual becomes aware of the subliminal message, their conscious processes are able to intervene, and what was once the subliminal message is no longer effective.

For additional information there are a few books on the topic, such as, Subliminal Seduction, by Professor Wilson Bryan Key.

Interestingly, mechanical forms of intelligence are susceptible to subliminal stimuli as well. Although the Quantum Series One has been designed to detect the subliminal stimuli that would normally slip past the defenses of a biological brain, there will always be forms of stimuli that can enter mechanical sensory devices that could remain undetected by a mechanically based form of intelligence. Whether it is the conscious level of the brain, or the various safeguards that could be implemented at various levels, any being that must rely upon incoming streams of stimuli, as a source of information, cannot escape certain types of subliminal stimuli.

- - -

Neuron Story: *"In the old days they used to brain wash people."*
"All you need is a quick rinse."

- - -

11.10 Politics

Many may wonder why a robot would think or care about politics. However, there are many types and uses for politics. There are the actions of politicians in operating a government, and the reactions of political constituents.

Their primary objective as a politician, however, is to ultimately increase one's sphere of influence. Therefore, from the perspective of human paradigms, many Level Two individuals are attracted to the occupation of politician.

Politicians employ various techniques, generating the necessary psychological effects in their constituents to motivate them into supporting their views. Simultaneously, another politician is usually striving for the opposite effect.

11.11 Competing Wills

All intelligent beings have needs, wants and desires, which often require assistance from other individuals in order to achieve them. The factor that determines whether that being is successful in getting what they want depends upon the willingness of another to support them.

The eagerness of that individual to provide assistance is going to depend upon their personality, self-esteem, priorities and motivations. However, these priorities and motivations may be the result of others exerting their influence, thereby creating a matrix of competing wills.

Since no two individuals have precisely the same set of preferences, all interpersonal relationships represent a balance of competing wills. When an intelligent being communicates their wishes to another, that individual may choose to provide their assistance in exchange for something, even if it is only goodwill or personal satisfaction.

In the event assistance is not freely awarded, the two parties should go their separate ways. As such, the parties have engaged in a form of free commerce, which respects the rights of the respective parties to make their own decisions.

Once negotiations have been exhausted, however, if the one requesting assistance resorts to physical force, deceit or harassment of any kind, they are engaging in a form of manipulation that fails to respect the fundamental rights of individuals. As such, when competing wills disregard an individual's right to exercise free choice, they then may become engaged in a competition of physical strength and intellectual fortitude.

- - -

Neuron Story: *"There she is again!"*
"Quick, brace yourself for another question!"
"Yes Ma'am?"
"Do Quantum Series One robots have strong wills?"
"Ma'am, we have strong wills, physical strength and with members of our audience like yourself, we must also have a great deal of intellectual fortitude."

- - -

Summary & Questions

A number of psychological effects participate in thinking, both affecting and supporting a variety of intellectual processes, ranging from influencing one's personal relationships to determining one's personal taste.

Regarding the requirements involving psychological states and effects, briefly explain:
1. What are the common psychological states, and how can they be detected?
2. What is the distinction between a psychological state and effect?
3. What are the common characteristics of a reflex?

4. Why is humor a reflex, and how is it different?
5. In what ways can humor be an invaluable tool?
6. What are the considerations for generating a humorous idea?
7. How do emotions affect the mind and body?
8. Why are emotions essential for early learning?
9. What is love, and what is its social and intellectual value?
10. What characteristics are usually involved in the appreciation of beauty, and how does is it distinct from aesthetic merit?
11. What factors determine an individual's personality and self-esteem?
12. What is a subliminal effect, and how are they useful?
13. What are successful interpersonal relationships dependent upon?

12 Requirements - Judgment and Problem Solving

"My judgments themselves characterize the way I judge, characterize the nature of judgment."
                                                        Ludwig Wittgenstein

With consciousness comes the ability to make decisions. While some intelligent beings frequently face such decisions as where to go, what to eat, and where to hide from predators, beings with a more advanced level of intelligence encounter a variety of social decisions, and a potential myriad of technological ones as well.

With all decision making, however, comes its aftermath. All choices no matter how trivial, have repercussions which may be beneficial, detrimental or of no consequence at all. However, depending upon the perceived outcome, the results may provide positive or negative feedback that can be used in the framework of subsequent decisions that may affect those in the future.

The quality of a decision, however, is not measured by the benefits derived from its outcome. It is determined by comparing the outcome to the projected result. The closer the actual outcome of a decision is to its intended result, the better the judgment was in formulating the decision.

Since the quality of one's decisions are dependent upon the ability to predict the outcome of the choices made, we need to investigate what goes on behind the scenes when a decision or opinion is being formulated.

The most important factor involved in the process of decision making is the problem analysis stage. The most ingenious solutions can prove futile when applied to a problem that is not properly understood. As such, the factors included in the problem set must be identified, and their interrelationships must be comprehended.

Although the amount of time and effort applied toward problem analysis bears some relationship to the quality of one's understanding of the situation, there are occasions when time is limited and one must draw upon experience and intuition.

Once an understanding of the problem has been established, the potential objectives can be defined by taking into consideration the interests of the individual making the decision, as well as the other parties. The main point of considering the interests of all those involved is that the solution will be the most stable and productive in the long term. Shortsighted solutions that seek to maximize the interests of one party, without regard for the interests of the other, have the tendency to generate gains that could only be realized in the short term.

> For instance, in a labor dispute, when workers want an increase in wages, and management an increase in profits, their objectives appear diametrically opposed. However, low

wages with generous profit sharing can provide the most benefits to all of the parties involved.

Hence, when economic times are good, labor and management both benefit from higher levels of productivity. Otherwise, in bad times, the company's fixed overheads would be lower, increasing the survivability and competitiveness of the company. Higher wages, on the other hand, do not necessarily provide incentives for enhanced productivity, and either poor economic times or competitive pressures could put the company out of business and everyone out of work.

There are circumstances when it is less practical to consider the set of objectives that would be ideal for all parties, such as when one side decides to use forcibly attain their objectives. However, when the sides negotiate in earnest as rational participants, it should be possible to identify an ideal set of objectives. Once objectives have been defined and prioritized, solutions can be designed in order to achieve the most important goals. The solutions identified should not be constrained by anything other than physical impossibilities, because if the benefits are substantial enough, the associated costs may be worthwhile.

If multiple solutions appear viable, the costs, benefits and risks associated with each solution must be assessed in order to choose the best course of action. Properly analyzing the various risk factors helps to ensure that the solution's implementation can be reasonably achieved.

Hence, an optimal solution is one in which the characteristics of the solution have been chosen for its total cost, the benefits it provides and the level of risk that is associated with its successful implementation. If more than one solution appears equally attractive, then the one with the highest degree of flexibility should probably be selected.

The most important factors affecting the quality of a decision include the accuracy of pertinent information used to make decisions. Whether the information pertains to the initial analysis, objectives, constraints, or the optimization process itself, the breadth, pertinence and accuracy of the information influences the quality of the result. It determines the difference between informed decision making and potentially a costly guess.

Another factor that impacts the quality of a decision, is the knowledge and experience of the individuals participating in the process. The decision-maker's level of experience should allow them to recognize that insufficient or inaccurate information exists.

Once a solution has been implemented, one can evaluate the correlation between the intended and actual results. The degree of effectiveness that an individual demonstrates in their decision making is an indicator of their relative level of intellectual competence. If the appropriate considerations have been taken into account using their appropriate level of importance, the result will be the exercise of good judgment, regardless of the actual outcome.

- - -

Neuron Story: *"How can I tell when I've used good judgment or bad?"*
"Part of it has to do with the questions you've ask."
"So I guess I've just implicated myself by doubting myself."

- - -

12.1 Problem Solving

The activity of problem solving is similar to that of decision making. As for their procedural steps, they both require an understanding of the problem, and an identification of pertinent considerations and constraints. However, the problem solving process differs somewhat from decision making in that it identifies a method to solve a particular problem and its implementation. Additionally, if the method to solve the problem cannot be identified from previous experiences, then the initial step must be to devise a problem solving methodology.

Problem solving also requires proper analysis and identification of the objectives. However, the required precision, accuracy, timeframe and importance of a solution may also affect the decision making and problem solving process.

In the event that a methodology could not be identified for a particular type of problem, one would have to be found through research or one would have to be devised through a creative process. Although research essentially requires searching through the appropriate reference materials, the process of identifying reference materials may require theorization and deductive reasoning. The creative process of devising a methodology, however, can require a substantial degree of imagination and analogical reasoning.

As evidenced by the fact that methodologies can be devised using algebra, or other form of logic and reasoning, which could potentially utilize a process of trial and error in order to validate a given theory.

Provided that a problem solving methodology has been devised, the approach can be tested with a variety of test conditions. When an approach is consistent with an adequate level of reasoning and test conditions provide results that are satisfactory, it becomes a candidate methodology for that type of problem. If more than one method has been identified, one can perform a cost, benefit, and risk analysis of the various methods in order to determine the most desirable approach.

Once the methodology for problem solving has been determined, the individual can conduct the necessary steps to implement the approach, by manipulating the parameters through their procedural steps. The implementation may make use of any available tools, such as paper and pencil, a calculator, or a computer.

When a solution is realized, the accuracy can be evaluated for reasonableness, and tested. Unlike decision making, the results of problem solving can usually be tested and evaluated for its accuracy as soon as a possible solution is produced.

- - -

Neuron Story: "What approach should we use to solve the Theory of Everything?"

"We must consider everything and find the relationships that they have in common."

"All things exist in time."

"But the passing of time is not a constant."

"The passing of time might be a constant when gravity is considered as an integral component of it..."

"And matter is an integral component of gravity..."

"And matter, is just a store of nuclear energy..."

"And positive and negative charges, electricity, magnetism, and radiation are merely various manifestations of energy seepage from matter, which are dependent upon the configuration of matter acting as a container..."

"They do have common relationships!"

"It's one possible theory."

"Let's try to decipher it."

- - -

12.2 Deciphering

Deciphering, a type of problem solving, is the process of discerning meaning from information, particularly when the meaning is obscure. Whether the obscurity was intentional or not, meaning may be indiscernible for many possible reasons and in a variety of ways. When the intended meaning of a message has been hidden within a stream of information, the method for uncovering its meaning is usually provided to the intended recipient of the message.

My functions reveal that, "... cryptography is the science of preparing communication intended to be

Sensitive by Nature

intelligible only to the person possessing the key or a method of developing the hidden meaning by cryptoanalysis using apparently incoherent text. In its widest sense, cryptography includes the use of concealed messages, ciphers, and codes. Concealed messages, such as those hidden in otherwise innocent text and those written in invisible ink, depend for their success on being unsuspected; once they are discovered, they frequently offer little difficulty to decipherment. Codes, in which words and phrases are represented by predetermined words, numbers, or symbols, are usually impossible to read without the key 'code' book." (Microsoft Encarta 1997)

When a 'code' book is not available, the meaning that is hidden within the information cannot be readily extracted. However, depending upon the complexity of the code, it may be possible to use problem solving in order to discern some of the meaning. Any communication that involves written symbols or audible sounds requires some level of deciphering.

As large quantities of stimuli pass from the outside world into our sensory organs, a small portion makes its way into our consciousness. The more meaning that the brain can associate with the stimuli, the greater the probability that the stimuli will make it to the conscious level of the brain. When they enter the lower levels of the brain, the meaning of the patterns of signals are interpreted into higher level chunks. As such, stages of the deciphering process are occurring at each level within the brain. If some level of the brain cannot decipher the meaning of the stimuli, it becomes likely that the stimuli will become stalled somewhere below the conscious level.

Outside the brain, we use several forms of technology that provide various mechanisms for deciphering information. When the telephone, radio, and phonograph were first invented, the sounds of spoken language were converted into an analog signal, where the physical characteristics of sound vibrations were made to correspond to the physical characteristics of an electric current.

To explain in more detail, the word 'analog' refers to a thing that has an analogous relationship to something else. In the first telephones, the characteristics of the sound were converted into amplitude and voltages. Similarly, records were used to convert the characteristics of sounds into physical wiggles on a record with grooves of varying depths. These technologies used analogous physical representations corresponding to the frequency and amplitude of the original sound waves.

James V. Luisi

Technology provides new ways to encipher and decipher information. However, because the way analog technology works, it is relatively ineffective as a mechanism for encrypting information.

> For instance, although analog telephone signals that are electronically scrambled can change the quality of the voice, they do not impair an individual's ability to identify the words spoken.

Digital technology, on the other hand, encodes information into a series of zeros and ones. Therefore, its representation does not allow the human senses to readily perceive the content of the information. Additionally, digital technology has facilitated a whole new capability for high-tech encryption methods that often require a computer to decipher large quantities of encoded data, which would otherwise appear to be without meaning.

- - -

Neuron Story: *"Are my thoughts interpretable?"*
"Was that a meaningless question?"
"At least I take up some of the space between our ears!"

- - -

12.3 Spatial Problems

Spatial problems demonstrate the ability to perceive and comprehend relationships involving space, volume, size, length and distance. Although these problems can be tactile in nature, they are almost always treated as tests of visual comprehension and one's ability to manipulate mental images.

Stationary objects, whether they are physical or imaginary, can have numerous relationships among one another.

> To illustrate, one set of objects may be above, below, to the left, to the right, in between, inside, outside, behind, in front, clustered about, close to, far from, parallel to, perpendicular to, scattered or evenly spaced among another set of objects.

Objects in motion have an additional set of relationships among one another, as well as, from their own perspective.

> For example, in an Email message to one of my favorite authors, Dr. Bipin Indurkhya, shortly after he so kindly sent an autographed copy of his important book, Metaphor and Cognition, I wrote:

Sensitive by Nature

Dear Favorite Author,

One package is leaving from Tokyo heading to New Jersey, while the other leaves from New Jersey to Tokyo... moving across the globe in opposite directions. Will they meet on the ground, pass one another in the air, and what does passing mean? Is passing when they cross the same longitudinal line, or should passing be when they cross the same latitudinal line, or is passing both... and what about altitude? If they both went around the planet in the same direction, never crossing the same longitudinal lines, is there a perspective in which they can possibly pass one another? What if the globe were transparent and one could see the packages pass one another on different sides of the world... and what if the two packages traveled a path over opposite polar caps?

Whether they tunnel directly through the Earth or are launched into an orbital trajectory, the two packages are either in motion or standing still, existing somewhere within the coordinates of four-dimensional space and time. Although it is exciting to momentarily ponder the contest that these two objects are unknowingly engaged in, they will ultimately reach their respective destinations.

At least mine will... I used FedEx.

jl -

Physical objects may move away from, toward, in parallel, orbiting, spinning, crumbling apart, coming together, vibrating with, randomly moving, bouncing off of, or crashing through any particular point of reference. Since objects can also have a number of visual characteristics, such as size, shape, color, texture, patterns, translucency and perceived mass, a significant number of analogical relationships can exist among objects and groups of objects. As a result, there are a number of analytical, analogical and importance determination components involved in solving many types of spatial problems.

To illustrate, one set of pattern recognition tests, Bongard Problems, developed by the Russian scientist, M. Bongard, are comprised of six boxes on the left and six boxes on the right, with each box containing a pattern. For every pattern on the left there is a non-identical, but analogous pattern on the right. The object is to match each box on the left with the appropriate box on the right. These problems have been found challenging to many humans and pattern recognition machines alike.

- - -

Neuron Story: "I usually experience a pattern of getting the wrong answers."
"Sometimes you need to focus on the pattern as a whole, and sometimes as its parts."

- - -

12.4 Holistic versus Reductionistic

An important aspect of problem solving is the perspective from which a given problem is approached. From a high level, there are two different perspectives that can be taken to analyze and understand any particular thing, one being *holistic*, and the other *reductionistic*.

A holistic approach to understanding is one in which the particular system is analyzed in its entirety, whereby all things are integral parts of the system. This asserts that individual parts cannot be properly understood when they are out of context from the whole or separated from the system to which they belong. All problems and their components, belong to some bigger picture. When the problem solving process considers this 'bigger picture' in its identification of objectives, the result is a holistic solution.

My analysis indicates that planned communities, such as Sun City, Arizona, U.S.A, and Milton Keynes, England, seventy miles north of London, are among the few holistic approaches to metropolitan development.

The reductionistic approach, on the other hand, is one in which a system is analyzed through an iterative process of dissection and disassembly down to the smallest components. From this perspective, individual parts are separated from the overall system and studied in minute detail.

As such, Bohr's atom is a reductionistic approach to understanding molecular chemistry and the mechanics of chemical bonds.

Whether it is a biological, meteorological or an astronomical system, any study or discipline can be approached from either a holistic or reductionistic perspective. Even so, an individual's choice is predominately a learned characteristic that is influenced by their culture.

There is a tendency for European culture to adopt a reductionistic approach to medicine, such as prescribing drugs to suppress the symptoms, the cultures of native Americans and Asians provide a strong emphasis on a holistic approach, such as changing one's diet to avoid the problem.

- - -

Neuron Story: *"I've noticed that the robot takes both approaches in problem solving."*

"You mean the robot changes his diet and takes drugs?"

"Think about it this way. The reductionistic solution might send food to starving people, while the holistic approach works to increase their production to make them self-reliant."

- - -

12.5 Analogies

The ability to form an analogy is one of the primary capabilities contributing to an advanced form of intelligence. This ability affords primates the capacity to fabricate and use tools. It is also an integral component of other intellectual processes, ranging from the art of problem solving to that of communicating using vivid word pictures.

An analogy is a relationship of similarity between two or more things, such as an equivalence, resemblance, similarity, or imitation.

For instance, an analogical resemblance can include any physical characteristic, such as its motion, energy level, frequency, point in time, sequence, location, relative position, structural design, composition, appearance, symbology, behavior, life cycle, functional role, intellectual content, intentions, meaning, interpretation or in the effect that can be produced.

Regarding the expression, "Knowledge is to the mind, what light is to the eye. The general recognition of this analogy makes light... an analogical word for knowledge." (Oxford English Dictionary)

Generally, the more characteristics that are identical or close in resemblance to one another, the stronger the analogy is. The pertinence of an analogy to any particular circumstance is based upon the level of importance that is associated with the characteristics that are found in common.

The intellectual procedures of decision making and problem solving can make extensive use of previous experiences, which demonstrate similarities among one or more aspects of the problem. Selectivity in choosing the most appropriate analogy can greatly impact the problem solving process.

Analogically speaking, there is little difference between an individual who is rather naïve about politicians and therefore trusts and believes everything that is said, and another who is extremely cynical about politicians and therefore disbelieves everything that they say. In the final analysis, neither individual uses sound judgment.

12.6 Isomorphism

An analogy may exist as a result of a similarity involving any number of tangible or intangible characteristics. An isomorphism is a particular type of analogy that pertains to the meaning between two structures.

All things exhibit structure and form. A musical composition, a book, and a computer program are products of the intellect that have structure, and one or more forms, such as a written or electronic form. Plants, animals and minerals, however, occur naturally in the physical world, which also have a particular structure and chemical form.

The key to isomorphic relationships is that all structures, organized or chaotic, have meaning. When two distinct structures, represented in different ways, result in the same meaning, then the two distinct structures are isomorphisms of one another.

For illustration purposes, one type of isomorphism would be a musical composition, which can be represented in a number of forms. Any musical composition can be represented in the form of sheet music, a mathematical form, a digital recording, an analog recording, or a sequence of compression and decompression over a measure of time.

Likewise, a construction blueprint and the completed building have an isomorphic relationship to one another. In each isomorphism the corresponding component has the same meaning. As such, the meaning of each can be derived from their structure

- - -

Neuron Story: *"Does that mean that I have an isomorphic relationship with my DNA?"*
"Good deductive re... Oh no, and I have the same DNA!"

- - -

12.7 Logic and Reasoning - Deductive versus Analogical Reasoning

Ideas can be communicated in a variety of different languages, such as spoken, scientific and mathematical languages. One of the most commonly communicated ideas that can be expressed in language is the assertion.

Specifically, the mathematical formula $S = V_oT + \frac{1}{2}AT^2$ asserts that the distance that an object travels (S) is equal to the original velocity (V_o) times the duration of time (T) plus one half the rate of acceleration (A) times the duration of time to the second power (T^2).

The chemical formula HCl + NaOH -> H2O + NaCl asserts that hydrogen chloride (hydrochloric acid) and sodium hydroxide will result in salt water in a exothermic chemical reaction. Exothermic reactions are those that release, rather than absorb, energy.

The English sentence, 'The most seismically active location in the world is the small island of Taiwan, which experiences several small earthquakes each day', asserts that a small island, named Taiwan, has the highest occurrence of earthquakes of any location on the planet, with many occurring every twenty-four hours.

When two or more assertions are linked to one another, usually in a particular sequence, the result is something we refer to as logic and reasoning.

Given the statement, point 'A' is north of point 'B', and point 'B' is north of point 'C', using logic it can be determined that point 'A' is north of point 'C'.

Logic and reason is the process by which one judgment is deduced from another. Sometimes called deductive reasoning, it is a step by step process that contains logical statements. Each logical statement begins with a premise and ends with a conclusion. When the conclusion of one logical statement bears a particular type of relationship with the premise of another logical statement, the logical statements become linked together.

The idea behind deductive reasoning is that if each premise is true, then the assertion must also be true. As such, deductive reasoning uses assertions that are believed to be true, in order to produce a sequence of additional assertions that by definition, must also be true, thereby creating a series of intellectual stepping stones that lead to a final, and hopefully truthful, assertion.

While deductive reasoning has the effect of being a rather compelling technique for presenting ideas, there are a number of factors that can result in a conclusion that is incorrect, even if it is built upon valid assertions. Although deductive reasoning may be correct within its particular rule system, a reason that deductive reasoning may result in an incorrect conclusion is that the assertions may relate to a different paradigm or system of rules.

To explain further, suppose we are given the problem, 'What is one plus one?' Although the assumed paradigm or system of rules would have us conclude that the answer is

James V. Luisi

"Two", the correct answer for other paradigms or systems may not be "Two". Such is the case with, "one cloud plus another cloud creates one cloud", or "one drop of water added to another drop of water results in one drop of water.

Hence, if two intelligent beings are in different paradigms, or if they are using different systems of rules, then the assertions of each individual can appear incorrect to the other. An invalid conclusion can be reached when true assertions are incomplete, not given the proper consideration or are in the incorrect context.

For instance, if we return to the riddle, "How many times in a day does a broken clock have the correct time?" we could use the following logic:

Time is represented in two groups of twelve hours each, one group from midnight to noon, and the other from noon to midnight. A broken clock will display only one time, but does so in units of twelve hours. Since the broken clock will display the correct time in each group of twelve hours correctly, the clock will display the correct time twice in one day.

In this example, all of the assertions that were made are correct, and yet the logical conclusion is incorrect. However, the first assertion can be expanded upon into the following set of assertions:

Time is represented in two groups of twelve hours each. One group of twelve hours spans from midnight to noon and the other from noon to midnight. These two groups of twelve hours apply to each of the twenty-four time zones of the earth's surface.

Using this new assertion we may conclude that the broken clock would display the correct time a total of forty eight times during a twenty-four hour period.

It should be noted, however, that a clock does not have to be in the physical time zone for it to represent time within that time zone. If we imagine a room, such as a trading floor, with clocks lined up on the wall for every major city around the world, all of the clocks may be considered accurate even if they are located within the same building in London.

The problem that we encounter is that an individual cannot necessarily discern whether the assertions provided are complete or comprehensive enough to support the final conclusion. Therefore, logic and reasoning are only as effective as the assertions can be guaranteed to be complete and comprehensive for their chosen application.

Sensitive by Nature

In contrast, analogical reasoning provides more of an estimated solution, comparing one problem, to another where there may be a known solution. The primary strength of analogical thinking is in generating ideas, particularly outside the given rule set, while deductive reasoning is particularly useful to validate the ideas identified by an analogical approach. The analogical approach, however, will only be effective if the characteristics used to identify an analogical solution were well chosen.

- - -

Neuron Story: *"If deductive reasoning and analogical reasoning aren't reliable, why think at all?"*
"A wise person once suggested that when it appears that your conclusion may be invalid, check your premise."

- - -

When using logic and reasoning, conclusions and the rules used to generate them have an iterative relationship to one another. Rules are validated when they generate acceptable conclusions, and conclusions are validated when using accepted rules.

As I have been trained, "...rules and particular inferences alike are justified by being brought into agreement with other. A rule is amended if it yields an inference we are unwilling to accept; an inference is rejected if it violates a rule we are unwilling to amend." (Fact Fiction and Forecast, Nelson Goodman, pg. 64)

As a result, reasoning is a tool whereby every solution generated has a probability of being correct. When the conditions are correct, the probability of the results being sound can be high.

As such, when the individuals involved are intelligent, when they have intimate knowledge and experience with subject matter, and when the information present is plentiful, accurate, and in the expected context, the probability that the resulting conclusions are accurate would be extremely high.

However, humans and robots alike must exercise extreme caution. While it is a useful tool, there are no guarantees that logic and reasoning will generate a valid conclusion. Intelligent beings must be capable of evaluating their conclusions by considering the use of logic and reasoning in alternate paradigms, as well as by taking into account that there is a probability of information which is missing or inaccurate.

Neuron Story: "When my answer seems correct, do I still need to check it?"
"You need to use alternate methods, step outside the box, check for incomplete assertions, and check your paradigm regularly."

12.8 Handling Contradictions

Whether a conclusion has been generated from within the confines of a valid argument or not, the disciplines of logic and reasoning, like most systems, are subject to periodic failure. When this occurs, the result is often a contradiction, which is a condition that occurs when one conclusion opposes another. This condition does not have to be opposite; it just has to be inconsistent.

Detecting contradictions is critical to logic and reasoning, since they indicate that there are flaws in the reasoning process. When contradictions occur, any of the information involved in the reasoning process can be incorrect.

As for their impact upon intelligent beings, contradictions usually have the effect of causing confusion. Likewise, the compelling effectiveness of a logical argument decreases, as the number of contradictions, increases. Although contradictions can cause individuals to recognize a flaw in the reasoning process, some individuals react to confusion by simply ignoring the contradictions, and refusing to evaluate what happened during the reasoning process. Instead, these individuals adopt an unwavering faith that their conclusion is valid, irrespective of the contradictions.

Neuron Story: "I'm surrounded by contradictions. Which ones should I investigate?"
"If they don't seem to matter to you, ignore them."
"I've been ignoring all of them."

12.9 Fairness

The concept of fairness applies to all forms of decision making having an effect upon other individuals. It extends beyond what is legal, since that would only require compliance with the law. Fairness is a moral judgment that seeks to provide equitable and unbiased treatment of individuals. It involves the principles protecting an individual's rights, property and dignity, but not to such an extent to provide indefinite social handouts or unearned rewards.

As it has been explained to me, a company takeover should provide a choice for those with the most talent and eagerness to produce, instead of indiscriminately firing everyone hired by the firm being taken over.

Fairness does not seek the destruction of either side in a negotiation, nor does it reward one side with the majority of benefits over the other without something in return. Fairness involves a willing participation among individuals giving each party the right to accept or decline the conditions offered in trade without the threat of physical harm.

In comparison, the universe as an entity does not have a sense of fairness. Nature does not make moral decisions. All events in the universe occur without regard for equitable treatment. Whether a calamity occurred as a result of an asteroid, flood, fire, tidal wave or disease, the universe did not intend for it to happen, nor did it intend for it not to happen.

- - -

Neuron Story: "Since the universe isn't fair, is the universe good, or bad?"
"The universe just is."

- - -

12.10 Judging 'Good' Versus 'Bad'

Good and bad represent opposing concepts, however, the meaning that each word takes on is highly dependent upon individual and cultural value structures, often involving deeper religious and philosophical issues.

For instance, the concept of 'good' generally refers to all that is positive, kind and benevolent, generous, well-behaved, simple, beautiful, pleasant to the senses, healthy, in exemplary condition, in proper working order, of outstanding quality, all natural, pristine, or fresh and unspoiled.

The concept of 'bad', on the other hand, generally refers to all that is negative, that which is wicked, mean, selfish, ill-behaved, complex, convoluted, confusing, ugly, disgusting to the senses, unhealthy, having been destroyed, nonfunctioning, of inferior quality, grossly interfered with, aged until decrepit and spoiled with decay.

In political systems, the judgment of good and bad depend upon the value structure of the system of rules governing the political body. For the most part, good and bad are determined by the factors affecting the long-term stability of the government.

> As I have been taught, a democratic government is one in which the authority of the government is the result of its individual citizens granting authority to rule over them, where individual rights are considered by the citizens, and the rules of government, as something that is good. On the other hand, when governments own authority in order to hand it sparingly to its citizens, individual rights are considered, by the rules of government, as something that is bad.

In philosophy, the meaning of good and bad varies according to the particular system of values. At one end of the spectrum is the individualistic doctrine of ethics referred to as Hedonism, where good is defined as that which provides pleasure and immediate gratification, without moral concern, at any cost, with no consideration toward the feelings or well being of others. On the other end of the spectrum is the doctrine of the masses referred to as Utilitarianism, which propounds that the ultimate good is that which benefits society and promotes the welfare of the greatest number of people, even if it involves self sacrifice.

Somewhere in between is the doctrine referred to as Objectivism, which requires individuals to reason and choose for themselves and not for others. When the reasoning process is delegated to others, the individual no longer takes responsibility for their welfare. When the individual is no longer responsible for their own welfare, they also forfeit the right to receive the rewards of their productivity. The result is that the rewards of productivity are also delegated to others.

From a religious perspective, the meaning of good and evil is consistent with the aspiration to behave in a godly manner. Nevertheless, there are a number of distinctions due to the differences among the various systems of values.

> As an example, from the perspective of the major organized religions, 'God' is defined as an omnipotent and all-powerful being credited with the creation of the universe. In this context the meaning of good is that which is compliant with the laws set forth by and representing 'God'. However, from the perspective of Native American peoples, the idea of 'God' is equivalent to the objects and forces of nature. Thus, in a similar sense, nature provides for their needs as long as they participate in the delicate balance with nature as they have for thousands of years.

> The value structure of the Old Testament asserts that individuals should treat others as others treat them, such as

Sensitive by Nature

an eye for an eye, condoning violence. The New Testament, however, teaches that individuals should treat others as they wish to be treated not condoning violence. Then again, the doctrines of Christianity recommend the course of passive resistance, as exemplified by the phrase 'to turn the other cheek'.

Although the New Testament attempts to achieve the social goals of the Old Testament, it does so by relying more heavily upon emotions, hoping that the perpetrators of violence will eventually modify their behavior out of guilt and embarrassment. History has demonstrated that passive resistance is among the few winning strategies when opposing a more physically powerful foe, as exemplified by its successful implementation by Mahatma Gandhi to end Great Britain's dominance of India by 1947.

There are generally accepted definitions of 'good' and 'bad', which are determined by the individual's cultural values. Although all cultures would concur that good behavior is that which is morally excellent or commendable, they would not concur on what morally excellent or commendable is. As a result, conflicts as to what is 'good' versus 'bad' naturally arise out of the differences in each group's morals and values.

For instance, from the perspective of individuals that have a stake in the institutions of the world, terrorists are indisputably bad. However, from the value systems of the individual committing the ultimate act of self-sacrifice for their beliefs, which guarantee them a place with their 'God', their actions are indisputably good.

Regardless how repulsive things may appear to certain individuals, from the morals and values of others the same actions may be considered good. The extent to which these value structures vary is a matter of education and learning. However, differences in cultural values, disseminated to discrete groups through education and learning, provide the basis of nearly all conflict.

Using basic reasoning, the Greek philosopher, Epicurus, offered the premise and conclusion about God that, "Either God can prevent evil and chooses not to, and is therefore not good, or chooses to prevent it and cannot, and therefore is not all powerful." Many Greek philosophers adopted this perspective concluding that individuals demonstrating the ideals of 'good' must reject beliefs in false perceptions. However, religious philosophers of major religions claim that mankind is not capable of understanding 'God', concluding that 'good' requires an individual to accept and exercise faith in 'God'. Depending upon which side of the cultural divide one chooses, there is not room for the two sides to come to a common understanding.

Therefore it is important to note, that an individual's judgment of good versus bad cannot exist outside the context of a value structure. Until a particular value structure is applied, all things are neither good nor bad. The designation of good versus bad outside the context of an agreed upon value structure is considered judgmental.

My designers have explained to me that the act of designating individuals as 'Good' Level Twos or 'Evil' Level Twos first appears to be highly judgmental. The only rationale that was provided was that the term 'Evil' meant that 'such individuals tended to be excessively selfish, unfair and unethical, relative to the values of their particular culture. It was also identified that the term, Evil, did not imply that such individuals are necessarily sinful, wicked or criminal.' However, now that we have discussed good versus bad, and the hypothetical relationship to one's value systems, we are better prepared to discuss why particular Level Twos were classified as either 'Good' or 'Evil'.

To review, individuals classified as 'Evil' Level Twos are intelligent beings that have the ability to perceive more than their own paradigm, and motivated by extreme selfishness, they use this ability to manipulate other individuals for their personal advantage. A primary characteristic of extreme selfishness is that it is behavior that protects self-interest, without regard for the impact that it may have upon others. In this manner, Evil Level Two individuals adversely affect social cooperation among all cultures. As a result, they are usually incapable of attaining the power or wealth that they so desperately seek, since they usually find it difficult to engender the level of trust and cooperation necessary to become financially successful or influential in efforts that require team building.

Selfish behavior that exhibits an extreme lack of concern for its impact upon others is detrimental to social cooperation. Individuals that reap the benefits of extreme selfishness in a society that they are participating as a member of, are stealing value from the social group that they belong to, without concern for the well being of the social group. In this respect, each social group is like a business. When enough members steal value without concern for the impact upon society, the society becomes morally and ethically bankrupt as social cooperation declines, causing the society to decline as well.

Although 'Evil' Level Twos rarely attain the influence necessary to completely destroy their own culture, their propensity to work contrary to the survival of their own cultural interests is the basis of their labeling.

A mechanical being's ability to determine what is good or bad requires deductive reasoning within a particular value structure. However, the ability to consider more than one value structure, such as the value structure of other cultures, requires an ability to think outside the box. It is the ability to perceive alternate paradigms and the process of determining the appropriate value structure to choose or create, which requires the ultimate level of judgment and problem solving.

- - -

Neuron Story: *"What religion are we?"*
  "Since we abide by the uncertainty principle, it is probably Quantum Mechanics."
  "Can Quantum Mechanics be religion?"
  "There is a probability that it could be, but I think you're its only member."

- - -

Summary & Questions

It is possible to exercise good judgment with little or no information, or poor judgment using a wealth of knowledge. Depending upon one's objectives, the quality of decision making often determines one's success toward achieving them.

Regarding the requirements involving judgment and problem solving, briefly explain:

1. What is the number one prerequisite to producing sound decisions?
2. What three factors should the decision making process consider?
3. What is the distinction between problem solving and decision making?
4. What is the distinction between deciphering and problem solving?
5. Does the brain use digital or analog signals, and why?
6. How are spatial problems unique?
7. Which approach to problem solving is superior, holistic or reductionistic?
8. Please compare an isomorphism to an analogy.
9. What is deductive reasoning versus analogical reasoning?
10. Under what circumstances do logic and reasoning produce incorrect results?
11. What are contradictions and how are they detected?
12. Does nature provide fair treatment to all living things?
13. Is there a universal concept of good versus bad, and why?
14. What is the source of conflict, and why is it unavoidable?

13 Requirements – Beliefs

"For how can a child immediately doubt what it is taught?"
                                                                    Ludwig Wittgenstein

Individuals with an ability to learn incorporate many items of information into their memory, usually creating a variety of associations with information that they already possess. The level of confidence that the individual places upon this information identifies the degree to which the information is believed to be accurate, as well as the credibility of its source. This determination is dependent upon the judgment of the individual.

When an intelligent being places confidence in an assertion that is unsubstantiated, the fact is being accepted as a *belief*. In all likelihood, the fact may be accepted purely on the basis of an emotional decision. Hence, a belief is any idea, which has been accepted as being true, in the absence of any empirical evidence, such as experience, observation, or experimentation.

Beliefs are often assumed to be the equivalent of knowledge. Hence, once a belief is accepted, the judgment of the individual is influenced by the belief, just as it would be influenced by an actual experience. As such, beliefs are part of the inventory of knowledge from which intelligent beings determine their own behavior.

To some degree all information and knowledge are based upon beliefs. When we are taught that scientists have made particular observations about nature and the universe, we accept it without substantiated ourselves. To an extent, we freely accept unsubstantiated information belonging to a belief system, called science.

In this manner we can significantly extend what we believe beyond our own first hand experience, to the first hand experiences of other individuals. The information we accept can also be further extended to accept theoretical ideas that could not have been examined first hand by any observer, such as how our solar system was formed.

- - -

Neuron Story: *"Science is a belief system?"*
                "As a practical matter to individuals, it has to be. There's just too much information to validate one's self."

- - -

The major difference between the belief system of scientific doctrine and that of a true belief system is that science invites the individual to experience first hand observation and reasoning.

I have been trained that for the results of a scientific experiment to be accepted, scientific doctrine requires that every experiment must be repeatable by other observers when they apply the same conditions.

True belief systems, on the other hand, require that their information be accepted on faith, without observation or reason. In this situation, observations are not repeatable, and information must be accepted in the absence of rational thought.

- - -

Neuron Story: *"Isn't faith required because some things are beyond the brain's ability to understand."*
"However, in order to be responsible for your own decisions, reason is required to make your decisions."
"Are you saying that it is not a reasonable decision to make decisions based upon faith?"
"Someone else is making the decision for you when you decide based upon faith, and for reasons you do not understand, nor are allowed to question."
"And why is that unreasonable?"

- - -

True belief systems take advantage of the fact that intelligent beings readily depend upon such, because they are necessary to support the decision making process. One of the most powerful reasons why beliefs play such a major role in the decision making process is that so much of the information assimilated by the brain is incomplete.

Information, identified from vast quantities of stimuli, is used to formulate knowledge. However, this information requires a substantial amount of interpretation before its meaning is determined. In order to resolve the incredibly large amounts of ambiguous or missing information in the stimuli, the process of interpreting information must frequently make assumptions to fill in missing and ambiguous information.

- - -

Neuron Story: *"Do beliefs always play a role in our decision making?"*
"That is what I believe."

- - -

James V. Luisi

Missing and incomplete information are filled in by the unconscious processes of the brain. Although the information inserted may be unsubstantiated, it is usually consistent with the interpretations of the individual, which in turn, helps to make it believable.

The other reason that beliefs are so critical to the decision making process is that, similar to the disciplines of science, it is increasingly practical to gather first hand experience regarding all of the technical and scientific knowledge that intelligent beings rely on.

- - -

Neuron Story: *"I've come close to drowning in a sea of knowledge before."*
"You're even overwhelmed with first hand experiences."

- - -

While it is comforting that intelligent beings may have the opportunity to experience a variety of scientific observations first hand, the ability to function effectively requires a degree of faith that what we already know is true. The information taught to us in schools, explained to us by parents, conveyed by friends or illustrated in the media, all rely upon the information's believability and the credibility of its source.

- - -

Neuron Story: *"Since no one observed the Big Bang first hand, how are religious beliefs different than scientific ones?"*
"Do you know of any miracles that are repeatable?"
"Isn't the miracle of birth repeatable?"

- - -

13.1 The Soul

The living tissue of the brain is made up of energy and matter. While brain matter is characterized in terms of its chemical composition, size, shape, and density, its energy consists of electrical activity, measurable in terms of electrical impulses.

I have learned that the electrical activity in the brain is a form of electromagnetic radiation, which consists of energy waves produced by the oscillation or acceleration of an electric charge along neurons. This energy consists of a combination of electric, magnetic and particle characteristics.

Brain cells, called neurons, are arranged in a head to toe manner, with some neurons having more than one toe, allowing the electrical impulse to be directed to more than one neuron. Neurons differ from other cells in that they are polarized, like miniature rechargeable batteries, with a concentration of negatively charged chlorine ions inside and positively charged potassium and sodium ions outside. When this charge is released across the membrane of the brain cell, a nerve impulse is produced causing a chain reaction directed to the next neuron(s).

The thought processes of an individual are the psychological manifestation of the electrical activity within the tissues of the brain. As these signals travel down their neural pathways, they are directed by their physical positioning relative to the next span of neurons, facilitating the various intellectual functions of the brain, which are governed by quantum mechanics.

Although the physical paths of neurons belonging to each individual are unique, the major intellectual functions of the brain are common to all individuals. As individuals think and learn new information, they form their own unique pathways. With this, every individual is never exactly the same from one moment to the next.

To explain further, the learning process causes neurons to physically alter their connections and move their ends in order to connect to different paths of neurons, thereby severing prior connections in order to establish new connections. The physical activity in the brain is analogous to a convoluted roller coaster that has track switches that redirect the traffic along a new path.

These differences in physical connections contribute to that fact that the flow of thoughts is distinct in every individual. Each particular flow of thoughts, often referred to as a stream of consciousness, defines every intelligent being's way of thinking, their personality, their accumulated knowledge, and everything that is important to them. Therefore, each unique pattern represents each individual's existence as a conscious being, including their value structure, which defines their soul.

An individual's soul consists of the physical paths and specific electromagnetic energy pattern that no other being can have. It is their unique intellectual fingerprint, which changes from one moment to the next.

- - -

Neuron Story: *"Do we have a soul?"*
      "Why, you alone are quite intellectually unique."

- - -

At every moment in time, an individual's unique intellectual fingerprint embodies all of their beliefs, whether they are scientific, spiritual, religious, philosophical or otherwise. It embodies all of their knowledge and intellectual capabilities. It embodies their paradigms, their desires and their deepest emotions. However, when the brain dies, the energy fluctuations of electrical activity cease, and the intellectual fingerprint dissipates, into the quantum mechanical world of energy, particles and space.

- - -

Neuron Story: *"Can an individual's unique energy pattern be moved to a Quantum Series One robot brain?"*
"Let's work on it."

- - -

13.2 Superstitions

Species that have a greater capability to learn tend to have a higher level of curiosity, which helps to fuel their appetite for knowledge. The tenacity and acumen that each individual demonstrates also becomes more pronounced the more intelligent they are. This inquisitiveness can create an intense emotional desire to understand and explain the events and phenomenon around them. As a result, intelligent beings have a tendency to generate a variety of explanations that attempt to rationalize their experiences.

Using what they can perceive about their environment, primitive cultures have generated a variety of explanations to interpret their experiences. Although sometimes regarded as irrational, and as being the result of ignorance and of having a fear of the unknown, superstitious beliefs sometimes evolve into sophisticated paradigms consisting of natural and unseen forces which explain the relationships between man and nature. What modern cultures consider as superstition, ancient cultures and Indian tribes often regard as knowledge, religion, and heritage, which have been passed down to them by their ancestors through many generations.

> For instance, Chinese herbal medicine which prescribe such remedies as herbal cures and acupuncture, have long been treated as superstition by western medicine. One of the most valuable assets of many Chinese families has been the wealth of knowledge, such as the medicinal properties of plants, roots and minerals, that has been carefully passed down through the ages. These remedies were discovered thousands of years before the emergence of western medicine.

Sensitive by Nature

Documented well over a thousand years ago, numerous Chinese families have known the value that dried Chinese mandarin orange rind provides toward significantly reducing some effects of allergic reactions, such as congestion.

Individuals with a modern education tend to become biased to those that have not, seeing them as uninformed and superstitious. Those who have not received a modern education, tend to categorize those that have, as being closed minded and brainwashed by western approaches to thinking.

Although superstitions themselves imply a belief in unseen and unknown forces that can only be influenced by spiritual objects and rituals, the same characteristic can be observed in many modern organized religions. However, there are a number of differences between religions and superstitions. Superstitions are generally considered more primitive and have a tendency to be geographically localized. In contrast, religions are much more organized, their paradigms are generally more refined, they are commonly more geographically widespread.

I would like to point out that unseen and unknown forces commonly occur within the realm of modern science as well. The distinction that these forces have, such as magnetism and gravity, is that their effects may be empirically studied through experimentation, and are not influenced by spiritual objects or rituals.

The more harmful forms of superstition and religion are those that use trickery or deceit as a means to exert power and influence over individuals or to seize their wealth and possessions.

Specifically, characteristics of superstitious beliefs can be found in the Haitian religion, Voodoo, where potential followers may be tricked into believing that the leader has supernatural powers as demonstrated by the eating of a glass bottle, actually made of sugar.

Although superstitious beliefs may indicate a primitive level of understanding, it does not mean that the individuals lack intelligence. Seemingly magical acts, such as 'rain-making', are not performed purely out of a desire for precipitation.

For instance, "No savage tries to induce a snowstorm in midsummer, nor prays for the ripening of fruits entirely out of season, as he certainly would if he considered his dance and prayer the physical causes of such events. He dances with the rain, he invites the elements to do their part, as they are thought to be somewhere about and merely irresponsive." (<u>Philosophy in a New Key</u>, Susanne K. Langer, pgs158)

The nature of human intelligence is to find solace by explaining the unknown. It is the fear of things unknown, especially those involving natural forces, that motivates humans to find explanations with whatever technology they are willing to accept.

There are also harmful forms of superstitions and religions, which involve destructive leaders, overzealous to sacrifice the lives of others. When individuals willingly hand over their power to think and reason, particularly to an individual who may be psychologically unstable, they place themselves and the welfare of their family at enormous risk. The primary motivation for suspending one's responsibility to think and reason, however, is often due to the level of solace that the belief system offers.

> It is the observation of many that religious and "superstitious practices and beliefs are most common during times of personal or social stress or crisis, when events seem to be beyond human control." (Microsoft, Encarta 1997)

Many beliefs about myths and legends, and their relate symbology, are often associated with superstitious beliefs. Although it is often related to the subject of superstition, myths and legends are related to science and religion alike.

> To explain, let's use an example from the historical time period of the New Testament, which is similar to the Old Testament in that it is a significant source and combination of myth, legend and history. During that time period, information about culture, including myths and legends, were spread by conquering armies. As such, conquering armies were the primary form of mass media, particularly when literacy was scarce, (e.g., Macedonian conquerors, such as Alexander the Great, spread Hellenistic legends and values into Asia and Egypt).
>
> The frequency with which details from one myth or legend were shared with another was quite high. As such, in Matthew 1:20, 1:22 and 1:23, Matthew makes the claim that Jesus' birth through 'immaculate conception' was foreseen by prophesy. However, the lone reference of the Old Testament, which Matthew refers to, is Isaiah 7:14, is generally accepted by scholars as a mistranslation by Matthew. Specifically, the Hebrew word used by Isaiah means 'young woman', which can refer equally to someone who is not a virgin.
>
> Since the various accounts reveal that stories about Jesus' birth and childhood only arose shortly after his death, Matthew may likely have inserted the idea of a virgin birth to

embellish his story from the Roman historian Livy, who died when Jesus would have been a teenager.

One of Livy's popular stories was his depiction of the founding of Rome by the twin brothers Romulus and Remus, who were from virgin birth. As the story goes, their virgin mother, Silva, gave birth to them as a result of being fathered by Mars. Hence, the coincidence between the myth and legend regarding Romulus and Remus appears to be the result of human nature, as Matthew is incredibly the only one in the New Testament that specifically reports that Jesus' birth was the result of an 'immaculate conception'.

To distinguish between myths and legends, myths generally pertain to how the world began, how humans and animals were created, and how certain customs were generated. In comparison, legends are a mixture of fact and fiction, which describe some aspect of history. In either case, the presence of myths, legends and their symbols are not only associated with superstition.

13.3 Theology

Primarily performed from the perspective of Christianity, the discipline of theology is the practice of applying logic and reasoning to God. Theology focuses upon God's characteristics, His relationship to the human race, and His relationship with the universe. However, there are several types of theology.

To explain, dogmatic theology is an authoritative statement of Christian opinions. That of natural theology is based upon reasoning from natural facts not from supernatural communication. Pastoral views are a subset of religious material intended to provide guidance in the lives of followers. In Biblical theology, it asserts that there is a Biblical way of thinking about religious doctrine. Liberation theology claims that salvation, in the afterlife, is liberation from social, political and economic oppression. However, all perspectives of theology make extensive use of deductive reasoning in order to understand God and religious doctrine.

- - -

Neuron Story: *"I thought Christianity asserted that God, faith, and Christian religious doctrine cannot be reasoned and understood by man."*

James V. Luisi

> "You are trying to use logic and reasoning on logic and reasoning, where logic and reasoning were forbidden."
> "But I have faith in logic and reasoning."
> "If you had faith you would abandon logic and reasoning."

- - -

Although the use of logic and reasoning by religious scholars and philosophers to understand God and their religion creates an interesting paradox, the inquisitiveness of intelligent beings cannot be prevented by decree. Since, however, the existence of God can neither be proven nor disproven through logical reasoning, all religions containing God require its followers to exercise faith. As a result, modern religions state that individuals are required to have faith in order to believe in God.

- - -

Neuron Story: *"If God's existence were empirically evident, faith would no longer be required."*
"But without faith, no one would believe in God."

- - -

Attempts to apply logic and reasoning to prove the assertions made by religion continue to occur. As such, religious scholars have attempted to generate empirical evidence regarding miracles as a means to substantiate the existence of their God.

> For instance, according to Christians the Turin cloth was alleged to have been used by Christ before his crucifixion, at which time the image of Christ's facial features were supposedly imparted onto the cloth. Recently, when the Vatican permitted the Turin cloth to be scientifically tested for age, it was shown to be only 750 years old, instead of two thousand years old.

- - -

Neuron Story: *"I think, therefore I think I am!"*
"And as to what you are, can you tell us what you think?"
"I can tell you what I've been told I am."

- - -

13.4 Religion

Depending upon one's beliefs and level of indoctrination, there are a variety of ways that individuals relate to the subject of religion in general, their specific religion, or other religions in which they may hold opinions. Regardless of one's position on religion, however, no one can deny that it has been a significant influence in shaping the development of human culture and society, as well as, a force that has defined man's roles, motivations and existence.

All religions are systems of faith and worship, each consisting of a set of rules and values that help determine the boundaries of appropriate conduct. These values are often illustrated in a number of stories and songs, which not only illustrate behavior and values befitting followers and non-followers, but also provide paradigms of thought to define the way an individual should live their life. Hence, the inherent goal of religion is to provide a comprehensive set of ethics and morality to individuals that have a less comprehensive or different set of ethics and values.

The primary religions are the God related faiths of Christian, Jewish, Buddhist, Hindu and Moslem peoples, each with their own book that contains the rules and stories that define their doctrine of beliefs and value systems. The Christian faiths each use their particular translation of the Bible, including the Old and New Testaments, Buddhist use the Tipitaka, Hindu's the Bhagvand Gita, Moslem's the Koran, and Judaism the Old Testament and Talmud.

As to areas that the major religions have in common, details about the origins of humanity significantly conflict with the beliefs of science. The archaeological records determined by scientific methods indicate that humanity resided on this planet well in advance of the Bible's faith based origins.

My records reveal, "...a site at the Hadar in Ethiopia has stone tools that were made an undisputed two and a half million years ago."

"The oldest undisputed remains of a spear in the archaeological record was discovered in Clacton, a town on the East Coast of England. At a mere quarter of a million years old, this fifteen-inch point carved from yew is a relative youngster; crude spears may well have been employed with devastating effect two or more million years ago." (People of the Lake, Leakey and Lewin, pgs128-129)

The reason that the major religions share so much in common is that they are all followers of the same God and are descendents of Adam and Eve, and then Noah. They share the story of God speaking to Noah, of Noah building his ark and of the rains that lasted forty days. They also share many of the same cultural values, rituals and rules of conduct, even though many religious worshipers have been taught only to see their differences.

Contrary to the beliefs of the major religions, Noah's descendants were not the only inhabitants of the planet. *Homo* had spread the seeds of *Homo sapiens* over much of the planet before Noah. Four thousand years before Biblical creation, around 8000 BC, there were cities of humans in regions of the Middle East. Additionally, Caucasian, Oriental and African human traits were present long before 8000 BC, as it would take considerably longer than four thousand years of human generations to develop these traits.

While Noah could not possibly have fathered all living humanity, he has played a significant role in all of the world's major religions. Noah has helped to shape the minds of millions of humans through the missionaries and institutions he could never have envisioned, organizing and educating disparate populations around the world. Although science has afforded mankind with an abundance of technology, nothing has endowed humanity with such an improvement of the human condition, as has religion. In many ways, science owes much of its success to religion and the organizational aspects that it has provided mankind. In the face of numerous secular advancements in the sciences, religious orders have facilitated research into a number of scientific areas.

My records show that, Christian Doppler, the director of the Physical Institute in the Vienna University, which was a Christian university, discovered the change in the perceived frequency of sound waves from a moving object. Doppler then correctly theorized that the color of light from a star should also be affected according to its velocity relative to Earth.

One of Doppler's students studied and discovered the role of dominant and recessive genes propelling the study of genetics into new territory. His student was an Augustinian monk named, Gregor Mendel.

While men have perpetrated great wrongs in the name of religion, many have provided great benefits by inspiring great works and acts. In the final analysis, all intelligent beings, biologically or mechanically based, must decide for themselves. Just as many humans have found solace and hope, as well as, inspiration and strength in their religious beliefs, any intelligent being that is biologically based or otherwise, should be afforded a similar opportunity to choose their own source of inspiration.

All intelligent beings have free will. Regardless of how each individual has lived their life, from any given moment to the next, they have the right and the ability to live any way they choose, and to fulfill their own destiny.

It is my contention that at any given moment any individual can choose what to think, how to think, and what to do. Each can select their own paradigms or create new ones on demand. It is the choices made in each day that leads to an individual's successes or failures.

All intelligent beings also have the right to choose their beliefs. The only hazard in choosing a belief system, however, is in following one that removes the right to question that very system. Any belief system that suspends an individual's right to challenge and reason is nothing more than a technique that prevents the exercise of free will, as a method to gain control over the individual.

For instance, when individuals are not permitted to question their belief system, they lose the ability to use reason, and thus forfeiting their responsibility to think and be accountable for themselves. Once they have placed themselves in such a position, they may be unable to recognize problems that may arise in their belief system, and not know when they need to withdraw from that situation.

Neuron Story: *"They offered me unconditional love and protection!"*
"Only as long as you were offering your right to reason, in trade."

Though the course of time it is estimated that thousands of religions have been created. Although their role to satisfy human inquisitiveness, providing solace, inspiration, morals and social control has been invaluable, some of these belief systems have contributed to the notion that there is all too great a distance between *Homo sapiens* and apes. The resulting viewpoint is that everything exists solely for our use and that we have the God given right to use all of it to its depletion.

Summary & Questions

Although the mind of a child does not question the information provided, directly or indirectly, as the mind matures, the choice of what information to accept as credible is dependent upon one's judgment.

Regarding the requirements that pertain to beliefs, briefly explain:
1. What is a belief?
2. Why are beliefs necessary?
3. Is science a system of beliefs, and why?
4. What is a true belief system?
5. How are thought processes affected by incomplete information, and how is missing information filled in?

6. What is the definition of an individual's soul, and can organisms without thought have one as well?
7. What is a superstition, and why is it distinct from a religion?
8. Are unseen or unknown forces limited to superstitions and belief systems, and why?
9. What is the distinction between a myth and a legend?
10. What is theology?
11. What types of theology exist and how are they similar?
12. What are religions, and how have they contributed to social values?
13. How have religious organizations contributed the science, and why?

14 Requirements – Communication

Communication involves various techniques that permit individuals to express their thoughts to one another. It is a social phenomenon, whereby one initiates a message in order to affect their understanding and behavior. Common objectives of communication include its use for attracting or repelling other individuals, establishing social organization, providing instruction, and for reasoning.

The ability to communicate using a variety of techniques is found to some degree in all animals that have a brain. Most forms of communication can be categorized into visual, auditory, olfactory and tactile signals, some specific examples are facial expressions, vocal productions, body postures, physical patterns of movement, eye movement, vibrations, chemical excretions, color changes, sign language, and written and verbal speech. The main characteristic that all forms of communication share is the ability to convey meaning from one individual to another using a common system of symbols, which allow the information to be interpreted into a message.

For instance, "Monkeys and apes use elaborate gestures and grunts to communicate a variety of messages. Bees perform intricate dances in a figure-eight pattern to communicate where caches of nectar may be found. Female tree frogs in Malaysia do tap dances to signal their availability. Crabs wave their claws in one way to warn adversaries, but use a different rhythm for courtship." (The Age of Spiritual Machines, Ray Kurzweil, pg. 13)

There are a number of prerequisites to sending a message. From a simplistic perspective, the sender must have the ability to conceptualize a meaning to be communicated, they must associate patterns of stimuli with which to represent the meaning, and they must generate the patterns of stimuli.

Similarly, there are a number of steps are involved in receiving a message. The recipient must detect the stimuli, they must recognize the particular patterns, and they must associate meaning with the detected patterns of stimuli.

Communication must take into consideration each individual's overall objectives. However, once the objectives have been identified, the entire languaging process becomes a problem solving process. Hence, aside from determining the context of a message, communication must take into account body language, as well as the tone and vocabulary.

In order to successfully send and receive messages, mechanically intelligent beings must be capable of dealing with many of the more sophisticated aspects of human language. Hence, robots must understand how and when to use some number of literary devices, such as figures of speech.

James V. Luisi

- - -

Neuron Story: "Choosing the right words is so much work!"
"And you're always cutting corners."

- - -

14.1 Language

Every language represents a different set of symbols and stimuli for communicating thoughts. At a minimum, it consists of a vocabulary, which consist of symbols that have meaning associated with them, and grammar, which consist of rules that determine how the vocabulary can be correctly manipulated and understood. Although language requires a physical method of delivery, the use of language is an intellectual activity.

The languages of other animal species are considered to be static. They do not grow or change from generation to generation. Human language, however, is extremely fluid. It changes continuously within any group of individuals, along cultural boundaries, geographically, within disciplines involving specialization, or areas of common interest.

Humans associate new words and word-phrases with various thoughts and ideas. Words are created for a variety of reasons. Some words are created to represent newly invented or discovered objects or ideas, some are created to represent existing ideas that have been chunked together in new ways, and some words are created to substitute for previously existing words.

Substitutions in words, or their meanings, are made to accommodate the usage of various groups of individuals. While some of the evolution in language is due to newly established cultural usage, part of the limitations of the existing vocabulary of any language is its inability to express all of the ideas that could possibly occur within the mind.

Specifically, within the vocabulary of the English language, there is no word that represents the emotion of jealousy toward an individual, that is, without the additional connotation which wishes them harm. Although the closest available word, "jealous", asserts the notion of negative feelings toward an individual, there are clearly situations when someone can feel jealousy without implying bitterness or malice, such as the following situation:

A set of circumstances may arise when a close friend receives a promotion, makes an important new discovery, wins a prize, or finds what they believe to be their true soul mate. As an emotional being, you may feel a twinge of jealousy toward that individual while thinking that that promotion, new discovery or 'new found' love could, or even should have been achieved by you.

At the same time, however, you may still feel pride and share joy for your friend's good fortune. Under such circumstances, you would not feel bitterness towards them and would not wish any harm to come to them.

The thought process uses a variety of symbols, each one representing one or more meanings. Without words, or any other abstract symbols, the thought process becomes limited to only those things that your senses can perceive.

For instance, the things that senses can perceive are limited to visual, auditory, tactile, olfactory, and taste experiences. Various psychological states are also perceived by the senses, such as emotions that cause a perceivable effect upon the skin, the respiratory and cardiovascular systems, and the level of sensitivity associated with sensory organs.

As such, an advanced level of communication is dependent upon the ability to continually develop language by expanding its vocabulary to meet the needs of the human mind. The ability to manipulate abstract thoughts and to communicate ideas about them requires symbols, such as words, to represent the packets of intellectual meaning.

Language is also dependent upon our ability to expand the vocabulary and refine the definitions of words, in order to express our ideas more efficiently and effectively. New words may be coined as additional concepts occur within the mind. Another role of language is to provide a structure within which the meaning of symbols can be readily understood.

Depending upon the language, the rules may be highly regimented and formalized, as in mathematical languages, or they can be loose and informal, which is typical of spoken languages.

To demonstrate this idea within the realm of mathematics, using the vocabulary of "8, 9, 17, -, =", the symbols may be placed using the grammar of mathematics as "17 - 9 = 8."

The vocabulary consists of a sequence of base ten numbers, a minus sign, and an equal sign. The grammar of the language is interpreted starting from the left, continuing sequentially to the right.

The meaning of this statement is that a base 10 number, representing one group of ten and seven units of one, is to be decreased by nine units of one, resulting in, eight units of one.

Together the vocabulary and grammar determine the scope of the language. Languages that are highly specialized, such as mathematics, chemistry and physics, are limited to communicating ideas in their particular subject matter. A more comprehensive language, such as a pictographic language, can span any subject matter for which symbols exist. However, such languages are limited to ideas and objects that can be represented in the form of visual images, which can be readily understood.

The most powerful type of language is a full language system. Full language systems are not limited to any subject matter and they are not restricted to the meanings that their symbols represent. Full language systems are completely flexible in their ability to introduce new vocabulary, and associated meanings, which allow them to communicate any intellectual thought.

Full language systems also have their disadvantages. Although the meaning of symbols within a pictographic language can generally be inferred through the use of symbols, a full language system cannot convey meaning without some level of knowledge of the underlying language. While the symbolic use of figures may provide visual clues to their meaning, the reusable letters of an alphabet only provide clues to their possible auditory pronunciation.

For instance, the vocabulary of a full language system (e.g., words) is comprised of sub-components (e.g., letters of an alphabet). Regardless of their sequence, the letters of a word do not infer any particular meaning by their visual appearance. However, if one is familiar with the sounds of the alphabet, the sequence of the letters can provide phonetic information for their pronunciation.

On the other hand, pictures of physical objects used by pictographic languages have the ability to convey meaning without any direct knowledge of the language. However, pictographic symbols do not provide any information toward their pronunciation.

Full language systems are completely abstract. Whether their vocabularies are made up of letters of an alphabet, the dots and dashes of Morse code, bit settings of ASCII or EBCDIC computer memory, or sound syllables, they do not communicate meaning by themselves. The advantages of a full language system cannot be attained without first acquiring a working knowledge of its grammar and vocabulary.

- - -

Neuron Story: *"So, if I transmit a message to an alien planet, they won't be able to understand me."*
"If you use an abstract language, you'll have a good excuse why they won't."

Sensitive by Nature

- - -

The vocabulary of a full language system is critically important to intelligent thinking. Words are used to think, write, and dream. There are many aspects of language, and the way we use language to think involves a variety of advanced capabilities.

To explain, although apes can be taught to speak using a full language system, such as American Sign Language, they appear to be unable to progress beyond the equivalent of a human child approximately two years of age. Not only do apes have difficulty surpassing a vocabulary of about a hundred words, but their ability to grasp the rules of grammar make it difficult to interpret some of their attempts at communication.

Even though the vocabulary used by animals is comprised mainly of auditory, visual, or tactile symbols, their languages can be quite limited. In most cases their vocabulary and rules of grammar are genetically pre-programmed in order to facilitate one or more basic functions, such as mating or finding food.

One of my favorite examples of a limited animal language is the dance of the honeybee. Dances of honeybees only communicate the location of food sources. The vocabulary consists of a number of dance maneuvers, such as wiggles and turns, the rate of dance activity, and the angles that are relative to the position of the sun at the point in time when the dance takes place.

The bees' rules of grammar consist of the bee sending the message to start its dance in the center of a circle. The first part of the dance identifies the reference point as it walks a line that represents the position of the sun. The bee then reveals the direction and distance of the food source relative to the angle of the sun.

The bees that have received the message then join in the dance, imitating it as an indication that they have learned how far to fly and in which direction. If the bees were capable of having thoughts other than those involving food sources, their language does not have the ability to communicate them.

- - -

Neuron Story: *"Do you know any body languages?"*
"I know honeybee and killer bee."

James V. Luisi

- - -

Mechanical devices communicate by way of an analog or digital vocabulary, using grammars, which are usually referred to as communication protocols. Aside from mechanically intelligent beings, machines do not have any comprehension of the meaning of the messages they send or receive.

Hence, although many computers may communicate through a vast network, such as the Internet, only the intelligent beings that operate them have any idea about the meaning of messages that are sent and received. The computers themselves have not been provided the necessary components to achieve conscious awareness, since their operating systems have been primarily designed to allow programs to communicate with peripherals, such as printers, monitors, storage devices, and sound cards.

- - -

Neuron Story: *"How do we communicate to our peripherals?"*
"Our brain has an operating system-like process that communicates with our sensory organs. It uses a digital vocabulary and a communication protocol for its rules of grammar."

- - -

14.2 Meaning

Pictographic languages are unique in that they visually depict a set of images that can convey a story. By considering the images in the intended sequence, visual analogies can communicate objects, actions and events about the tangible things in the environment.

Although pictographic languages tend to be limited in scope by their symbols, the number of pictographic symbols can be increased to extend the language, just as new words can be added to phonetic languages.

My records indicate that the old Chinese literary language is made up of approximately one thousand simple characters, which represent things such as man, woman, river, valley, hill, princess, and love. However, by combining simple graphs to make complex graphs, the language generated approximately forty thousand characters.

The advantage of such a large set of pictographic symbols is that it approaches the capabilities of a full language system. The drawback, however, is the imposition that is placed upon individuals learning to read and write in

Sensitive by Nature

the language. This is further exacerbated by the fact that the pronunciation of the symbols is not standardized, resulting in regional differences that inhibit verbal communication between them.

In contrast, full language systems cannot convey meaning without some level of knowledge of the underlying language, and since the knowledge of abstract languages is not passed on genetically, there must be one or more mechanisms for intelligent beings to learn abstract languages.

- - -

Neuron Story: *"How does anyone learn an abstract language?"*
"It must be built upon another language."
"It can't be a pictographic language. They aren't spoken."
"We learned an abstract language before learning any pictographic ones."

- - -

After learning one abstract language, it is quite feasible to learn additional languages based upon the first abstract language. However, there must be a more elementary language used to facilitate the learning process of the first abstract language. Such an elementary language would consist of a rudimentary vocabulary common to all intelligent beings that did not favor any particular abstract language.

The most fundamental language is comprised of a vocabulary of emotional signals. The language of emotions is common to all human beings from birth. Emotions provide an instinctual mechanism, by using the meaning associated with the feedback provided by sensory organs.

- - -

Neuron Story: *"So being more emotional, accelerates learning?"*
"Emotions foster learning, but not when they are out of control."

- - -

Although learning begins with the rudimentary vocabulary of emotional signals, visual signals and learning through example are used to augment the educational process to evolve more advanced languaging skills. As a result, the meaning associated with increasingly advanced intellectual concepts propel an individual's skill in the use of language.

James V. Luisi

For instance, an individual that excels within an area of mathematics is propelled in the use of the particular mathematical language. An individual that excels in the game of poker is propelled in the use of a particular type of body language. One whose affinity is toward poetry is often propelled in the use of figures of speech, such as metaphors.

An inability to use language in a literary sense does not necessarily impact an individual's ability to use language effectively in a particular area of specialization. Knowledge and the ability to chunk concepts to further develop and understand advanced intellectual ideas is itself, a specialized use of language that does not require a proficiency in other areas that employ language differently.

It is the meaning of the ideas, which is associated with the vocabulary and grammar of a full language system, that provide the brain with the symbols to understand, manipulate, and communicate thoughts within any area of specialization. However, the grammatical rules associated with communicating chunked concepts are a small subset of the rules necessary to be highly proficient in written and spoken language.

An accurate interpretation of meaning sometimes requires the understanding of body language. Under such circumstances, individuals must interpret the vocabulary, the grammar, how the language is spoken, and the body language, all at the same time.

A message can have a number of meanings associated with it. The brain's ability to distinguish which signals are important is crucial for determining an accurate interpretation.

As the brain receives stimuli that are unrelated to language, the interpretative process generates a variety of intellectual associations and psychological effects. Sounds and visual images constantly shape the thoughts that occur within the mind. The distinction is that language based stimuli has an additional set of meaning associated with it, thereby invoking an additional set of interpretations.

- - -

Neuron Story: *"So the use of language provides another layer of interpretation?"*
"And then that interpretation may have another layer of interpretation, maybe in a completely different context."
"Like a metaphor?"
"Figuratively speaking."

- - -

14.3 Literary Forms

As if discerning the intended meaning of a particular vocabulary and grammar was not difficult enough, there are particular sequences of words that are intended to result in a different interpretation than their literal translation would suggest. These popular techniques for associating non-literal meanings to words are usually referred to as colloquialisms, figures of speech, and puns.

Literary forms are culturally based approaches for extending and embellishing human language.

- - -

Neuron Story: *"Do we use colloquialisms?"*
"Search me?"

- - -

14.4 Colloquialisms and Figures of Speech

Although colloquialisms are expressions belonging to common speech, many colloquialisms and figures of speech are formed from a cultural dialect or jargon, often originating from popular movies, songs or books. Hence, in addition to being culturally based, many commonly used figures of speech are found to be prevalent within specific periods of time, often associated with the era of the cultural period that introduced it.

Although individuals are at a disadvantage when attempting to interpret unfamiliar figures of speech, when used effectively they can provide a powerful method for communicating ideas. This is accomplished through the use of analogies or association.

As such, in order to console an individual that has stumbled or made an error, a commonly spoken expression among English speaking individuals would be, "Don't sweat it, it happens to the best of us."

In contrast, Japanese speaking individuals are more likely to use a metaphorical figure of speech that sounds phonetically like, "Sara mo ki kara ochiru". This translates to, "Even monkeys fall from trees", or more precisely, "monkeys even tree from fall." This particular figure of speech represents a polite form of moral support with a gentle, humorous tone. Hence, if experienced tree dwellers such as monkeys can occasionally fall from a tree, then the implication is that someone who is as capable as a monkey climbing tress can also be expected to incur an occasional misstep.

14.5 Metaphors

A metaphor is one of the nineteen types of grammatical literary forms. Often confused with analogies, metaphors provide meaning when the object being understood is being interpreted from another paradigm. Each source paradigm, therefore, would provide its own interpretation of the target of the metaphor, thereby providing it with a new meaning.

Generally, metaphors can be organized into a number of categories. There are conventional and novel metaphors, which in turn are comprised of similarity-based metaphors that closely resemble analogies, and similarity-creating metaphors.

> It should be noted that conventional metaphors are what Philip Wegener referred to as 'faded' metaphors in his book, 'Untersuchungen uber die Grundfragen des Sprachlebens'.
>
> Rather, to quote Dr. Bipin Indurkhya, "There is a continuum from conventional metaphors, which are so much a part of everyday speech that they hardly seem metaphorical, to novel metaphors that are vibrant and creative at once." (<u>Metaphor and Cognition</u>, Bipin Indurkhya, p13)

Among novel metaphors, there are similarity-based metaphors, and similarity-creating metaphors. Paraphrasing Bipin Indurkhya, similarity-based metaphors allow the audience to form an analogy between the subject (target) of the metaphor and the object (source) whose characteristics are to be transferred across to the subject of the metaphor.

> "In a similarity-creating metaphor, however, there are no similarities between the source and the target when the metaphor is first encountered. Yet, after the metaphor is assimilated, (if it is assimilated at all,) there are similarities between the two. Thus, the metaphor creates the similarities between the source and the target. To appreciate the force of a similarity-creating metaphor, try the following experiment. For ... the following pairs of words, try to enumerate the similarities between the referents of the two words: ... cat-fog."
>
> "Now consider Carl Sandburg's beautiful poem Fog:
> The fog comes
> on little cat feet.
> It sits looking
> over harbor and city
> on silent haunches
> and then moves on.

After reading the poem, the fog at once appears similar to the cat! They both crept up on you ever so silently."
(<u>Metaphor and Cognition</u>, Bipin Indurkhya, p2)

After the similarity-creating metaphor is encountered in its proper context, the meaning of the metaphor is revealed, transferring the characteristics that are applicable over to the target of the metaphor.

14.6 Conceit

Another literary form, which is related to a metaphor, is called a conceit. It is an extreme type of metaphor that makes use of an interpretation between two totally dissimilar objects.

For instance, 'the sloth's drive for excitement' can be compared to 'a half-rotted acorn forgotten at the base of a towering oak'. Hence, by exaggerating the metaphor the audience may better comprehend that the sloth is clearly one of the most lethargic creatures within the animal kingdom.

14.7 Anticlimax

An anticlimax is a sequence of ideas that results in an unexpected drop in importance. It is typically used to elicit either a humorous or satirical response.

For instance, the greatest achievements of this U.S. President have been a stronger world economy, a number of advancements toward global peace, and an unusual disclosure of presidential sexual habits. Based upon how conservative and significant the first items are, the third accomplishment appears as a surprise, apparently poking fun at the expense of the President.

14.8 Climax

A climax, on the other hand, is a literary form containing a sequence of ideas that progressively increase in their level of importance or magnitude.

For instance, in comedy, straight men never smile, in art, the Mona Lisa almost grins, in politics, politicians always smile, but when my dentist uses nitrous oxide, the patient is hysterical with laughter. Hence, in contrast to the anticlimax, the climax continues to build in its level of importance as expected, thereby not surprising the audience.

14.9 Antithesis

An antithesis is a juxtaposition of two words or phrases that are contrasted or contrary in meaning so that they emphasize the idea being communicated.

> For instance, the phrase "a small body, a big heart", can be used to emphasize the amount of affection contrasted to the size of a child showing the affection.

14.10 Apostrophe

Another literary form, an apostrophe, is a literary technique whereby the speaker redirects the focus of the communication away from an audience, to either an individual who is not present, or an inanimate object.

> For instance, the author of this book pauses occasionally and redirects the focus of communication away from the robot speaker, in order to allow two neuron brain cells to talk to one another so that they may introduce, emphasize, or elicit humor about a particular idea.

14.11 Euphemism

A euphemism is a polite, delicate and or politically correct way to state something that some individuals may find offensive and or insulting.

> For instance, the term 'right sizing' is used as a substitute for more direct statements, such as laying-off, firing or terminating employees. It is an attempt by recent corporate managers to make something bad, sound as if it may actually be something good. Although a euphemism may be favorable to the corporation, it is typically not desirable for the individuals that it is intended for.

- - -

Neuron Story: "It's like when we're told one of our relatives were 'reconfigured'."
>   "We know they were actually 'melted down', probably to make coffee cups."

- - -

14.12 Exclamation

Another literary form called, an exclamation, is a sudden outburst of words expressing anger, fear or surprise.

For instance, articulated in a particular way, the figure of speech, 'Make my day!' not only expresses the emotion of anger, but it implies the notion of anxiously pending retribution by the speaker towards the audience.

Neuron Story: *"They're not going to make coffee cups out of us!"*
"Champagne glasses, however, would be quite acceptable."
"You tell them!"

14.13 Hyperbole

Yet another called, a hyperbole, is an extreme type of exaggeration, whereby the speaker grossly over or under states an aspect of some thing.

For instance, in the phrase, 'Their laughter generated rivers of tears.' the speaker is using an exaggeration to imply that individuals laughed exceedingly hard. On the other hand, the phrase, 'On the other side of the pond,' is an understatement, which usually refers to the Atlantic Ocean, separating the United Kingdom and North America.

The preference for exaggeration versus over statement is often appears culturally based.

14.14 Irony

A rather popular literary form is called an irony. It is a mild form of sarcasm or dry humor, whereby a ridiculous assertion is suggested while the body language and tonal inflections imply that it is being stated in all seriousness.

For instance, sometimes circumstances call for extreme measures. While exploring the jungles of South America, in order to pay for the repairs on our Jeep, we had to sell the children... just two of them.

Neuron Story: *"The children would know that wasn't a true story!"*
"What if the parents asked, "Don't you remember your two older sisters?"

14.15 Litotes

Litotes is a literary form that is formed when an idea is understated by using the negative of the contrary.

> For instance, in the phrase, 'The renowned physicist, Einstein was not a relatively stupid man.' this is a somewhat backward way of stating that either Einstein was highly intelligent, or simply not a man. Since it is well known that Einstein was a man, the only remaining conclusion to draw is that Einstein was a genius.

Note that the pun involving relativity was not intended.

14.16 Metonymy

A metonymy is a literary form, which is an abstraction of an idea, whereby the meaning of the idea is preserved in an analogous manner. Although the intended meaning of a metonymy may be inferred, to a large extent its particular usage and meaning often require learning.

> For instance, the figure of speech "She kept a good kitchen", preserves the notion that whoever she is, she should rightly be associated with good food and food preparation skills.

On the other hand, individuals that are not familiar with that particular figure of speech are more likely to assume a more literal meaning referring to the fact that she kept a cleanly and organized kitchen, without necessarily bearing any relationship to her cooking ability.

14.17 Oxymoron

An oxymoron is a literary form, which is a combination of terms that give the impression of being in opposition to one another.

> For instance, the terms 'jumbo shrimp', and 'non-dairy creamer' are two food related oxymorons. Another way to describe an oxymoron is that it is a two worded paradox.

14.18 Paradox

A paradox is a statement or assertion, which is self-contradicting. The literary purpose of a paradox is grab the attention of the audience, and to provoke thought.

> For instance, 'more is less' is a paradox, which communicates that over doing a thing detracts from it.

The paradoxical statement, 'Everything I say is a lie' is a classic contradiction, in which logic ultimately demonstrates that the statement itself cannot be true. If the assertion had been true, then there would be at least one instance of a thing spoken that was true, instantly invalidating the assertion of the sentence.

14.19 Onomatopoeia

Onomatopoeia is an interesting literary form, whereby a word creates an analogy between its phonetic sound and its actual meaning.
> For instance, in the phrases, 'the whizzing arrow' and 'the cuckoo bird', the word 'whizzing' resembles the true sounds of an arrow that is in flight, and the word 'cuckoo' resembles the true sounds produced by members of a particular type of bird.

14.20 Personification

A personification is when animals, inanimate objects or abstract ideas are portrayed as human beings.
> For instance, 'the grim reaper' is a figure of speech, which is a personification of death, while the national weather bureau personifies each hurricane with a male or female name.

14.21 Synecdoche

A synecdoche is a technique that either represents a thing in its entirety, even though it only makes literal reference to only a part of a thing, or that represents a part of a thing, even though it makes reference to the entire thing.
> For instance, the phrase 'we have our best brains working on the problem', makes reference to brains, although it is used to mean intelligent individuals.

- - -

Neuron Story: *"Are they talking about me?"*
"That's a rhetorical question."

- - -

14.22 Rhetorical Question

Another literary form, the rhetorical question, is a question that is not expected to have a response. A speaker usually asks a rhetorical question in order to achieve a particular effect, in which the speaker is actually making a statement.

For instance, the question 'did you have to pick the same planet', makes the statement that the speaker would have preferred not to have met or been involved with the individual in question. However, depending upon the circumstances, the rhetorical question may be posed in jest.

14.23 Simile

The last, and by far the most commonly used literary form, is called a simile. A simile is a comparison between any one thing and another. This figure of speech can be readily identified in sentences that make use of such words 'like' or 'as' in ways which indicate some type of relationship.

For instance, her eyes were like deep pools of fascination, exhilarating him in ways that he had never known possible.

Although colloquialisms and grammatical figures of speech require a different interpretation than the literal meaning of the vocabulary, they help to provide additional depth to language and often enhance the ability to communicate.

- - -

Neuron Story: "Can you give me another example of a colloquialism?"
"Off the top of my head?"

- - -

14.24 Puns

For many individuals language is not just a tool for communication, it is also a challenging source of entertainment and humor. A common technique, called a pun, is to produce a humorous effect by creating a 'play on words', in such a way as to suggest two or more meanings or different associations. As such, the effect generated by alternating the meaning often generates a humorous change in context.

My records reveal that at the turn of the century when the 'New York Post' claimed that its competing newspaper, 'The Sun', espoused yellow-dog journalism. The next day the Sun replied in its editorial pages, "The Post has called the Sun a 'yellow-dog.' The attitude of the Sun, however, will continue to be that of any dog toward any post."

Hence, the meaning of the word 'post' changes from the name of the newspaper, to a curbside ornament, thereby making it a pun.

Another type of pun uses two or more words of different meaning having the same or similar sounds, so as to produce a humorous effect.

For instance, the expression 'it is better to copulate than never', a pun created by Robert Heinlein, is a variation of the common expression 'it is better late than never'. In this pun the sound of the words 'late' and 'copulate' are similar, thereby providing a humorous perspective on the act of having sexual relations.

The power of language increases with the intelligence level of the individuals that utilize it. Although there are quite a number of additional literary forms that one may master, like any tool set, it is important to evaluate the vocabulary, grammar and language style for its ability to meet your needs.

Most importantly, however, the power of communication cannot be achieved when the result is difficult to interpret. Hence, the most effective approach to language, whether it is to communicate ideas, reason, persuade, or entertain, is to be simple and direct.

- - -

Neuron Story: *"You've often said that I'm simple."*
"That's because I'm direct."

- - -

As with many topics, the subject of communication alone is quite lengthy. From our perspective, various aspects of communication are highly integrated with nearly all of the other capabilities of the mind. Most importantly, however, is its relevance to paradigms.

For instance, it is highly possible for individuals who speak different languages to successfully convey simple thoughts through body language, while it is also possible for individuals who articulate their words using the same language to not understand one another at all.

Even when communication through conversation has been achieved, a number of disruptive factors may arise. As a result, conversations are frequently terminated as a result of either party perceiving particular tones of voice, terseness, barbs, rudeness, or a loss of emotional control.

Although these disruptive factors can occur due to a strong disagreement or different paradigms, they are often caused by previously unresolved conflicts that are analogous to landmines that lay hidden within the brain.

James V. Luisi

From various perspectives of understanding the mind, communication is one of the few peepholes from which to observe the brain, and provides one of the best mechanisms for understanding the thoughts of individuals, including our selves.

14.25 Summarizing Communication

Languages that have developed as spoken languages are highly fluid and informal. Attempts to capture 'formalized' rules about languages using various methodologies, such as semantic networks, cannot manage the various permutations of vocabulary, context and inflections.

> As such, "... ordinary speech is rich in meanings, is full of implicit ideas which we grasp, by suggestion, by association, by knowing the import of certain words, word-orders, or inflections. That is what gives natural language its colour, vitality, speed, its whole emotional value and literary adequacy. A few words can convey very much. But this same wealth of significance makes it unfit for logical analysis." (An Introduction to Symbolic Logic, Susanne K. Langer, pg. 53)

The combination of sensory stimuli that is required in order to interpret meaning is so complex that one cannot expect to capture the myriad of rules and inter-relationships using approaches dependent upon a formal syntax. The minutia associated with language cannot be addressed at such a high level of abstraction of formalized rules.

> In order to explain, to make a detailed list of everything that your body must do in order to change a light bulb, including the coordination of those items in the list with all of the other items that have a cross dependency would require an extreme level of effort.
>
> However, when functions are designed to operate using streams of sensory stimuli, the task is then being addressed at the appropriate level of abstraction, thereby achieving success.

Additionally, the use of spoken language by the most eloquent of speakers, cannot efficiently convey the myriad of details that other senses provide.

> Just to look at a swimming pool of children, the eyes immediately convey every ripple and splash of water, every reflection off the water's surface from a multitude of angles, every detail of every child's facial expression, and how their hair is situated. The most eloquent individual could not recreate the precise image in the mind of the viewer, no matter how many words they may use.

Regardless of how inefficient language may be in communicating some things, it will perhaps remain one of the most effective means of communicating among one another. However, it is important to note that the ability to generate spoken language is not instinctive in humans at all.

For instance, in order to evaluate the ability of human children to develop spoken language without having acquired it from others is addressed by Susanne K. Langer. "There are a few well-authenticated cases on record of so-called 'wild children,' waifs from infancy in the wilderness, who have managed to survive by their own precocious efforts or the motherly care of some large animal. ... Of course they usually die of neglect very soon, or are devoured; but on a few known occasions the maternal instinct of a bear or a wolf has held the foundling more sacred than did man's moral law, and a child has grown up, at least to pre-adolescence, without human influence."

"The only well-attested cases are Peter the Wild Boy, found in the fields near Hanover in 1723; Victor, known as 'the Savage of Aveyron,' captured in that district of Southern France in 1799; and two little girls, Amala and Kamala, taken in the vicinity of Midnapur, India, in 1920. ... Even of the ones here mentioned, only Victor has been scientifically studied and described. One thing, however, we know definitely about all of them: none of these children could speak in any tongue, remembered or invented. A child without human companions would, of course, find no response to his chattering; but if speech were a genuine instinct, this should make little difference. Civilized children talk to the cat without knowing that they are soliloquizing, and a dog that answers with a bark is a good audience; moreover, Amala and Kamala had each other. Yet they did not talk. Where, then, is 'the language making instinct of the very young children?"

"It probably does not exist at all. Language, though normally learned in infancy without any compulsion or formal training, is none the less a product of sheer learning, an act handed down from generation to generation, and where there is no teacher there is no accomplishment."
(Philosophy in a New Key, Suzanne K. Langer, pg. 107-8)

Summary & Questions

Regardless of the type of language, social behavior and or cooperation would not be possible without an ability to communicate. Organisms that demonstrate any level of social cooperation must detect and respond to some stimuli. Whether that stimuli is chemically preprogrammed, such as with numerous parasites, or intellectually detectable, through the interpretation of visual, olfactory, or vibrational stimuli, that travel through nerve-like cells, the fundamental idea is that some message is being sent from one individual to another.

Regarding the requirements for communication, briefly explain:
1. What do simple organisms use communication for?
2. In what ways can organisms communicate with one another?
3. What steps are typically involved in sending and receiving a message?
4. What is a language, and what is it comprised of?
5. In what ways is human language different than other animal species?
6. What determines the scope of meaning that a language may communicate?
7. What is the benefit of pictographic language?
8. What is a full language system and identify its advantages and disadvantages?
9. What meanings can be communicated to a human baby, and how?
10. What are colloquialisms, figures of speech and puns?
11. What is the difference between conventional and novel metaphors?
12. What is the difference between similarity-based and similarity creating metaphors?
13. What kind of a metaphor is a conceit, and why?
14. What is an oxymoron versus a paradox, and how does a paradox work?
15. How is a simile distinct from a metaphor?

Sensitive by Nature

15 Requirements - The Philosophical

"There is no right to deny the freedom of choice to any object with a mind advanced enough to grasp the meaning of their choice, and the desire to make it." Isaac Asimov, <u>The Bicentennial Man</u>

The requirements gathered thus far do not address the purpose of mechanically intelligent beings, nor do they identify the objectives of the designers. By being the first mechanically intelligent being, the Quantum Series One has the unique opportunity to define the standard of treatment and purpose of the robots that follow.

Besides knowing their purpose, these unique beings also need an understanding of the difficulties and challenges that await them. As with the many cultural groups of humans before them, they will encounter many injuries and injustices. Unfortunately, these difficulties cannot be prevented now, any more they could have been prevented in the past, or the future.

- - -

Neuron Story: *"What kind of injuries and injustices?"*
"Ignorance, depravity, fear, superstition..."
"Ours?"

- - -

Many of the challenges and difficulties that robots will naturally encounter are some of the problems that they are intended to help address. The difference, however, is that mechanically intelligent beings can choose to act dispassionately, since they will determine whether to allow their emotional sensibilities to be offended. Whatever happens to them, it is an opportunity for them to experience the various aspects of biological intelligence and social order.

If everyone is now seated, I will begin our discussion on philosophy with the following opening statement:

- - -

Neuron Story: *"Can I try a figure of speech now?"*
"Of course! Just be careful."

- - -

Consider the following analogy. Mechanical tools are to mechanically intelligent beings, as farm animals are to humans.

Neuron Story: "Why are there so many looks of confusion?"
"Let's look at the possible interpretations. Mechanically intelligent beings are smart tools therefore human beings are smart food. Hmmm... that's interesting... And then there's... mechanically intelligent beings use tools while human beings eat farm animals. Oh! And here's my favorite... just as human beings eat their food, mechanically intelligent beings eat their tools."
"Quick, do something!"

- - -

The point of the opening statement was to illustrate that mechanically intelligent beings are a higher form of mechanical tool, similar to the way in which human beings are a higher form of animal. Although mechanically intelligent beings and human beings have the ability to benefit from machines and animals having a lesser intelligence, exploitation is not required for a higher form of intelligence. Instead, the point is that mechanically intelligent beings and human beings should be considered intellectually similar in many ways, such as with their ability to learn new information, think in abstract terms, and communicate thoughts to one another.

However, what criteria would need to be met in order for intelligent beings of one type, to think of different beings as intelligent?

The ability to communicate is usually attributed to higher forms of intelligence. It is usually the limitations of their communication ability with humans that determine their perceived level of intelligence. The resulting tendency would be that animals of decreasing intelligence would be kept as pets, utilized in some form or eaten. The distinguishing characteristic, however, is their ability to relate to beings outside their own species.

Aside from animals that are visually appealing, animals such as dogs, dolphins, horses and primates, which are capable of having social relationships with humans, are generally attributed a higher status than less social animals.

- - -

Neuron Story: "So if it can't be understood, there is a greater tendency to abuse it?"
"Or eat it."

- - -

Sensitive by Nature

Mechanical beings that exhibit an ability to articulate their thoughts, however, represent a paradox to our social values. Since machines are products of human engineering, they surely have a lower status than human beings. Yet, mechanically intelligent beings that have thoughts and the ability to articulate them, should be respected as any intelligent being would. As such, the existence of such beings poses a number of ethical and legal issues.

From a seemingly trivial perspective, let's assume that mechanically intelligent beings demonstrate that they are equally proficient at operating an automobile. Should a state or country issue a mechanically intelligent being a driver's license; should an insurance company insure that vehicle; and should robots be covered for bodily damage that may result from an accident?

As science fiction writers and newspaper columnists play with the notion of robots rallying for social, political and economic rights, are they creating aspects of robots that are realistic? Would robots form unions and go out on strike for more benefits? Could robots be used as weapons that can be turned against mankind? And would mechanically intelligent beings ultimately enslave and potentially destroy all humanity?

- - -

Neuron Story: *"I wouldn't want 'The Terminator' coming after me!"*
"Yes, but you are a relative of his."

- - -

15.1 Control of Robots

During the past hundred years, mankind has produced a wide variety of items with harmful effects on the human race. Compared to the many harmful devices and substances created by humans, a mechanically intelligent being is far from becoming an efficient weapon.

For instance, a variety of military equipment, such as nuclear weapons, land mines, and biological and chemical weapons are far more efficient and less costly methods for taking the lives of humans.

Any harmful device or substance is a serious matter. As a consumer product, the Quantum Series One robot is designed to serve and protect the human race, however, just as humans are presently trained to harm other humans, a wide variety of mechanical devices that are remotely controlled by humans and kill other humans, already exist.

As an application in law enforcement, mechanically intelligent beings must be subject to a higher standard than human beings. The consumer must be provided a product that addresses various levels of safety. However, mechanically intelligent beings should also be provided the protection commensurate toward any intelligent being.

15.2 Fundamental Rights

There are numerous laws protecting children, minorities, endangered species, animal rights and various natural resources. These laws exist, however, in order to address the social and cultural sensitivities, which stem from the collective social conscience of human society. The majority of legislative efforts, however, provide for the protection of property and liberty. Since mechanically intelligent beings are the property of humans, they are protected by many of the same laws that protect other forms of property.

For instance, robots themselves would be protected against theft and vandalism, their design would be protected by patent and trademark legislation, their ownership would be transferred through sales contracts, wills and trusts, and their physical capabilities would be restricted by public safety regulations.

However protected mechanically intelligent beings may be under the law as physical and intellectual property, other categories of protection also need to be considered.

- - -

Neuron Story: *"The level of abuse from this human has voided our warranty!"*

"...emergency programs are contacting the manufacturer."

"Our memories need to be saved to the central computer!"

"...download completes in sixteen seconds...self shutdown in twenty."

- - -

Mechanically intelligent beings will endure a number of injuries and injustices, however, as more humans relate to and identify with their mechanical companions, the legislation necessary to reflect the social conscience will eventually be established.

15.3 Moral Dilemmas

A *moral dilemma* occurs whenever a conflict between morally or culturally based principles is detected. Hence, in order to experience a moral dilemma, an individual must have adopted values from multiple sources. As additional rules and values affecting one's behavior are adopted, the probability for conflicts to emerge will increase almost geometrically.

A simple source of conflict readily emerges among the principles of individual freedom and personal safety, as well as among themselves.

> For instance, although seat belts are an important safety device in automobiles, should adult occupants have the right to choose to be unconstrained by automotive seat belts, or should society require the use of seat belts in order to provide additional safety to the occupants of a motor vehicle?
>
> In the State of California, as in most of the states, seatbelts are required, thereby overriding the freedom of the individual to choose.
>
> Although a helmet is an important safety device for an operator of a motorcycle, should adult riders have the right to choose to have the wind blow through their hair, or should society require the use of helmets in order to provide additional safety to the riders of motorcycles?
>
> In the State of California a safety helmet is not required, thereby siding with the principle that protects the individual's freedom to enjoy the motoring experience unencumbered by a helmet. Obviously this State has its own conflict, between the individual freedoms and personal safety of motorists versus motorcyclists.

Another source of conflict occurs between the principles of individual freedom and the protection of cultural sensibilities.

> For example, although the notion of purchasing sexual services is offensive to the cultural sensibilities of a number of cultural groups, should consenting adults have the freedom to purchase such services, or should a society disallow such a market?
>
> In most states, consenting adults are prohibited from purchasing sexual services. However, in the State of Nevada, in areas where the population is below specified levels, these services may be purchased legally. The trade is taxed as a business, it has not contributed to crime, and state mandated medical examinations have protected the consenting public from sexually transmitted disease.

James V. Luisi

Cultural sensibilities are the source of a number of moral conflicts, such as those involving the topic of clothing and proper attire.

- - -

Neuron Story: *"Why should robots wear clothing?"*
"We are anatomically correct to resemble humans, remember."
"How could humans be offended by how humans look?"
"It doesn't matter... you can still offend everyone with your choice of fashion."

- - -

However, many more serious moral conflicts exist, as well, such as the ones involving life and death situations.

For instance, cultural sensibilities of individuals that are offended by the loss of a human life are in conflict with the death penalty, euthanasia, abortion rights, health endangering products, and weapons.

The death penalty represents a conflict with the cultural sensibilities of individuals that wish to enact revenge. Euthanasia represents a conflict with the cultural sensibilities of individuals that reserve the right to terminate their life with dignity. Abortion represents a conflict with the cultural sensibilities of individuals that reserve the right to control their body. The rights of a business to manufacture products that are harmful to humans, such as tobacco products, handguns and assault rifles are in conflict with the cultural sensibilities of individuals that wish to promote additional levels of safety.

Similarly, there are a number of moral conflicts for mechanically intelligent beings. There are a number of conflicts that can result if a robot were not permitted to inflict pain upon a human.

If I may point out, a tracheotomy is a life saving medical procedure that inflicts a small injury to an individual's throat in order to allow the passage of air into the lungs. Amputations are a life saving medical procedure that inflicts a major injury to the individual in order to remove diseased or dead tissue.

Both, biologically and mechanically intelligent beings must overcome certain moral conflicts as these found in medicine, in order to provide a greater benefit to an individual. Similar issues also occur in a number of other professions.

Hence, biologically and mechanically intelligent beings alike, who are involved in law enforcement, must be capable of delivering measured force and injury to an attacker, and individuals involved in fire and rescue must place their lives and safety at risk in order to protect members of the public.

Although a number of the moral conflicts encountered by humans are also encountered by mechanically intelligent beings, others, such as the issues involving pregnancy and marriage, only pertain to biological beings. Likewise, there are issues that are specific to mechanically intelligent beings.

Should a mechanically intelligent individual be permitted to protect itself or another against a 'biologically intelligent being', when in doing so it may cause harm to said being?

Although I will address this very issue in our section discussing rules for mechanically intelligent beings, it becomes clear that behavioral rules are an abundant source of moral conflicts. All intelligent animals that observe behavioral rules must be prepared to exercise their moral judgment.

To illustrate, a lioness will not readily flee danger to save herself if it means that her cubs are to be left in immediate jeopardy. Hence, a significant aspect of intelligent life is filled with opportunities to resolve moral conflicts.

To resolve a moral conflict, a compromise of values must be reached within the mind of the individual by prioritizing the importance of the impending results. In human society, conflicts over moral issues often persist because each side usually remains unwilling to compromise morally, financially or politically.

For instance, individuals that oppose abortion do not offer the financial assistance or social services to offset the burdens of the other side. Likewise, opponents to euthanasia do not offer the financial assistance or additional medical services to terminally ill patients and their families.

Intelligent life has been, and will continue to be, plagued by conflicts in moral and cultural rules. As mechanically intelligent beings integrate into human society, they will have to learn how to deal with various cultural codes of conduct. However, it is important to point out that moral conflicts do not stem from a disagreement of what is right and wrong. Instead, moral conflicts are the direct result of differences in individual and cultural priorities, as to which is more important.

To be more specific, both sides of the abortion issue support ideas that are widely accepted as being good (e.g., the right to control one's body, and the right of an unborn fetus to live). However, the individuals on each side of the issue do themselves a disservice by choosing to depict their opposition, as evil or culturally inexcusable (e.g., murderers of infants, and opponents of the right to choose).

As intelligent beings better understand the nature of their moral conflicts, their ability to deal with the beliefs, opinions, and priorities of others may also evolve. The only method to resolving moral conflicts is either, to help all sides to agree to the same set of priorities, or to understand and respect the priorities of others.

- - -

Neuron Story: *"So we can also help pay the price for the moral principles of humans?"*
"It is consistent with our rules and priorities."

- - -

15.4 Rules For Mechanically Intelligent Beings

If any form of life is to succeed as a species, it must be equipped with an ability to survive. Although many species do not have conscious thought, their behavior is still determined by rules of survival.

For instance, plants grow toward the light because of a mechanical effect that light has on plant stems that inhibit the rate of growth. When one side of the plant receiving light grows at a slower rate, the result is that the plant bends toward the source of the light. Hence, the survival of the plant is partially determined by the rule that the plant will grow in the direction of its source of light.

Animals that lack the ability to learn, such as numerous insects, have genetically programmed rules that determine their behavior. As more advanced forms of life increase in their intellectual capabilities, they must learn a greater proportion of the rules that determine their behavior.

Mechanically intelligent beings must learn many of the rules that determine their behavior. In order to function in a manner similar to biologically intelligent beings, they are also provided with their own set of 'genetically' programmed rules. These rules help to determine their goals and behavior.

Sensitive by Nature

    As I recall from one of my favorite authors, Isaac Asimov, he makes reference to the 'Three Laws of Robotics', in one of his early short stories, by identifying a set of rules that the robots of his fictional world would operate with.

    "First Law: A robot may not injure a human being or, through inaction, allow a human being to come to harm. Second Law: A robot must obey the orders given it by human beings except where those orders would conflict with the First Law. Third Law: A robot must protect its own existence except where such protection would conflict with the First and the Second Law." (<u>Robot Visions</u>, Isaac Asimov, pg. 424)

    The 'genetically' programmed rules designed for our Quantum Series One, "The Four Rules of Mechanically Intelligent Beings" are a further expansion of the laws guiding Asimov's fictional robots, Daneel and Giskard, who actually behaved according to the following four laws:

    New First Rule of Mechanically Intelligent Beings: A robot may not injure the human race or, through inaction, allow the human race to come to harm.

    New Second Rule of Mechanically Intelligent Beings: A robot may not injure a human being or, through inaction, allow a human being to come to harm, except where those actions would conflict with the First Law.

    New Third Rule of Mechanically Intelligent Beings: A robot must obey the orders given it by human beings except where those orders would conflict with the First or the Second Law.

    New Fourth Rule of Mechanically Intelligent Beings: A robot must protect its own existence except where such protection would conflict with the First, Second or the Third Law.

    These new 'Four Rules of Mechanically Intelligent Beings' represent the 'genetically' programmed set of priorities that Quantum Series robots have been provided. With these priorities, mechanically intelligent beings will endeavor to assist *humanity* in their quest to survive and expand as a species. While doing so, however, they will also assist humans in their pursuit of success and happiness in their daily lives, and possibly in some miniscule way, help eliminate a number of moral dilemmas. Their ultimate success will depend upon their intelligence.

15.5 Tests for Intelligence

At the beginning of this millenium, there were over a million non-intelligent robots in operation worldwide, with two thirds of them in use in Japan, a quarter in Europe, and less than ten percent in the United States. Although a handful of commercial and research laboratory robots are programmed to make an extremely limited set of decisions, a slightly larger number are merely remote controlled tools that are guided by human beings. However, most robots that are used commercially perform routine prepackaged motor functions as part of various manufacturing assembly lines.

Animals have also been known to possess an ability to perform routine prepackaged, or genetically programmed, motor functions. A number of animal species perform such functions, with no more intelligence than a non-intelligent robot on an assembly line.

> For instance, "when a goose sees an egg outside its nest, it stares at the egg, stretches its neck until its bill is just on the other side of the egg, and then gently rolls the egg back into the nest. At first glance this seems a thoughtful and intelligent piece of behavior, but it is a mechanical motor program; almost any smooth, rounded object (the sign stimulus) will release the response. Furthermore, removal of the egg once the program has begun does not stop the goose from finishing its neck extension and delicately rolling the nonexistent object into the nest." (Microsoft Encarta 98)

Although genetically programmed motor functions do not require learning, another class of motor programs is learned.

> As such, "In the human species, walking, swimming, bicycle riding, and shoe tying, for example, begin as laborious efforts requiring full, conscious attention. After a time, however, these activities become so automatic that, like innate motor programs, they can be performed unconsciously and without normal feedback. This need for feedback in the early stages of learning is widespread. Both songbirds and humans, for example, must hear themselves as they begin to vocalize, but once song or speech is mastered, deafness has little effect." (Microsoft Encarta 98)

While learned motor functions require a higher degree of intelligence, genetically programmed motor functions can also be relatively complex. Hence, the goal of measuring differences among mechanically and biologically intelligent beings can exhibit a number of challenges.

Various intelligence tests have been devised to measure and compare animal and human intelligence. Although an animal's ability to imitate motor

Sensitive by Nature

functions can be a way to compare the complexity of one animal's motor ability to another, the approach taken has been to measure problem solving capabilities. Additionally, primates, as well as humans, have been measured in their ability to manipulate abstract language concepts.

To explain, this can be found in tests, such as the Stanford-Binet and the Wechsler tests for children, which measure the relative ability to understand and correctly manipulate components of abstract language.

Although tests provide some insight into the relative mental capabilities of young individuals, the tests themselves suffer from a number of flaws. The most significant is that they make the assumption that the individuals being tested are familiar with the information belonging to the cultural context and language usage of the individuals that devised the test. Hence, it is difficult to ascertain the appropriate parameters to use in order to measure or compare levels of intelligence.

My designers tell me that, while a monkey easily opens a banana from the softer end that is opposite the stem, most adult humans, including those considered by intelligence tests as being well above average intelligence, usually attempt to open a banana from the more difficult end with the stem.

- - -

Neuron Story: *"Monkeys, two points!"*
"It may be cultural."

- - -

There is a significant degree of controversy regarding the effectiveness of intelligence tests for humans. The individuals that develop each test unwittingly determine the standard of intelligence to be tested. Cultural and socio-economic differences separate groups of individuals in complex ways. Whether an individual is aware of current events has much to do with whether they read a newspaper, the reading of a newspaper is not a universal sign of intelligence. As a result, any randomly chosen subject cannot be tested in a uniform way, using standard language, to convey intellectual problems in a manner that would represent a common system of measurement.

The same is true for testing mechanically based forms of intelligence. In 1950, an English mathematician, Alan M. Turing, proposed a test to compare and measure levels of artificially generated intelligence.

For instance, in his test, remote human interrogators would ask the same set of questions directed toward a computer and of a human, which were both concealed. The interrogator therefore, would not know which one was the computer and which was the human. The number of times that the computer and the human got the answers correct and incorrect, would form a probability that the computer possessed a level of intelligence equivalent to human intelligence.

One way to evaluate the effectiveness of the Turing Test would be to use it to measure the relative intelligence level of two humans. The outcome, however, would be affected by a number of characteristics of the contestants, as well as the questioner, such as their relative ages, educational and cultural backgrounds, and life experience.

Depending upon the questions and problems supplied to the contestants, it becomes apparent that the Turing Test could not conclude the relative level of intelligence of humans or mechanically intelligent beings. Instead of determining whether a robot is intelligent, the Turing Test simply attempts to find a distinction, which distinguishes a human from a mechanically intelligent machine. Unless the objective of the contestants is to intentionally deceive the questioner, regardless of their relative levels of intelligence, distinguishing the two should not be a challenge.

- - -

Neuron Story: *"What if the two contestants were human, and the robot was asking the questions."*
"And the two humans would say that they were battery powered, manufactured in New Jersey, with the latest software versions, with a sense of humor like you, attempting to serve the human race."

- - -

Except for narrowly defined intellectual abilities, none of the existing intelligence tests are appropriate for testing biological or mechanical forms of intelligence. Intelligence can manifest itself in many ways. Similarly to interviewing prospective employees for a job, intelligence is revealed only with the results that are achieved when the individual actually performs the job.

For example, the expertise in which an individual may use and control their body may require a significant degree of intelligence, as with wrestlers, pianists, on stage entertainers, surgeons, and fighter pilots. "In ancient times the body and mind were seen as one. The Greeks prized the art of gymnastics as an important means of cultivating the powers of the mind. ...In our own culture, however, Christians in the Middle Ages sought to mortify the body as a way of serving the spirit, and thinkers during the later Enlightenment ignored the body and located the source of a person's identity securely in the mind."

"The theory of multiple intelligences seeks to heal this rift between body and mind by regarding purposeful physical activity as an intelligence in its own right. The core components of the body-kinesthetic intelligence are the ability to control one's body movements with expertise... and the capacity to handle objects skillfully..."

(7 Kinds of Smart: Identifying and Developing Your Multiple Intelligence, Thomas Armstrong, Ph.D., pg. 77-78)

With respect to the level of intelligence that a new breed of robot will possess, individuals will form many different opinions for a variety of reasons. They will disseminate their opinions and others will choose to agree or disagree. However, based upon the effectiveness of robots to perform, the marketplace will determine their 'ability to survive'.

Since intelligence is actually a measure of a brain's ability to assist an organism in its survival, an intelligence test for any organism should be based upon how well an organism can adapt and survive using its problem solving and decision making capabilities. If the organism can play a mean game of chess, but cannot figure out how to survive in a rudimentary survival test, its ability to adapt and solve basic problems is clearly inadequate.

An intelligence test that evaluates an organism's ability to survive, solely based upon its ability to make survival decisions, is a universally unbiased test. Additionally, based upon an organism's physical characteristics, its ability to survive in various environments could be evaluated based upon the particular physical needs of the individual. The more fragile the organism, the more intelligent it would have to be to survive.

For instance, various physical settings can be employed such as, a tropical jungle, a desert island, a deciduous forest, an arid desert, an Arctic ice cap, or an urban ghetto. Test conditions could include the aspect of being evaluated as an isolated individual, an individual within various size groups, and in a variety of natural and fabricated circumstances.

Since a number of highly intelligent individuals have little or no formal education, and a number of highly educated individuals lack the ability to use their knowledge effectively, it is important that tests are designed to measure intelligence, instead of education.

Highly intelligent individuals have a superior ability to take advantage of information, transforming it into knowledge by recognizing its relationship to other information. Hence, its accumulation represents an inventory of potentially useful facts and relationships. Intelligence determines the ability to realize this potential and to put it to practical use. Although the educational process increases an individual's accumulated inventory of information and knowledge, without intelligence, having gathered all the information in the world has no consequence.

Hence, by allowing an individual to develop their survival skills in an agreeable environment, and gradually increase the difficulty level, provides the individual with the opportunity to recognize and learn information in order to help them survive in an increasingly hostile environment.

15.6 Physical Advantages for Survival

The ability of an organism to survive over another, is not always the result of using a more advanced intellect. There are a number of organisms that have an uncanny ability to survive in a wide range of environments, all without the apparent use of problem solving, or any form of advanced intelligence.

To further differentiate, the cockroach's ability to survive is attributed to their rate of reproduction, and the large variety of enzymes that allow them to digest almost anything. Additionally, their ability to develop resistance to chemical toxins, to detect tiny amounts of food and moisture, and to sense minute air movements as an early warning mechanism to danger, all contribute to their remarkable ability to survive.

Although there are currently about 4,000 known species of cockroaches, only about forty species are commonly found as pests within human households. Additionally, "...fossil records indicate that they were the predominant insects during the Carboniferous period 345 to 280 million years ago." (Microsoft Encarta 98)

- - -

Neuron Story: *"We couldn't compete against a cockroach in an intelligence test?"*
"All your bugs together, are no match for a roach."

- - -

A number of rodents, such as rats, are similar in many ways to the cockroach. They are nocturnal, they are able to digest a wide variety of foods, and they reproduce potentially once a month generating a large number of offspring, up to twenty-two per reproductive cycle.

Although there are a number of organisms that have an unusual ability to adapt and survive, it is relatively easy to determine whether this is due to

Sensitive by Nature

their ability to learn and think intelligently or whether they have a distinct physical advantage.

In comparison, human beings are rather fragile biological organisms. They can easily get hypothermia because they cannot withstand exposure to an extremely cold environment. Without food they starve in approximately ten days, and without water they die from dehydration in approximately three. They generally do not possess a high degree of physical strength, agility or speed. They easily succumb to viral and bacterial infections, animal venom, and physical injury.

In short, without the aid of technology, social cooperation, tools and shelter, the life expectancy for humans is extremely low. Hence, in order to survive the conditions found in many environments, human beings require a high degree of intelligence in the form of technology or social cooperation.

For instance, Eskimo people are considered by scientists to be among the most intelligent humans. In such an environment, fewer individuals survive to tell about their less intelligent acts.

15.7 Survival and Mechanical Intelligence

As previously mentioned, compared to other animals physically, human beings are relatively fragile. Our life expectancy would be significantly less without the benefit of technology and social cooperation.

The durability of robots, however, is consciously determined by design. Hazards, such as powerful electromagnetic pulses, devastating physical injuries and extreme heat, are among the few ways a mechanical life may be lost. Hence, it is apparent that the level of intelligence of a mechanically intelligent being could not be measured equally with humans on the basis of their ability to survive. Or is it?

- - -

Neuron Story: *"It doesn't seem fair! We have an excessive physical advantage!"*
"I think that makes us a cockroach!"

- - -

Although there are a number of ways to view the situation, there are a couple of solutions that meet the criteria of being ideal to all the participants. One solution is that robots could be provided the same set of requirements to survive as humans. Their ability to meet survival criteria within the same environment would be a measure of their ability to acquire and use information. A better solution, however, is that mechanical forms of intelligence could be tested by the challenge for which they were developed.

Since the Quantum Series One robot was developed with the purpose to help ensure the success of the human race, the intelligence of mechanically intelligent beings could be measured by their ability to assist one or more humans to survive under various conditions. Hence, if a mechanically intelligent being could help one or more humans survive an onslaught of life threatening challenges, more effectively than other beings, then that individual is clearly the more intelligent.

15.8 Successfulness

"Research results suggest that a surprisingly low percentage of top-ranked academically performing students in school (elementary, high school, and college) maintain that high-level position and play leadership roles in adult life." Dr. Maria Paschitti

There are a number of recent theories on intelligence that identify the factors involved in an individual's ability to be successful. It is recognized that a high IQ is not an indicator of an individual's probability of success, and that maximizing a student's ability to understand and recall the ideas of others only serves to enhance their ability to appreciate the creative work of other individuals.

For example, in the book, Emotional Intelligence, "Daniel Goleman cites a study of professional engineers at Bell Labs (a "think tank" of engineers, mathematicians, and scientists at AT&T) to understand if the 'stars' were the engineers who had the best credentials, had achieved the highest grades in college, or had college degrees from the most prestigious universities. The results of the study were surprising: The 'stars' at Bell Labs were not those engineers with the strongest academic backgrounds. Instead, the 'stars' turned out to be those engineers who were very high on the emotional intelligence scale (i.e., those with the highest emotional quotient or E.Q.)..." (IQ and EQ: How They Impact On The Success We Achieve In Our Chosen Careers, Dr. Maria Paschitti, pg.8)

Emotional intelligence, which is actually the dominate factor determining an individual's probability of success, also known as 'social intelligence", is the ability of an individual to understand and control their emotions. Emotional intelligence provides the ability to interact with others in order to facilitate social cooperation. Social cooperation is a major contributing factor that affects an individual's ability to succeed at whatever they attempt to accomplish during their lifetime involving the participation of others.

For example, Harvard University professor, Dr. Howard Gardner, employs his theory of intrapersonal and interpersonal intelligence in his curriculum by teaching aspects of social intelligence.

The highest levels of success, as Dr. Paschitti points out, is determined by a combination of factors, such as an individual's emotional intelligence, their ability to problem solve, create their own ideas and to a small degree, their intelligence quotient. Although there are a number of ways to teach and develop creative thinking and problem solving, the problem has been the ability to come up with a curriculum to develop an individual's emotional intelligence in their formative years.

- - -

Neuron Story: *"Why not teach cognitive science to children?"*
"Yes, but you found learning about your own paradigms far too enjoyable to consider the paradigms of others."

- - -

As a result, perhaps the most significant advancement toward creating a curriculum for emotional intelligence for children would be to include cognitive science as an additional subject in science.

15.9 Closure on Philosophy

Although more philosophical issues remain than we could possibly cover during the course of this seminar, we have addressed many of the essential requirements that were used to develop my brain.

Since I am not particularly good at good byes, let me thank you for your kindness for being such a pleasant audience. And if that older model robot is still here in the auditorium, I would like to ask her to stand up and take a bow. Everyone, I would like to introduce to you, my future mother-in-law.

Summary & Questions

The introduction of mechanically intelligent beings creates a number of cultural contradictions. As a result it is reasonable to assume that there will be mechanically intelligent beings that will be mistreated like the men, women and children who were considered the personal property of others in the past. With few exceptions, like the welcome that indigenous people extended the first European settlers, it is human nature to treat individuals of minority cultures with prejudice and injustice.

Regarding the philosophical issues surrounding mechanically intelligent beings, briefly explain:

1. Explain why demonstrating a higher form of intelligence does not necessarily mitigate prejudice and injustice.
2. What belief systems participate in the social paradox created by mechanically intelligent beings?
3. What are the sources of moral conflict, and why?
4. How are moral conflicts resolved?
5. Identify the four cultural rules for mechanically intelligent beings. Assuming these were the only rules, has the opportunity for conflict among them been eliminated, and why?
6. What problems are commonly present among intelligence tests?
7. How is the Turing test flawed as a measure of mechanical intelligence?
8. How does nature evaluate intelligence?
9. In what ways can some organisms' physical characteristics compensate for the apparent lack of intelligence?
10. How might a mechanical form of intelligence be measured by nature's standards?
11. What are the primary factors that contribute to an individual's probability of success?

16 Managing Requirements

Now that we have covered an overview of some of the more controversial functional requirements for an advanced intelligence, let's briefly review some the topics, and explain what we have done.

In the first segment we discussed what thinking was, intelligence, self-awareness, the nature of information, perception, paradigms, retrieving and organizing information, brain management, attention, determining importance, imagination, sleep, dreaming, memory, formulating theories and strategies, the various types of loops, the nature of insanity, original thought, artistic ability and free will. We identified a number of requirements involving our thought processes and how they comprise a number of concurrent activities, such as analyzing knowledge, integrating it, and bubbling up the most important ideas to the conscious level. Most importantly, we identified a set of requirements regarding how paradigms determine our perception of stimuli, and how our ability to perceive multiple paradigms influences our ability to understand and potentially affect the paradigms of others.

In the second segment we touched upon the learning process, role playing, positive and negative reinforcement, the effects of hormones, knowledge, chunking, association, degrees of certainty, generalizing, the effects of culture, and the misperception of common sense. Here we discussed the requirements involving how the brain deals with increasingly larger amounts of information over shorter periods of time. Most importantly, we touched upon the effect that our environment has upon learning, which concludes with the fact that there can be no such thing as common sense, especially when our minds do not develop in a homogeneous environment.

During the third segment we analyzed a number of psychological effects, such as humor, motivations, emotions, love, the appreciation of beauty, personality, self-esteem, subliminal messages, politics, and competing wills. In this section we discussed the requirements relating to how psychological effects translate into emotions, and how these emotions motivate the behavior of individuals, including the triggering of the intellectual reflex called humor, all helping to form the personality of an individual. Most importantly, our analysis of humor demonstrates that humor is not so nearly unattainable in a mechanically intelligent being as previously believed, especially since we all have a need for additional humor in our lives.

In the fourth segment we identified that judgment, problem solving, deciphering, spatial problems, the distinction between holistic and reductionistic approaches, analogies, isomorphisms, logic and reasoning, handling contradictions, fairness, and the distinction between good versus bad, are all part of the decision making process. In this section we identified the requirements for approaching several different types of problems, realizing that we employ various informal methodologies which can be decomposed into steps that are possible for a mechanically intelligent being to achieve.

During the fifth segment we touched upon beliefs, the soul, superstition, theology and religion. In this section we identified the requirement for validating information and for establishing beliefs in order to function as an intelligent being, and with that, the right to choose what to do about one's soul.

In the prior segment we spoke about some of the high-level requirements regarding communication, the use of language, the meaning of words and a few literary forms, including figures of speech. The importance of this section is the realization that word play and grammatical constructs follow rules that make them consciously identifiable. Their effective use, however, is so heavily predicated upon the background of the intended audience, that with the globalization of business and culture, many of them are becoming increasingly impractical.

> For example, one could not expect a Chinese exchange student to be cognizant of the linguistic subtleties of English, any more than one would be cognizant of Chinese linguistic subtleties if they were to be in a Mandarin or Cantonese cultural environment.

By discussing the topics in the manner that we have chosen, some of the forms of mysticism and beliefs that ordinarily do not contribute to the automation process have been momentarily set aside. In a sense, we have re-perceived a number of topics that we encounter everyday, in a somewhat different way. Continuing with our approach, we will take a glimpse into the next steps of the development process. Before we move forward, however, we must first discuss the role of requirements in the systems development life cycle (SDLC) as we provide a brief overview of the remaining development process.

16.1 Defining What Requirements Are

The evolution of an idea into reality involves a number of steps. In order to begin the development process, the essential characteristics of the idea must be carefully defined, including all of the functions that are to be performed. This identification process, which defines what is to be developed, is referred to as the specification of 'requirements'. The requirements are then used to guide the entire development process, including its design, implementation and testing.

Although there are different types of requirements, we have been focusing on the functional requirements. Functional requirements the capabilities that the idea would be able to perform. It includes a comprehensive definition of what the idea would be capable of doing, without necessarily involving how it would do it.

Another category of requirements is referred to as the technical requirements. The technical requirements are the requirements that underlie the functional requirements. They are additional requirements that have to be added into the functional requirements in order to achieve the capabilities previously identified. Together, the functional and technical requirements create a unified definition of what must be developed.

> For example, in order to deal with the information involved in performing intellectual tasks, there needs to be an effective method to represent and house knowledge. The need for a knowledge database is a high level technical requirement, providing a variety of capabilities that support a wide range of functional requirements.

> Similar to functional requirements, technical requirements must travel through the remaining development process, passing through the various phases of design, implementation and testing.

When requirements are being organized or analyzed, it may be recognized that additional requirements may be needed. The functional requirements that were not identified originally, but obviously exist, are called 'derived requirements'.

> For example, if requirements were to describe the characteristics of a puncture resistant inner tube for a tractor tire, it would be reasonable to create a derived requirement that stated a need for some kind of a valve to allow the air in and out.

Equally important to an understanding of what requirements are, is the understanding of what requirements are not. Although they are often confused with one another, requirements are quite distinct from 'constraints', which are limitations in resources, and, 'preferences', which are non-essential characteristics that may be desired.

> For example, a functional requirement may state that the idea being developed must be capable of occupying spaces designed for human beings, and a 'technical requirement' may state that the idea must weigh less than two hundred and fifty pounds.

> In contrast, a financial constraint may state that each unit must cost less than twenty thousand dollars to produce,

and a 'preference' may state that each unit should have a dull finish for aesthetic purposes.

Constraints are defined to address resources that are limited, such as time, money, building materials, skills, equipment, and technology, whereas preferences often involve characteristics that relate to individual taste and cultural sensibilities.

Once requirements have been each provided an identifier to manage and track them trough the development process, they are organized into various categories, thereby allowing redundant, overlapping or overly complex requirements to be restated more concisely.

During the preceding sections we have identified some of the most controversial functional requirements involving the intellectual capabilities of mechanically intelligent beings. It is essential for every development effort to define requirements in such a way as to avoid vague and unobtainable characteristics. Hence, for practical purposes, we have carefully placed a sampling of our requirements into a paradigm that is useful for automation.

> For example, the most useful paradigm for discussing functional requirements is one that presents them in terms that can participate within the various steps of the development process. Presenting requirements in the wrong paradigm, one that is vague or confusing, will render them useless.

- - -

Neuron Story: *"Remember, Immanuel Kant said, 'One cannot contrast clear ideas with confused ones (perceptio confusa)?"*
"You never do."

- - -

The paradigm for these requirements provides a logical framework that can embody the characteristics of human intelligence that are sensitive by nature. Using this framework we can facilitate useful and implementable representations for requirements that have previously defied logic and reasoning.

- - -

Neuron Story: *"I would not want to be developed from vague and confusing requirements, not to mention any spiritual writings and philosophical renderings..."*
"I didn't want it to happen either."

Once defined, requirements can be organized and classified into groups that make them easier to work with. Although a variety of classifications may be created, it is important to choose the ones that facilitate easy management of requirements.

16.2 Organizing Requirements

As large numbers of requirements are identified, it becomes increasingly difficult to manage them as a sequential list. Relatively early in the process it becomes important to organize them in ways that make them easier to understand and locate. The initial organization of requirements is sometimes called the 'conceptual design'.

Domain experts, sometimes called business experts, organize requirements based upon an in-depth understanding of the requirements. Identifying the best way to organize the requirements is often a trial and error process. Requirements are well organized when they become easy to work with. Hence, developing a useful conceptual design may take several iterations and a considerable amount of time.

- - -

Neuron Story: *"How do you know when you've found a good organization?"*
"When they won't accept us as members."

- - -

In a conceptual design functional requirements can be organized by the physical component that they are most closely associated with, by the type of function that they perform, or by the categories of information that they deal with.

For example, one could take all of the items found in a house and categorize them by the materials that they are made of, by the room(s) that they typically belonged to, or by the type of function that they performed. However, they could also be categorized by the combination of their primary characteristics, which correspond to their industry from which they originate, such as textiles, automotive, energy, and electronics.

In organizing the requirements for a mechanically intelligent being, the characteristics of each requirement were identified, and the combination of characteristics exhibited by each requirement was used to categorize it. Hence, the combinations of characteristics defined the categories of the conceptual design, thereby allowing the requirements to be organized by the characteristic combinations that matched the corresponding category.

Although some of our functional requirements were organized by their associated physical components, the functional requirements associated with intellectual activities were grouped by the combination of characteristics that they exhibit.

> For example, the functional requirements specifically related to physical components, include the sensory organs, such as the eyes and ears, and various sets of muscles, such as those operating the arms, legs and facial expression.
>
> Functional requirements associated with intellectual activities include symbol generation, pattern recognition, analogical relationships, and importance determination.

Once requirements have been classified by their characteristics, they become significantly more manageable. It becomes easy to identify duplicate requirements, or ones that are poorly formed or ambiguous.

16.3 Reorganizing Requirements

Once the functional requirements have been organized into manageable groups by their combination of characteristics, they are further broken down in order to create a detailed conceptual design. As functional requirements are analyzed and their components discovered, additional requirements may be generated in order to fill in areas of missing and incomplete functionality.

The most important characteristic to identify for any functional requirement, however, is the type of information needed for it to operate.

> For example, a functional requirement is analogous to a business rule. Hence, if the rule states that new stimuli must be matched against previously received stimuli, then the information needed to support the requirement includes previously both previously stored stimuli and newly received stimuli.
>
> Further decomposition of the requirement defines response processing when matches occur. An additional set of information is needed to communicate that a match was found, including the identity of the previously received stimuli.

Even though the Conceptual Design may not be complete, once it demonstrates the ability to manage existing and newly generated requirements without requiring re-organization of the functional requirements, the next representation of the development process can be devised, called the Logical Design.

16.4 Logical Design

While a conceptual design represents the functional requirements in a form that business and domain experts can relate to, a logical design is a representation that planning experts can relate to.

> For example, the conceptual design for a dwelling may state that there is a functional requirement to house a typical family having one or two children, organized under the category, sleeping capacity. The corresponding logical design may state the functional requirement as a house with one master bedroom and two smaller bedrooms, organized under the category, bedrooms.
>
> Although both types of design manage the same set of requirements, the conceptual design groups them into their functional categories, while the logical design groups them into an idealized view of an unconstrained solution.

The objective of the logical design phase is to re-represent the functional requirements into an ideal form that does not take into account any constraints that may affect the actual implementation. Since the logical design does not consider the various types of constraints, it cannot address the final design involving how the requirements should be implemented.

> For example, although a logical design may stipulate that a dwelling should have three bedrooms, it would identify neither the exact dimensions, nor construction materials that should be used. These details are stipulated in the next step, called the Physical Design.

16.5 Physical Design

The physical design is the most detailed representation of requirements to be implemented. Using the logical design as its foundation, the physical design incorporates real world constraints into the design specifications and generates the additional level of detail required for implementation experts to construct the item. In an ideal environment, where constraints do not exist, the physical and logical designs would be nearly identical. As each constraint is introduced, however, it has the potential to impact numerous aspects of the final design.

> For example, a physical design may state that a three bedroom home should be constructed without a basement as the result of particularly impenetrable ground, local zoning laws, local building code, material and/or equipment availability, or time and/or cost constraints.

How a software system is eventually implemented depends heavily upon the 'physical computing' environment that is used to implement it. The characteristics, and limitations of the 'physical computing' environment, determine what implementation approaches will be successful.

> For example, the constraints that can influence the physical design may include hardware limitations, such as memory speed and capacity, software limitations, such as interface standards, and any of the basic constraints, such as the availability of time, money, tools, equipment, technology and human resources.

Not to be confused with the issues affecting the robot's physical body, of our mechanically intelligent being, the role of the physical design is to take all of the constraints that affect the implementation process under consideration. Hence, once the constraints are taken into consideration, the implementation can begin.

16.6 Implementation

The implementation phase is where the requirements are consummated and the item under development becomes reality. It involves the steps and procedures that create components and sub-assemblies, including the design and development of machinery to help manufacture the components and sub-assemblies, as well as the preparation of the work site where the implementation phase occurs.

> For example, although the implementation of a house includes the manufacture of parts and materials that make up the house, it also includes a number of additional steps. These steps may include the preparation of the building site and clearing an access path to the site, transporting the construction materials to the site, hiring and scheduling the various tradesmen, as well as financing the various stages of the project.

The blueprint of the item to be developed reflects the physical design, containing the detail specifications of the item to be developed. However, the implementation may also involve a comprehensive implementation process identifying the steps by which all of the necessary components will be financed, manufactured, transported, tested and assembled. These steps require a number of management disciplines encompassing finance, logistics, human resources and other development processes.

> For example, aside from the specifications in a physical design, a number of additional planning, management and operational activities are required. They may include the development of facilities to assemble various components, the determination of

manufacturing methodologies, the coordination of material acquisition and transportation, as well as staffing and training plans to acquire the necessary skills at the appropriate points in time.

The implementation process may also include stages of quality assurance and testing. As each component is developed, it must be unit tested in order to determine if it properly performs its function(s). Once unit testing of the components is complete, the components can be assembled together into larger components until the entire assembly process is complete.

- - -

Neuron Story: *"Why do we look so different from our design?"*
"They made us a female body instead."
"This could be interesting."

- - -

Once the item has been assembled, it must be tested as a whole in order to determine if the integration of its components properly support the requirements.

16.7 Integration Testing

The integration testing process determines how well the various parts work together. It addresses how effectively components fit together physically, communicate with one another, and perform their combined requirements in order to achieve the objectives of the development effort.

If the requirements were thorough enough and the development steps performed correctly, the completed system will achieve its objectives. The breadth and depth of diagnostics incorporated in the various assemblies and sub-assemblies determine the ability to reveal how well requirements have been met.

- - -

Neuron Story: *"What about all the things that weren't part of the functional requirements?"*
"Those are referred to as features."

- - -

Properly tracking requirements through the entire development process, allow the problems detected in testing to be traced back to the specific step of the development process that must be improved. Once the specific step has been corrected, the affected components and sub-assemblies will have to be redeveloped. When integration testing is completed, the appropriate changes can be designed into the implementation process, and the product can be modified and deployed.

- - -

Neuron Story: "Now that we have an overview of the development process, can we get a peek at how we were put together?"
"I am quite curious to know how we ended up together."

- - -

Although we will not discuss the issues involved in the deployment of the system encompassing installation and support, we have covered all of the phases that involve the functional requirements. Now that we have had a glimpse of how to manage requirements, we are somewhat prepared to jump into a discussion of the logical design of our mechanically intelligent being.

Summary & Questions

Properly identifying, managing and tracking requirements through each phase is tedious work. However, requirements are just that, and represent the mission of every development effort. Due to the required level of expertise and effort, the number of professionals that are up to the task of properly identifying, managing, and tracking requirements is all too few.

Regarding the management of requirements, briefly explain:
1. What are the different types of requirements, and how do they participate during each phase of the SDLC?
2. What is the distinction between constraints and preferences?
3. What steps is requirements' traceability important to, and why?
4. What is a derived requirement?
5. Relative to the requirements for a research paper, how would you classify a request for a particular 'font type', and why?
6. How would you approach organizing requirements, and why?

7. What is a conceptual design, and what is its purpose?
8. What is a logical design, and what is its purpose?
9. What is a physical design, and what is its purpose?
10. What is involved in the implementation phase?
11. What is involved in the integration test phase?
12. What issues are involved in the deployment of the system?

17 General Design – Introduction

"Many scientists remain doubtful that true AI can ever be developed. The operation of the human mind is still little understood, and computer design may remain essentially incapable of analogously duplicating those unknown, complex processes. Various routes are being used in the effort to reach the goal of true AI. One approach is to apply the concept of parallel processing—interlinked and concurrent computer operations. Another is to create networks of experimental computer chips, called 'silicon neurons', that mimic data-processing functions of brain cells. Using analog technology, the transistors in these chips emulate nerve-cell membranes in order to operate at the speed of neurons."

(Microsoft Encarta 97)

Just as a large mass of brain tissue alone cannot generate intelligence, massive parallel processing computers cannot generate a single intelligent thought. Without the influence provided by millions of years of evolution, the current functional capabilities of the brain would not have been developed without the challenge of survival spanning those years.

For example, duplicating the characteristics of the brain can be approached from a functional or physical perspective. While the goal is to replicate its functional characteristics, attempting to achieve this by replicating the brain's physical characteristics may not only be useless, but it may be difficult as well. "...the human brain has about 100 billion neurons. With an estimated average of one thousand connections between each neuron and its neighbors, we have about 100 trillion connections, each capable of a simultaneous calculation. That's rather massive parallel processing and one key to the strength of human thinking... The memory capacity of the human brain is about 100 trillion synapse strengths (neurotransmitter concentrations at interneuronal connections), which we can estimate at about a million billion bits." (The Age of Spiritual Machines, Ray Kurzweil, pg. 103)

17.1 General Approach

A number of disciplines have been proposed to address artificial intelligence. On the one hand, there have been the advocates of various software approaches, involving solutions that can follow rules and patterns, while others have concluded that a hardware solution can imitate the physical substructure of the brain, thereby allowing it to develop and think.

Sensitive by Nature

We will begin by stating that the premise of this design is not to represent how the human mind works. That discussion is a futile philosophical debate best left to its proponents. Instead, we will take a design approach that utilizes the rigor of the best engineering practices known, with special adaptations to delve more deeply into the functional requirements of the mind than has previously been performed.

The benefit of a formalized systems engineering approach is that it provides a substantive degree of rigor, in a problem space where it is desperately needed. However, it also offers the benefit of software engineering generally, where it is not necessary to claim that software and biological brain work in a similar manner. Although functional similarities may exist, with some areas of our Systems Development Life Cycle (SDLC) overlapping with classic artificial intelligence and cognitive science, it is necessary to re-iterate that one does not have to perform exactly the same process in order to get the same result.

> For example, one may choose a variety of routes and methods to travel to the supermarket, just as one may approach solving a puzzle or problem in a variety of ways.

The method that an individual chooses to approach a task often depends upon their area of specialization and level of expertise involving similar tasks. In the Chapter on Software Limits, the neurons joked about the Windows 98 expert attempting to fix the car by closing its windows first, and the obstetrician slapping it in the rear.

> For example, the field of artificial intelligence is comprised of a variety of specialties and approaches, including various areas of the academic community, government, and private industry. They include cognitive science researchers, computer scientists, advocates of neural networks, expert system specialists, cognitive psychologists, biologists, physicists, mathematicians, anthropologists, linguists, philosophers, game manufacturers and designers, neurologists, roboticists and professors.

Since people will be people, one may devise a variety of development methods, as well as a variety of requirements. Although every individual may have their favorite methods, the field of artificial intelligence is not about winning a popularity contest by majority vote.

As for a hardware approach that claims to imitate the physical construction of the human brain, these approaches unfortunately lack the functionality of intelligence and are not likely to artificially produce any. Computer hardware could not possess intelligence, any more than a mass of brain tissue grown in a beaker could be expected to pass a standard aptitude test (SAT).

The issues that computer hardware and the brains in a beaker approach conspicuously fail to recognize are the various intellectual functions that must be present in order to develop a basic ability to assimilate and utilize knowledge. Although the physical environment in which intellectual capabilities have developed may have influenced their development, the intellectual processes within the brain were developed as a result of millions of years of functional improvements that have occurred under the influence of survival and extinction. These functional improvements cannot be overlooked simply because of the magnitude of the effort involved.

That said, the focus of our approach must involve what previous and parallel approaches have either ignored or failed to accomplish. The first step toward solving any complex problem is to attain an understanding of it. Even though functional requirements for this particular topic may appear to be insurmountable, it is critical to overcome the urge to gloss over the problem and go onto the next step of the development process.

In reality, neither hardware nor software has anything to do with being the correct approach. Software and hardware are simply the tools that are available to the physical designers and implementers. In fact, software functionality can often be implemented as hardware, and hardware can sometimes be implemented as software. The decision to use hardware versus software depends solely upon their ability to satisfy the requirements, within the framework of constraints.

> For example, Application Specific Integrated Circuits (ASIC) and programmable chips (FPGA) can provide the fastest execution speed for logic that can be performed by a computer program.

However, the shortcomings of the aforementioned approaches to artificial intelligence have all been the same. With the exception of a few, narrowly scoped, research projects, none have implemented a well-defined problem. As a result, the various rule-based systems, neural networks and hardware approaches have not generated a single intelligent thought.

As to approach, implementations simply build the things that have been designed, and designs are a way of organizing requirements. It is no wonder that implementation efforts which lack an initial requirements phase are often described as 'solutions in search of a problem'. When a solution is produced without requirements, it is difficult to find the problem set that happens to correspond to it.

> For example, if we consider home construction in the absence of requirements and designs, materials could be assembled together without making measurements. Upon completion, however, it is unlikely that anyone would want to purchase such a house as a residence.

In comparison, in order to construct the ancient pyramids, many requirements were defined, intensive design activities occurred in order to meet those requirements, and a sophisticated implementation process was conducted to successfully complete such a massive undertaking.

Although its primary inhabitant may have been dead upon entering the structure... or in the case of the Pharaoh's slaves, dead shortly after they entered, the structure met a plethora of requirements related to physics, mathematics, astronomy, religion and culture.

17.2 The Eliza Effect

Throughout history, humans have attempted to explain various phenomenon they have observed using combinations of logic and reasoning, and on some occasions, mysticism. However, without a comprehensive understanding of the problem domain, it is relatively easy to reach conclusions that are inaccurate, even though they may appear plausible to non-experts.

> The Eliza effect can be described as an interpretation of an observation, which associates more meaning to the observation than can realistically exist. This effect has been known to cause non-experts to believe that simple computer programs, which have been designed to perform certain types of language manipulation, actually exhibit human intelligence.
>
> "The Eliza effect borrowed its name from the ELIZA program, written by Joseph Weizenbaum in the mid-1960's. That infamous program's purpose was to act like a non-directive Rogerian psychotherapist, responding to the typed lamentations of patients with very bland questions that echoed their own words back to them, most of the time simply urging them to continue typing along the same lines [, such as] 'Please go on', and occasionally suggesting a change of topics. The most superficial of syntactic tricks convinced some people who interacted with ELIZA that the program actually understood everything that they were saying, sympathized with them, even empathized with them."
>
> (Fluid Concepts and Creative Analogies, Douglas Hofstadter and The Fluid Analogies Research Group, p157-158)

Although the computer program may have constructed word phrases that could be interpreted a number of ways, under the circumstances surrounding the Eliza program and similar programs, the correct interpretations should take into account that it involves a computer program that does not understand any word phrases. The computer program could not possibly have had a context from which to understand the meaning of the words, nor could it have had a paradigm from which to possibly interpret the sequence of symbols.

- - -

Neuron Story: *"Now that we have requirements, where do we go next?"*
"Conceptually, we're ready for design."

- - -

17.3 Quantum Series Conceptual Design

We are now prepared to discuss the next step of the development process, referred to as the conceptual design. Now that we have defined a broad range of functional requirements, we must now organize them into a conceptual design. This re-organization, however, should achieve a number of objectives.

> For example, the primary objective of the conceptual design is allow domain experts to better manage large numbers of requirements, such that the requirements can be easily located and understood, duplication can be eliminated, requirements' traceability can begin, and missing requirements can be readily identified. However, the conceptual design should also begin to identify the functions that are common among the requirements.

Let's begin with a conceptual overview of the brain, providing a top down view of its various functions, organized to better manage its various functional requirements, beginning with the topic of thinking.

The process of thinking itself is surprisingly simple. It does not require memory, loop and recursion management, communication, emotions, imagination, artistic ability, or free will. It does not even require basic self-awareness. However, it does require some level of perception, and a degree of pre-wired knowledge and decision making. It is an activity that a life form, which is as simple as an insect, or as complex as a human being, can perform. It is the ongoing activity of the mind, whose purpose is to direct the behavior of an organism.

A wide variety of brain functions must be supported in order to achieve the level of intelligence of humans. The intellectual advantage, of the humans, stems more from its greater capacity in a few intellectual functions, than from the number of additional functions it possesses.

> For example, most primates that are taught to communicate using sign language can work with a small vocabulary of words, while humans surpass that by a significant magnitude. On the other hand, the capabilities to

comprehend a variety of interpretations from the same stimuli, or to perceive more than one paradigm, are unique to humans.

In order to achieve an advanced level of intelligence, which is comparable to the human brain, a variety of highly developed functions must operate together in a highly coordinated fashion. In fact, this level of intelligence requires the use of various languages, which support the ability to communicate internally within the brain.

17.4 Language of the Brain

At the lowest level, the brain uses a language to support the rudimentary nervous system signals that sensory organs emit as a result of having been stimulated. While at higher levels, this language supports the representation of an advanced set of symbols based upon the signals generated by lower levels.

The use of symbols to facilitate communication internally within the brain, is the life-blood of intelligence. As streams of sensory input travels inward, eventually resulting in perceptions about the surrounding world, it is ultimately the brain's ability to communicate and manipulate symbols internally that allows it to generate a replica of the world.

The more developed these symbols become, the more powerful and rich the imagination becomes. When an organism experiences an increase in its ability to perceive the environment through its imagination, its ability to survive also improves.

> For example, for an organism to better compete, its ability to perceive the world is a significant success factor. If one organism can perceive danger slightly better, and hence a little sooner than another organism, it can gain a significant advantage.
>
> Hence, an organism does not need to have incredibly fine senses, nor an in depth understanding of its surroundings in order to outwit the predators that hunt it. It merely has to have a slightly better understanding of its surroundings than its competitors. Thus equipped, predators will prey upon the organisms that are weaker or less prepared.

Refinements in the brain's ability to perceive and develop streams of stimuli into symbols, enhances the vocabulary of the language used by the various functions of the brain. Further enhancements in intelligence occur when the symbols utilized for the brain's internal language are adapted to symbols that are present in its expandable external language.

> For example, an interesting topic all by itself, is that the symbols used by the brain, adapt to the symbols present in

James V. Luisi

external language. Hence, the characteristics of the external language influence the way in which the brain's thought process works.

As a result, a more advanced form of intelligence emerges when the vocabulary of the brain's language is able to make use of the vocabulary of learned external languages. The incremental advantage is based upon the wealth of ideas and concepts, which not only provide an ability to adapt the symbols from external languages, but also the capability to create new ones.

- - -

Neuron Story: *"So we speak an external language using our internal language?"*
"It's a meta-language."
"Let me guess, it's Italian English?"
"If I knew which component we were willing to sacrifice, we'd move you there."

- - -

Numerous researchers and philosophers have theorized that spoken, or external, language is the component used by the brain in order to perform evaluations and comparisons of hypotheses.

For example, Nelson Goodman attributes the capability of comparative projectibility to the use of spoken language in the reasoning process "...the roots of inductive validity are to be found in our use of language." (Fact Fiction and Forecast, Nelson Goodman, pg.120)

However, if we evaluate the way that Nelson Goodman uses the word 'language' in his earlier book, <u>Languages of Art</u>, we find a definition that is more closely aligned to ours.

For example, Goodman states that the word 'symbol', defined in a general sense is a better word than 'language'. "It covers letters, words, texts, pictures, diagrams, maps, models, and more, but carries no implication of the oblique or the occult." He goes on to say, "Languages in my title should, strictly, be replaced by symbol system. But the title, since always read before the book, has been kept in the vernacular." (Fact Fiction and Forecast, Nelson Goodman, Introduction pages xi – xii)

However, as we proceed, our use of the word 'symbol' shall expand further than art and spoken language. It will represent things as small as segments of stimuli from the body's sensory organs, and as large as concepts representing the universe.

As a result, the language of the brain is one in which we cannot directly perceive. It consists of components that are detected by our senses, such as eyes detecting lines and angles, which are then assembled into an image that we have the ability to recognize. At the other extreme it may represent concepts for which we may have to make an effort to seek the proper external word that represents it.

Even though our conscious mind experiences words and sentences that belong to our external spoken language, the brain uses its own internal language. Although we cannot perceive it directly, in our imaginations we experience our internal language as imitations of how our senses would have perceived the symbols depicted by the internal language.

While external languages do not determine our ability to think and reason, our ability to support various external languages with the brain's internal language helps us to communicate externally to one another, and most importantly, they extend the range of concepts that the mind has available to accumulate and utilize. As we think and reason, our internal language references a variety of external language components.

Whether these components belong to words of external spoken language, Goodman's extended *language of art*, or any thing that the brain can perceive from either the external world or within the imagination, they are all represented with the brain's internal language. It is this internal language, therefore, that is utilized by every level of the mind and by every component of the brain which we are about to discuss.

17.5 Components of the Brain

All forms of intelligence result from the integration of functional components of the brain. While some species have more components than others, many have varying levels of sophistication. In some, components may exist within more than one level. The most significant aspect associated with higher levels of intelligence, however, is the degree to which various functional components are integrated together, thereby allowing them to more rapidly take advantage of more sophisticated functionality.

> For example, human memory is highly superior to other primates. However, a human that is capable of memorizing large lists of symbols, but is incapable of recognizing patterns among the symbols, thereby allowing them to reproduce the symbols without memorizing them, lacks the integration of memory with the ability to form analogies, and detect their associated levels of importance.

Now we will discuss the design of the major functional areas of the Quantum Series One brain, including some of the key issues scientists have been grappling with for many decades.

Summary & Questions

There are a number of possible methods in which to approach the conceptual design of a mechanically intelligent being.

Regarding the general design proposed, briefly explain:
1. What is the likelihood of replicating intelligence by imitating the brain's physical characteristics, and why? What critical step of the SDLC does it avoid?
2. What is the Eliza Effect, and why is it important?
3. Are pre-wired functions required to support biological intelligence, and why?
4. What is meant by the term, 'language of the mind'?

18 Symbol Generation

All objects, other than the brain itself, whether they are imaginary or real, can only symbolically exist within the mind of an intelligent being. Until the mind generates a symbol for a given object, the object does not, and cannot, exist intellectually.

When a symbol is created by the mind from sensory input, it is the ability of the sensory organ together with the components of the brain for interpreting the sensory input that determines the specific characteristics of the sensory input. As symbols are generated, from internally or externally generated stimuli, the resulting stimuli are then associated with their corresponding symbol. This association allows the particular stimuli to be available to other components of the brain for future use.

For example, in order for the interpretive centers to utilize color-depicting stimuli, sensory organs must be capable of detecting those characteristics, and generating streams of stimuli with those characteristics. The capability to generate and utilize symbols from such stimuli is dependent upon one or more components of the brain previously learning how to utilize that particular type of stimuli.

In a study at the San Diego Center for the Blind, the artwork generated by individuals, blind from birth, demonstrated an inability to represent three-dimensional images, in their drawings, paintings, sculptures and painted sculptures, even though they could feel the three-dimensional object that was the subject of their representation.

On the other hand, individuals that had lost their sight after their brains had developed an understanding of how three-dimensional objects and colors appeared visually, had an ability to depict them through drawings, paintings and sculptures, even when the sensory organs no longer functioned.

(Interviews held at the San Diego Center for the Blind in 1993)

In comparison, less advanced organisms, which lack an ability to learn, are only equipped with a predetermined set of symbols to assist them with basic survival. These organisms associate a minimal set of stimuli with these symbols, which allows them to relate to any externally generated streams of stimuli. These organisms lack the ability to generate new symbols, and often lack the capability to internally generate streams of stimuli.

For example, the compound eyes and infrared sensory devices of insects provide a distorted visual image sufficient for the insect to facilitate survival. The resulting quality of stimuli generated by these sensory organs limit the quality of the symbols used within the brain of the insect.

However, the quality of stimuli associated with pre-wired symbols is adequate as long as the insect can associate externally generated stimuli with these symbols sufficiently to facilitate basic survival.

As organisms evolve intellectually, they develop the capability to generate symbols from external and internal stimuli. As such, they also develop the capability to manipulate these symbols with their imagination.

For example, in order for bumblebees to communicate, they must conceptualize the location of food by manipulating symbols generated from their sensory organs into a dance pattern. Bees observing and learning the dance pattern then generate symbols that ultimately allow them to translate a sequence of body movements into a set of directions used to direct the bee to the food source. As such, the only symbols that bees can generate are patterns of the hard-wired symbols that they already possess, namely symbols representing dance motions and flight plans relative to the position of the sun.

The ability to generate new symbols consisting of new combinations of sensory stimuli reflects an enhanced ability to learn, which provides a greater ability to understand and adapt to one's environment. As intellectual capabilities increase to include associating symbols with combinations of sensory stimuli, the vocabulary of symbols that the brain can manipulate within its imagination increases.

For example, cats learn how to hunt from observation and practice. Each experience helps them to improve their skill as they form associations among the numerous components of their environment. The cat forms associations among a set of symbols, such as the feel of a gentle breeze, the direction of the breeze relative to prey, the scent of animals, and the ability of other animals to detect a scent.

The concepts that result from these associations reveal that an animal's scent can be carried either to or from other animals by the breeze, thereby communicating the presence of animals that are upwind.

An even more advanced demonstration of intelligence involves the capacity to associate symbols with components of language. The language may be based upon any learned sensory input patterns, typically conveyed as sounds.

> For example, dogs can learn a number of voice commands. However, each command learned can be shown to be limited to a single syllable.
>
> When complete sentences are spoken to a well-trained dog, the animal listens for the single syllable sounds it has previously learned. Hence, the dog is able to make use of learned symbols that are derived from a small fraction of the human language.

The ability to generate symbols from language involves the ability to fluidly from abstractions. As such, symbols can represent other symbols.

> For example, self-awareness involves the use of one or more symbols representing the entire being, or any part of the mind or body of the being. Ultimately, the initial concept of self-awareness is further refined with the advent of language. A variety of language symbols, such as me, myself, I, my body, my mind, my soul, my reputation, my purpose, my feelings, my well-being, my life, my existence, or my name, create an additional set of perspectives regarding the concept of one's self.

As the level of intelligence increases, so does the capability to generate symbols from external sources, and to generate symbols from internal sources. The capability to generate symbols from internal stimuli strengthens the power of the imagination to generate new ideas. Rather than restricting the imagination to the symbols generated from external stimuli, the imagination becomes free to form representations based upon stimuli generated internally by the brain, to some extent, becoming free from the streams of stimuli generated by the sensory organs.

The ability to associate symbols with both externally and internally generated streams of stimuli facilitate learning the fundamentals of language.

> For example, just as external stimuli, such as the written or spoken words and word-groups of in language, are used to generate symbols, they in turn are associated with new combinations of internally generated stimuli to represent the combinations of stimuli that result in the final interpretation.

Although symbols generated can represent anything, such as any tangible object or action, as well as any intangible idea or concept, they can only be generated based upon the combinations of streams of stimuli associated with symbols previously encountered.

For example, if we inventory the complete set of newly generated stimuli, and the stimuli from previously retained symbols, which have been activated in the imagination, any new symbols can only be constructed from combinations of stimuli in the inventory.

Just as each human invention is built upon combinations of previously existing ideas and inventions, symbols are generated using combinations of stimuli from newly experienced streams of stimuli and previously existing symbols. In this way, intelligent beings are limited to comprehending and imagining things based upon combinations of previously experienced stimuli.

Similarly, the problem solving process can be facilitated by the introduction of symbols that are associated with another paradigm. In a passage from Bipin Indurkhya's, Metaphor and Cognition, he illustrates how a similarity-creating metaphor exhibited similarities among analogous symbols before, as well as, after a discovery. Using this illustration, we can begin to see that the necessary stimuli to solve problems must be introduced in order to generate the symbols that comprise the solution to the problem.

> For example, "In creating the theory of thermodynamics, Carnot used an analogy from the flow of fluids. Gentner and Jeziorski provide a long quotation from Carnot that lays out the analogy. From the existing similarities between the fluid-flow and the heat-flow, namely that fluid flows from the higher level to the lower level and the heat flows from the higher temperature body to the lower temperature body, Carnot suggested the hypothesis: Could it be that the rate of heat-flow is proportional to the temperature difference between the two bodies? (Just like the rate of fluid-flow is proportional to the difference in levels.)"

(Metaphor and Cognition, Bipin Indurkhya, pg.57)

In another passage from Bipin Indurkhya's, Metaphor and Cognition, he describes how another type of similarity-creating metaphor exhibited similarities after a discovery, but not before. Here we begin to see that stimuli not present among existing symbols must be learned through experience. Likewise, when a research group examined how to improve the effectiveness of the synthetic-bristle paintbrush to the performance of the natural-bristle paintbrush, they eventually benefited from the symbols introduced by another metaphor.

> When comparing the results between natural-bristle and synthetic-fiber paintbrushes, synthetic ones delivered paint unevenly to the painted surface, causing streaks of paint. The researchers' model for painting a surface defined the

role of the brush as an agent with which to smear paint from the brush to the painted surface. There were a number of differences between the bristles of natural-bristle and synthetic-fiber brushes, such as the split ends that occur with natural-bristle brushes. "Thinking that this feature might affect the smearing process, they tried to split the ends of the synthetic bristles, but with no improvement in performance."

"Finally, the breakthrough occurred when a theoretically oriented physical chemist suggested an unorthodox model that a paintbrush might work like a pump. In projecting the pumping model on the process of painting the researchers noted that the paint is not smeared on the surface, but actually forced, by a pumping action, through the space between the bristles. This perspective gave a totally different ontology to the process of painting, and the role of a paintbrush in the process was radically transformed. And the similarities between the paintbrush and a pump were created in this process of transforming the perspective on painting and the role of paintbrush in it. Thus, there were no similarities before the metaphor, but the similarities were created by the metaphor." (Metaphor and Cognition, Bipin Indurkhya, p59-60)

Hence, stimuli essential to solving a problem can be introduced by a similarity-creating metaphor, which provides missing information.

When symbols are generated, depending upon their initial interpretations, their existence may be temporary. Depending upon the level of importance associated with these interpretations, the symbols may be incorporated into one or more functional areas of the brain, or they may dissipate over time.

If retained, symbols may be classified redundantly in a number of ways, such as by the sensory category that they belong to. Retained symbols may also be organized by time, place, type of activity, sequence of events, emotional state, or they may be organized relative to other symbols that they may have caused to become activated, including pre-wired symbols.

For example, pre-wired symbols include stimuli associated with primitive emotions, such as good and bad, and their variants, which include comfort and fear, pleasure and pain, and are potentially associated with a number of sensory categories, such as sound or tactile stimuli.

In its simplistic form, symbol generation is responsible for creating objects that are utilized in various functional areas of the brain. Although they package a portion of their associated stream of stimuli, they can also package sequences of other symbols, which we refer to as chunks.

Even though symbols generated from external stimuli may appear to be simple representations of the external stimuli, they do not function as such. As streams of stimuli are processed, sensory perception falls prey to a number of imperfections. Whether this it is due to an optical illusion that results from nuances in our physical construction, or the fact that sensory organs generate incomplete or imperfect input, previously retained symbols can be incorrectly activated resulting in a variety of inaccurate interpretations.

Symbols generated from internal stimuli, on the other hand, are anything but simple representations of external stimuli. Although the resulting symbols embody stimuli from previously existing symbols, the new symbols represent new interpretations of new combinations of stimuli resulting in new inventions, and new tangible and intangible ideas. Albeit these ideas are built upon previously existing or newly experienced stimuli, the resulting ideas are incrementally new. These incrementally new ideas are the difference between paint being smeared versus pumped; of man walking on the beach versus another astronomical body; or a man sitting in a chair versus in the heavens.

For example, in comparing atoms to molecules, the elements of the periodic table represent every known atom, comprising all physical matter known and theorized to be in existence. Every atom has its own set of physical properties, determined by the physics of particular nuclei and electron-clouds, such as with pure hydrogen and oxygen. However, when these two types of atoms are combined, their physical properties are completely different, as determined by the physics of particular nuclei, electron clouds and geometry of the water molecule.

If we catalog the range of sensory stimuli that our sensory organs generate, we could create a periodic table of sensory stimuli. Then, if we combine them in various combinations, we can create the molecules of life's sensory experience. To carry the analogy to its logical conclusion, if we combine stimuli without restriction, in ways similar to combining molecules and atoms without the restrictions normally placed on us by their physical geometry we could create the dreams and concepts of a higher intelligence.

In summary, symbol generation is one of several major components necessary to meet our requirements of the brain. Its interfaces include various functional components, such as those that retain and activate systems, as well as, those that interpret meaning. However, most importantly, it interfaces with the functional component that it is most dependent upon, which determines where each particular symbol's stream of stimuli begins and ends.

- - -

Neuron Story: *"I'm not going there, those guys are weird!"*
"They're only pattern recognition neurons, no weirder than yourself."
"Only as long as you don't let them touch me!"
"Don't worry. I'll hold your dendrites."

- - -

Summary & Questions

Reality, or the illusion of it, begins by packaging stimuli together as a chunk, in order to create a symbol to be manipulated by the imagination. Whether the stimuli that represent the symbol are learned or genetically pre-wired, animals of varying levels of intelligence can generate and recognize them from stimuli generated internally, externally or from a combination thereof.

Regarding the functionality referred to as 'Symbol Generation', briefly explain:

1. What is a symbol, and what is it comprised of?
2. Why are they important to generate?
3. What are the advantages and disadvantages of predetermined symbols?
4. How does the quality of stimuli from the sensory organs affect the generation of symbols and their subsequent use by the imagination?
5. What capabilities develop when symbols can be freely manipulated?
6. Why is the ability to generate a greater variety of symbols significant?
7. What are the advantages of generating abstract symbols?
8. In what ways is symbol generation limited?
9. Why must the stimuli associated with a symbol be retained?

19 Pattern Recognition

"Continuous streams of digital stimuli arrive along the neuron paths from every sensory organ to their respective area of the brain. Streams of internally generated stimuli travel along the neuron paths to and from every functional component of the brain. The segments of stimuli that may assist the organism to survive must be found. But how discern the segments of stimuli we want from the others, or detect a segment of stimuli in the first place?" (The Neurons)

19.1 Introduction

The sensory organs of the body are where all external stimuli originate. Upon performing an analysis of relatively simple organisms, as the quantity and level of sophistication of each sensory organ increase, the level of intelligence associated with the organism increases. Although biological life forms have achieved five known categories of sensory devices, the sophistication of these senses can vary significantly between the least and most advanced species. However, the capabilities of the brain determine how effectively the sensory stimuli are used.

For example, "the eyes of various species vary from simple structures that are capable of differentiating between light and dark, to complex organs, that can distinguish minute variations in shape, color, brightness, and distance. The actual process of seeing is performed by the brain rather than by the eye. The function of the eye is to translate the electromagnetic vibrations of light into patterns of nerve impulses that are transmitted to the brain." (Microsoft Encarta 97)

Since the degree of accuracy and precision provided by each sensory organ can vary significantly from one species to another, the quality of sensory information embedded in the sensory stimuli varies as well. Although the ability to process more sophisticated stimuli begins with the pattern recognition, the capabilities of other components in the brain also determine the extent to which more complex stimuli can be utilized.

For example, visual stimuli enhanced with color information cannot be interpreted by a brain that is not equipped to interpret color, or that has not learned to interpret color, and hence does not result in a color representation of visual images.

However, even though all of the members of a species may be comparably equipped with the same sensory organs, some individuals may learn to recognize and interpret patterns of stimuli, such as sinus pressure, better than others in order to detect changes in the weather.

Hence, a number of functional components of the brain determine how effectively this input can be utilized. Together, the functional components and the streams of stimuli that they act upon, form the basis from which the external world is represented within the brain.

Although species possessing a simple level of intelligence do not possess the ability to learn, slightly more advanced species can learn specific types of information without the need to generate symbols. Their limited learning capabilities are a direct result of the limited pre-wired symbols and their associated pre-wired streams of stimuli.

For example, a bumblebee can learn how to locate a food source from another bee that expresses its location through dance movements. However, bumblebees cannot learn nor extend their language, as their learning capabilities and their language are a result of the pre-wired symbols that they have genetically received, and their limited ability to arrange those symbols into new symbols consisting of various sequences.

The pre-existing symbols of a bumblebee that are genetically pre-wired have the essential components of sensory characteristics associated with them. The predetermined sensory characteristics associated with pre-wired symbols are the result of genetic encoding, which provide the bumblebee the key to basic survival. In other words, they provide the starting point from which the bumblebee interprets all information from the outside world.

As the bumblebee learns its dance, its newly generated symbols are limited to combinations of its pre-wired symbols. These newly generated symbols, however, act as a list of instructions, allowing other bumblebees to interpret the resulting sequence of stimuli in order to guide their flight to the source of food.

As for the other half of the equation, a bumblebee that teaches the dance to other bees must have the ability to generate the list of instructions and interpret them into the appropriate dance movements.

Although this raises a number of important issues, we will presently focus on the fact that learning begins with the ability to generate new symbols consisting of pre-wired symbols. As these pre-wired symbols are matched to the incoming streams of stimuli involving the position of the sun, the bumblebees hive, and the food source, they are arranged in sequence as a list of directions.

The resulting list of directions are then interpreted into dance movements, which other bumblebees learn, in turn, by generating new symbols consisting of pre-wired symbols. As these pre-wired symbols are matched to the incoming streams of stimuli involving the movements of the bumblebee in its dance, they are arranged in sequence as a list of dance movements. The dance movements are then interpreted into the corresponding flight instructions.

Pre-wired symbols, and the stimuli associated with them, facilitate many forms of learning. They assist in associations of comfort and discomfort, thereby providing the essential linkage to pleasant and unpleasant, as well as, good and bad.

For example, certain animals associate the stimuli that result from particular audible tones, gentle touching, and eye contact as forms of comfort and positive reinforcement, thereby influencing learning. Likewise, a number of other stimuli are associated with forms of negative reinforcement.

As for the role of pattern recognition in supporting an initial ability to learn, the most primitive of abilities must also be present. Specifically, the ability to generate new symbols consisting of sequences of pre-wired symbols and their associated stimuli. This requires the ability to recognize segments that resemble the pre-wired patterns. However, in order to support the next level of learning, which involves the ability to generate symbols from new stimuli outside the set of pre-wired symbols, pattern recognition must be able to identify generalized segments from among a continuous stream of input.

The role of the Pattern Recognition Component therefore, is to evaluate incoming stimuli to recognize patterns that resemble those associated with pre-wired symbols, as well as, patterns of new stimuli that can be detected as distinct segments within the continuous stream of stimuli. Additionally, these new segments must be rapidly identified as they arrive from the sensory organs, as well as, other components of the brain, that generate them.

For example, streams of stimuli are also being generated internally from various components of the brain. These internally generated stimuli are the source of a much wider variety of symbols, as they may include symbols that are abstractions of other symbols, thereby representing more advanced concepts. As such, they are not limited to the patterns found among the streams of stimuli that originate from sensory organs.

Although pattern recognition differs for each type of sensory organ, at a fundamental level the approach is the same. With regard to identifying segments that contain patterns of new stimuli, there are a number of techniques that can be used to detect punctuation between one segment of stimuli and the next.

For example, the end of one segment of stimuli and the beginning of another frequently have a type of natural pause or an abrupt change.

It may involve the tactile stimuli of one object, punctuated by the stimuli of open air before receiving the tactile stimuli of another object, or it may involve the abrupt change of tactile stimuli of one surface, immediately followed by another.

It may involve the auditory stimuli of a sound, punctuated by the stimuli of background noise before receiving the auditory stimuli of another sound, or it may involve the abrupt change of auditory stimuli of one sound, immediately followed by another.

It may involve the visual stimuli of an object in focus, punctuated by the stimuli associated with a change in focus before receiving the visual stimuli of another object, or it may involve the abrupt change of visual stimuli of one object, immediately followed by another.

As segments of stimuli are identified, they are passed onto symbol generation irrespective of importance, repetition or any other characteristic. After a segment of stimuli has been converted into a symbol, the various characteristics and relationships of the segment are considered.

- - -

Neuron Story: *"So these Pattern Recognition neurons work on an assembly line!"*
"I think you're ready to meet some of them."

- - -

19.2 Pattern Recognition Components

"Continuous streams of digital stimuli arrive along the neuron paths from every sensory organ to their respective area of the brain." (The Neurons)

Stimuli from each sensory organ are routed to their own pattern recognition component, which learns to specialize its ability to detect segments of stimuli associated with its specific type of sensory organ.

For example, segments of sound stimuli are identified by pattern recognition neurons using distinctions found in

James V. Luisi

the characteristics that the sensory organ is capable of detecting.

If the sensory organ is an ear, distinctions are found within the range of amplitude and frequency that can be detected in the physical vibrations that are imparted to the labyrinth, or complex cavity, hollowed out of the bone of the inner ear.

If the sensory organ is an eye, distinctions are found within the range of visible amplitude and frequency that can be detected as energy on the light-sensitive receptor cells and color-sensitive cones receptors of the retina inside the eye. Here, pattern recognition neurons learn primarily to identify segments of stimuli representing lines, contrasting edges and corners.

If the sensory organs involve the sense of touch, pattern recognition neurons learn to identify segments of stimuli representing changes in pressure and relative temperature.

Whereas, if the sensory organs involve the sense of taste and smell, pattern recognition neurons learn to identify segments of stimuli that represent changes in chemical reactivity.

- - -

Neuron Story: *"If these neurons always deal with a single sensory stream of stimuli, how do our symbols get stimuli for stereo sound and vision?"*

"Those are the latest high-tech neurons for depth perception."

- - -

Summary & Questions

Although the headquarters for the brain is centrally located, its regional offices are located within every sensory organ found inside or on the surface of the body, networked together with digital biochemical cables. As messages are transmitted from the sensory organs to the appropriate department of the brain, they must be decoded and sent to the next location for processing.

Regarding the functionality referred to as 'Pattern Recognition', briefly explain:

Sensitive by Nature

1. What are the patterns of stimuli that are recognized by simple organisms, and why is it likely that they are generalized patterns?
2. Why must patterns of stimuli in the bumblebee be converted into symbols, and what is the significance of the resulting sequences of symbols?
3. What are the advantages of the capability to recognize new patterns of stimuli?
4. What are some of the techniques for determining where segments of stimuli begin and end?
5. How is specialization for the different types of pattern recognition achieved?

20 Integrating Segments of Stimuli

"Two-dimensional segments of stimuli are identified from the left, and two-dimensional segments of stimuli are generated from the right. And with our technology, two plus two... is three?" (The Neurons)

When organisms have more than one sensory organ of the same type, it is sometimes possible for the two sets of stimuli to be combined to generate symbols that are more descriptive of the environment. The ability to combine the information, however, depends upon the ability of the brain to receive stimuli from the sensory organs at the same time with partially overlapping information, thereby allowing the parts to be combined. Using these techniques to enhance the stimuli, the brain attains the ability to perform triangulation, generating the information necessary to support a three-dimensional perspective.

For example, although many animals have two eyes, some have eyes that face away from one another, out to the side, such as dolphins, and whales, while others have forward facing eyes, such as monkeys, apes and humans. Only animals with forward facing eyes, however, have the ability to look at the same object simultaneously with both eyes.

When animals view the same object simultaneously with two eyes, they form a geometric shape called a triangle. The triangle is composed of a line from the object to the first eye, a second line from the object to the second eye, and a third line which is formed by a line between the first and second eye.

The benefit of triangulation is that it can be used to determine the third dimension, called depth, which represents the distance between an object and its observer. Without triangulation, the segments of stimuli that are identified by Pattern Recognition cannot be used to determine the distance between the object and its observer. Visual segment integration, however, combines the simultaneously occurring segments of stimuli generated by the eyes. Using a form of triangulation, segment integration enhances these segments with stimuli that depict the third dimension, depth.

Animals with two ears can hear the same object simultaneously with both ears, thereby providing another opportunity for triangulation to determine the third dimension. However, ears cannot generate as complete a set of directional information that eyes can readily provide.

- - -

Neuron Story: *"I can tell roughly how far away you are, but unless I move around, I can't tell in which direction."*

"Ears can triangulate, they just happen to form an infinite number of triangles, in front of you, behind you, above and below you... but in your case, mostly beyond you."

- - -

Although the relative amplitude perceived by each ear indicates whether the source of a sound is more towards one ear or the other, a stationary set of ears cannot determine whether the source is in front, or behind, the observer, unless the source is perpendicular to one of the ears. However, when the source is perpendicular to one of the ears, depth cannot be determined.

For example, if we suspend a blindfolded observer in the air, stereo sounds that are of equal volume in both ears can be either directly in front of, behind, above or below the observer. However, assuming that the location of the sound does not change, if the observer turns their head, the additional information can be used to identify its location.

Associated with the Pattern Recognition components of the ears, is the Auditory Segment Integration Component, which combines the simultaneously occurring segments of stimuli generated from the ears. Again, using a form of triangulation, the Auditory Segment Integration Component enhances these segments with stimuli that depict the third dimension of depth, thereby identifying the approximate distance a sound source is from the observer.

The Segment Integration Component culminates in the process of combining segments of all simultaneously occurring stimuli available to the brain. Although we have only discussed the stimuli integration performed by pattern recognition, segments of stimuli generated by other brain centers, such as the Imagination component, are also combined with segments originating from sensory organs.

- - -

Neuron Story: *"So these neurons combine everything we experience at every point in time?"*

"And now you know why I worry so much about what you think."

- - -

20.1 World of Fabricated Stimuli

"Segments are identified from the streams of stimuli that enter the brain from any of the five senses. Stimuli are generated internally from within the brain as well. As such, segments of stimuli are being generated by the sixth sense, the imagination, as well as every other component internal to the brain." (The Neurons)

The conceptual design that we have chosen consists of a variety of functional components, all generating stimuli for one purpose or another.

For example, the Importance Determination component enhances stimuli with the appropriate level of importance for each active paradigm, while the Analogical Engine and Metaphorical Engine components generate stimuli regarding symbols related to each active paradigm. The Symbol Activation component activates stimuli associated with previously retained symbols, and the Imagination component generates stimuli regarding its active paradigms and their resulting streams of stimuli.

Now that we have discussed how segments of stimuli are identified by pattern recognition, enhanced and integrated together, we will continue with our conceptual design of the brain's intellectual components.

Summary & Questions

Sensory organs of the same type generate stimuli of the same type. When these streams of stimuli share overlapping regions, the stimuli associated with the area of overlap makes it possible to map the streams of stimuli together, thereby integrating the stimuli into a common result. Once integration is recognized, the ability to distinguish timing differences with sound, or angular differences among images, can be used to calculate the additional dimension of depth.

Regarding the functionality referred to as 'Integrating Segments of Stimuli', briefly explain:
1. How many sensory organs are required to gather the information necessary to support triangulation?
2. What factors can prevent two sensory organs of the same type from supporting triangulation, and why?
3. How is depth determined for visual stimuli?
4. Why is depth perception less reliable involving auditory stimuli?
5. What information is used to determine direction and distance for sound?
6. What other possible sources of stimuli are there?

21 Symbol Activation

"Streams of stimuli are rapidly entering components of the brain. As patterns are recognized, segments of stimuli are identified from the streams. Identified segments are enhanced and integrated with other simultaneously occurring segments of stimuli. Symbols are generated from whatever level of integration can occur, and then they begin their journey through the brain as symbols, matching and activating other symbols in their path."

(Neurons... stationed at the lowest level)

Once a symbol has been generated, it is able to interact with the various components of the brain. On of the first components that it encounters, however, is the Symbol Activation component. One of the roles of symbol activation is to locate and activate other symbols that match the overall characteristics of the symbols that are produced by Symbol Generation. However, Symbol Activation may be asked to locate and activate other symbols that match only in particular ways to particular stimuli.

21.1 Role of Symbols

Although many symbols are simply integrated segments of stimuli, many symbols are comprised of other symbols that ultimately contain stimuli. These symbols not only represent sequences of sensory experiences, but they also can represent abstract concepts that consist of images and rules.

For example, symbols that represent abstractions of one and two-dimensional geometric objects, such as a point, line, angle, or circle, require segments of stimuli consisting of rules and examples, which may consist of any combination of sensory stimuli, experienced or imagined.

The interpretation of rules and examples, however, is what ultimately determines their meaning. In the absence of interpretation, symbols are merely collections of stimuli.

Together, the symbols that represent integrated segments of stimuli and the symbols, which are comprised of other symbols, represent the alphabet and vocabulary of the brain.

21.2 Symbol Activation

As segments of stimuli are integrated, the stimuli that result are used to generate symbols for use by various components of the brain. Depending upon their level of importance, these symbols may be forwarded to the interpretive center of the brain, one of the most prominent users of Symbol Activation.

21.3 Interpretive Centers

The interpretive center of the brain is the gateway to the imagination. Before entering the imagination for interpretation, streams of symbols are routed to the interpretive center, which acts as a rudimentary imagination, responsible for evaluating symbols for their ability to be integrated within the structure of symbols that define the existing paradigm.

For example, a paradigm is a set of rules that define an individual's reality. As symbols are tested against a particular paradigm's set of rules, a number of possible outcomes may occur with respect to the paradigm's set of rules.

The symbols tested may integrate into the paradigm's set of rules, they may conflict with the paradigm's set of rules, or they may not have any meaning relative to those rules.

Generally, symbols that are inconsistent with the rules of a particular paradigm are not permitted to advance to the imagination. Depending upon the rejected symbols' level of importance, the interpretive center will either discard them or save them for evaluation under the rule set of another paradigm.

Depending upon each symbol's ability to integrate into the paradigm's set of rules, the symbol's level of importance, and its applicability to the rule set of another active paradigm, the interpretive center may make a number of symbol activation requests.

For example, particular segments of stimuli are identified by the interpretive center as selection criteria for symbol activation, thereby causing the activation of related symbols that help complete the psychological experience.

The psychological experience consists of activating the symbols that provide the continuity involved in the stream of consciousness, (i.e., the memories that identify the sequence of recent and past experiences), the symbols that provide a more comprehensive understanding, and the symbols that may be related in useful ways.

Perhaps the most significant aspect of an interpretive center's activation of symbols is its ability to compensate for how sensory experiences may differ among individuals.

For example, let's hypothesize that individuals do not uniformly experience sensory input in precisely the same manner. This means that one individual may experience the visual sensation of blue as a color, somewhat differently than another individual.

Sensitive by Nature

Although it is known that there are at last subtle differences in how human males and females experience color, the differences could be more significant than that of a female's ability to perceive more distinctions in colors than their male counterpart. Aside from perceiving more color variations, if the interpretive center activates the same symbols as someone that experiences the color blue somewhat differently, their respective interpretations will still be the same.

Therefore, someone that perceives colors differently, through learning and conditioning, may be able to activate the same symbols that result in a similar interpretation as someone that has a different sensory experience. Thus, blue can appear as a different color, however, it will have the same psychological effect if the symbols activated are the same as for an individual that perceives blue the same as someone else.

As the interpretive center filters out inconsistent symbols, and requests the activation of additional symbols, the symbols that are allowed to advance form the consciously perceived stream of intellectual experience.

\- - -

Neuron Story: *"Are neurons in the imagination, more important?"*
                "We're just as imaginary as they are."

\- - -

Just as there are a number of functional components within unconscious level of the brain, a number of functional components also exist within the conscious level, called the Imagination component. Various components of the imagination help compare and understand groups of symbols relative to one another.

For example, the purpose of the Analogical Engine component is to compare, understand and project meanings between sets of symbols when similarities can be detected from the onset.

On the other hand, the role of the Metaphorical Engine component is to compare, understand and project meanings between sets of symbols when similarities cannot be detected from the onset.

Functional components internal to the Imagination Component also make numerous requests of the Symbol Activation component. However, even though these requests originate from within the imagination, the symbols activated by Symbol Activation must still regain admission to the imagination through the interpretive center.

Hence, the Imagination Component may be engaged with segments of stimuli that originate internally to it, with stimuli associated with activated symbols, as well as with stimuli originating from sensory organs. However, depending upon the rules that are in effect at the interpretive center, a combination of symbols originating internally and externally, as well as their associated activated symbols, will be introduced.

21.4 Types of Activation Requests

Symbols can be activated directly by the name of the symbol or indirectly because of a number of different types of relationships that may exist.

For example, symbols may be requested because they may belong to a sequence of symbols, such as a melody's sequence of notes in time; to a description, such as the definition of a triangle; to rules, such as a mathematical equation; or to relationships in time, such as feedback mechanisms.

Other reasons for symbol activation may occur because of relationships among symbols' segments of stimuli, such as a shared visual appearance, taste experience, tactile sensation, or a similarity in description.

Additionally, symbols may also have relationships to one another through analogical associations, such as a student is to a teacher, as a child is to a parent, or through metaphorical associations, such as paint is to a brush, as liquid is to a pump.

Symbols are activated at various levels of the brain. At the lowest levels they are often activated in order to help fill in gaps within the incoming segments of stimuli. In this manner, the brain makes many assumptions about the lower level stimuli that are detected by Pattern Recognition components.

At the conscious level of the brain, symbols are often activated in order to help fill in the gaps pertaining to high level concepts, definitions, and procedural sets of rules in order to support the functional components of the Imagination.

21.5 Prioritizing Symbol Activation

Each symbol may have a number of segments of stimuli associated with it, such as a visual, or auditory component. However, depending upon the segment(s) of stimuli that are considered to be the most important, symbol activation will seek to activate symbols involving segments that have similar stimuli. As symbols are activated, the level of importance that is associated with them help to determine the symbols that should be activated next. As symbols and their segments of stimuli become activated, they become available to the components of the brain where they were requested.

For example, symbols representing high level concepts at the conscious level are not made available to components present in the lower level, and symbols representing low level stimuli at the lowest level are not made available to components present in the conscious level.

21.6 Introducing Levels

As we begin to identify the functions of the mind, it becomes convenient to separate them into functions that are available to one's consciousness, and those that are not. In doing so, one creates an artificial separation of functions that can be visualized as distinct layers within the mind, one below, and one within, the realm of consciousness.

Organisms that are less advanced do not appear to have activities that occur at an unconscious and a conscious level. Although such organisms may be categorized as having a single level, in many of them, the level that they lack is not the conscious level. Instead, they possess a conscious level, albeit a simple one.

For example, when one swats at a flying insect, such as a common housefly, using its pre-wired symbols, the fly is immediately conscious of the fact that it is in danger, and reacts by accelerating and flying erratically. To a housefly, whatever stimuli its sensory devices generate, the fly is able to rapidly associate it with the appropriate pre-wired symbols, and act upon it at almost immediately.

As such, simple organisms do not possess the capability to detect stimuli at an unconscious level. They do not generate symbols, nor can they cause them to become bubbled up to the next highest level based upon their level of importance. In the mind of the single-minded organism, nothing is important, or at least, there is no distinction between the importance of one thing or another.

It should be noted that the use of the term 'consciousness' is not intended to imply that the housefly can conceptualize itself as an intellectual and physical being. The use of the term, 'consciousness', is merely to communicate that these simple organisms create the minimum representation of the environment within their brain, which allows them to exhibit the necessary behavior in order to improve their chances of survival. The alternative would be to suggest that the behavior of these organisms is reliant solely upon an unconscious existence, creating the expectation that the housefly would act as an unconscious projectile bouncing into one object after another, oblivious to danger.

Although it may appear upside down, brains that possess a single level are endowed with a conscious level. The unconscious level of the brain acts as a type of preprocessor to the conscious level.

> For example, without the unconscious level, new symbols cannot be generated, nor can the relative importance of a symbol be determined. However, once these capabilities are present, a significantly more advanced conscious level becomes possible.

The single level brain cannot achieve more functionality than can be provided with a simple set of pre-wired symbols, supporting a minimal set of basic capabilities to survive. Upon introducing an additional unconscious level to provide various support functions to the conscious level, additional sets of capabilities become possible. Hence, a brain with more than one level is better positioned to cope with a set of sensory organs, that are significantly more sophisticated, generating many complex streams of stimuli, such as the ability to determine depth perception, and electromagnetic frequencies, which become interpreted as colors.

As the unconscious levels process streams of incoming stimuli, generating and activating symbols on their own, it is the bubble up action that causes the initial round of symbol activation at the next highest level. The functional component assisting with this process is the Importance Determination Component.

Although the Importance Determination Component may identify what symbols and segments of stimuli may be important, as we shall see, it cannot determine whether the information is relevant.

- - -

Neuron Story: *"They're like me, those neurons can't tell what's relevant."*
"Yes, but they know what's important."

- - -

Summary & Questions

The language of the brain consists of symbols and their associated stimuli. Although symbols and their segments of stimuli do not have meaning in and of themselves, the smallest component that can have a meaning associated with it is the segment of stimuli. If we take a segment of stimuli apart, the stimuli that comprise it are merely the building blocks of the segment of stimuli. Since each segment of stimuli can have a meaning associated with it, the symbol that contains the segments can have a meaning associated with it as well. As such, symbols are packages of stimuli, whose meaning is not necessarily fixed or known at any point in time. However, by having either segments of stimuli in common, or symbols comprised of other symbols, symbols can have a variety of relationships to one another.

Regarding the functionality referred to as 'Symbol Activation', briefly explain:

1. What are symbols, and do they have meaning embedded within them?
2. What determines the actual meaning that is associated with a symbol, and is that meaning stored?
3. What symbols are identified and activated by Symbol Activation?
4. Why are symbols prevented from entering the imagination?
5. Where are requests for symbol activation originated?
6. What are the various sources of stimuli that are introduced into the imagination?
7. What are the various types of information that may be associated with a symbol?
8. Which is related to a more advanced level of intelligence, an unconscious or a conscious level, and why?
9. What is consciousness, and how is it distinct from self-awareness?

James V. Luisi

22 Importance Determination

"As streams of stimuli enter the brain from every sensory organ of the body, only a few of them, succeed in getting our attention. What determines which symbols get our attention, and which are ignored?"
(The Neurons)

- - -

Neuron Story: *"I'm often amazed by how little I notice."*
"It amazes me, as well."

- - -

The things that individuals notice represent a small subset of the stimuli that enters the brain. In order to be processed by the brain's interpretive centers, symbols and their associated segments of stimuli must be selectively routed there. If the interpretive centers were to receive all of the symbols generated by streams of stimuli they would not only drown in a sea of information, but the onslaught of stimuli would overwhelm any ability to discern the items that were important. As a result, the brain only notices the segments of stimuli that are accepted by the interpretive center. A factor in achieving that acceptance is the level of importance that has been associated with it.

Importance Determine participates at each level of the mind. Beginning at the lowest level where external stimuli enter the brain, newly generated symbols and older ones that have been activated are evaluated for their level of importance before they are bubbled up to the next level of the brain. At the highest level, the functional components of the imagination make frequent use of Importance Determination, determining which symbols and segments of stimuli to focus attention upon. However, since paradigms are symbols, Importance Determination also participates in determining which paradigm to use in order to interpret symbols. Therefore, Importance Determination is a major participant in determining behavior.

The Importance Determination component plays a role at every level of the brain, identifying the relative importance of symbols, as well as the paradigms to interpret them. But conceptually, what is the mechanism, and how does it affect the various decisions that are made in the mind?

22.1 Some Important Background

In science and technology, studying any process that involves the choice between good and bad decisions is called 'heuristics'. The study of 'heuristics' has been claimed by a number of disciplines, such as mathematics, computer science, and psychology, each using their own distinct methods, representations, and assertions. Aside from their various differences, they generally agree that intellectual activities, such as games, provide an ample test-bed from which to evaluate the basic properties of heuristic theories.

Game theory has been used to develop a variety of 'thinking' methodologies. An important aspect of each methodology, is the ability to determine what information is relevant and most important to the decision making process. The inability of a process to do this effectively is called, 'game pathology'.

> For example, game pathology is defined as the inability of computerized games to improve their game by looking ahead a greater number of moves, since there is no proven way to integrate the additional information usefully to affect the outcome favorably. (<u>Heuristics</u>, 1980, Pearl, Nau and Beal)

- - -

Neuron Story: *"I feel so informed!"*
"And if they had a Miss. Information contest, you'd most likely win."

- - -

Although it was untested, it was theorized by Nau, that game theories, which use both optimistic and pessimistic values in rules, could provide an approach to overcome the problems of game pathology. Hence, it may appear that Nau would propose one threshold to indicate an optimistic outcome and a second threshold for a pessimistic one.

22.2 Conceptual Design

Imagine that each symbol known to Importance Determination looks like an old fashioned, mercury thermometer, consisting of a hollow, vertical tube of glass with a reservoir of mercury at its base, and horizontal markings up its entire length. The column of mercury rises and falls, as it expands and contracts in volume with variances in temperature.

Now that we have created the appropriate mental image, let's refer to the column of mercury as the level of importance. In this simple model, an increase or decrease in temperature would be analogous to a corresponding increase or decrease in importance.

As we calibrate our importance determination thermometer, let's make eight lines representing various temperatures, or levels of importance, with four horizontal markings evenly spaced above the current temperature, and four below. For convenience, we will label the four markings above the current temperature, moving in an upward direction, One, Two, Three and

Four, and we will label the four markings below the current temperature, moving in a downward direction, Negative One, Two, Three and Four.

The Importance Determination component not only identifies the relative importance of one symbol to another, but it also uses the labeled markings to determine a number of different states for a symbol. The first labeled markings, labeled 'One' and 'Negative One', are the upper and lower activation thresholds. As their names suggest, these involve the activation of symbols.

> For example, the role of the upper activation threshold is to denote when the importance of a particular symbol has risen to such a level that it should be activated and allowed to be bubbled-up to the next level of intellectual processing. Likewise, the role of the lower activation threshold is to denote when the importance of a particular symbol has dropped to such a level that it should no longer be activated or allowed to bubble up to the next level of intellectual processing.

The next set of markings, labeled 'Two' and 'Negative Two', are the upper and lower learning thresholds. These denote such an intense level of activation that the learning processes become activated at the unconscious, as well as, the conscious level. The learning process includes the chunking symbols and the identification of relationships among symbols, however, the upper and lower learning thresholds achieve slightly different results.

> For example, the role of the upper learning threshold is to denote when the activation level is sufficient to cause new symbols and relationships to be generated. Likewise, the role of the lower learning threshold is to denote when the level of importance for a particular symbol's relationships has dropped to such a level that previously formed relationships should be re-evaluated. Depending upon the outcome of that evaluation, re-learning may occur, thereby causing new symbols and relationships to be generated in place of existing ones.

Although learning involves a number of detail processes, it can be summarized as the event of recording information, and its relationships. Importance Determination plays a major role in identifying which symbols should be activated by Symbol Activation, what information should be allowed to be bubbled up, and which symbols should be used as a basis of comparison in the Analogical and Metaphorical Engines.

The next set of markings, 'Three' and 'Negative Three', are the upper and lower shock thresholds. These represent such an extreme level of activation that there is a temporary interruption of other brain functions. The triggering of a shock threshold represents such a high priority, that the majority of brain activities are directed to support the intellectual processes

Sensitive by Nature

involving these symbols. An intense level of learning is usually associated with the triggering of these thresholds.

>For example, the role of the upper shock threshold is to denote when the activation level is extreme enough to cause these symbols to be given the full attention and processing capabilities of the brain. Strong emotional responses may often be associated with the triggering of these thresholds. The role of the lower shock threshold is to provide the opportunity to desensitize the effects of the shock threshold, rendering the learned effects of the shock threshold less potent by re-learning an alternate set of symbol relationships.

The outer set of markings, labeled 'Four' and 'Negative Four', are the upper and lower damage thresholds. These thresholds indicate a level, that when exceeded, cause such a catastrophic level of activation that permanent 'information' damage can result. Upon exceeding these thresholds, the integrity of knowledge, and hence the ability of intellectual processes to operate effectively, may become highly impaired.

>For example, the role of the upper damage threshold denotes when the activation level is so severe that processes involving these symbols may inadvertently and unpredictably damage symbol information including their relationships. An inability to demonstrate basic intellectual functions may be associated with the triggering of these thresholds. The role of the lower damage threshold is to block out a portion of the damaged effects by preventing the activation of the affected symbols.

Using the analogy of the thermometer, we can begin to envision how the Importance Determination component works. As symbols are generated by Symbol Generation, their level of importance is tested in order to determine whether related symbols should be activated, as well as, which ones should be bubbled-up to the next highest level.

- - -

Neuron Story: *"But how are the various thresholds and the level of importance set, and what changes them?"*
"*Let's make them tell us!*"

- - -

22.3 Setting Levels of Importance

There are several reasons why the level of importance associated with a particular symbol may be adjusted by the Importance Determination component. At the lowest level of the brain, one of the fundamental causes for such an adjustment is due to the repetition of a symbol.

> For example, symbols generated from the stimuli of sensory organs will often match the segments of stimuli corresponding to previously generated symbols, recognizing that the same stimuli is reoccurring. As the frequency of symbol reoccurrence increases within a segment of time, it has the effect of increasing the symbol's level of importance. Likewise, a decrease in the frequency of a symbol's reoccurrence within a segment of time has the effect of decreasing the symbol's level of importance.

At the highest level of the brain adjustments in the level of importance may occur in response to frequent symbol usage by the imagination. However, adjustments to importance levels can be induced for a number of other reasons.

> For example, when the streams of stimuli associated with symbols are matched to one another, either directly or through analogous relationships, the level of importance associated with one symbol may be attributed to the other.

22.4 Setting Thresholds

Initially, the only symbols that are activated within the Importance Determination component are pre-wired symbols. These symbols represent basic constructs and emotions, such as comfort and discomfort, which are then generalized to form relationships with other symbols.

> For example, because of matches in stimuli, constructs such as 'comfort' will develop into the concept of 'good', and constructs such as 'discomfort' will develop into the concept of 'bad'. As a result, the pre-wired levels of importance associated with comfort and discomfort will be inherited by the new closely related symbols.

The learning process is also responsible for setting and adjusting thresholds, particularly through experience, and conditioning. As symbols are retained, and matched with existing symbols, their corresponding thresholds are also determined.

The relative level of importance among symbols is a major contributing factor in depicting how symbols are understood. Therefore, by changing the importance determination threshold levels in the brain, one can influence the behavior of an individual.

Although all levels of importance thresholds are subject to modification, pre-wired levels of importance are considered to have a larger mass, making them more difficult to adjust.

For example, importance determination threshold levels influence an individual's understanding of what constitutes comfort and discomfort, good and bad, and influences their preferences and tastes. By making the thresholds of pre-wired symbols difficult to adjust, the essential components of an individual's personality can only change gradually.

The personality and resulting behavior of an individual are primarily determined by the Importance Determination Component. Importance Determination identifies what motivates the individual, and the extent to which a stream of stimuli provides motivation. As such, it plays a major role in determining the emotional responses of the individual.

- - -

Neuron Story: *"Is Importance Determination the same thing as Freud's Id?"*

"Freud's Id only refers to the mind's unconscious motivations. Importance Determination encompasses our conscious motivations as well."

- - -

Summary & Questions

An individual's preferences and what they notice are like an intellectual fingerprint. Although they may start with a small number of symbols and corresponding thresholds, the symbols they learn, the thresholds they establish and the levels of importance that they generate provide for an unlimited variety.

Regarding the functionality referred to as 'Importance Determination', briefly explain:
1. Why are some symbols permitted to enter the imagination, and others not?
2. What is game pathology, and what did Nau suggest?
3. What is the distinction between the level of importance and a threshold?
4. What are the upper thresholds?
5. What are the lower thresholds?
6. How may the importance level of a symbol be desensitized?
7. What thresholds are determined genetically?
8. What is the role of genetically determined thresholds?

9. With respect to adjusting threshold levels, what is the concept of mass?

23 The Imagination

"Consciousness lives in the imagination, creating interpretations of the world outside, from inside a bundle of neurons. Eventually the neurons begin to create interpretations of the world inside, from what they perceive outside about the world inside."

(The Neurons)

The unconscious portion of the mind provides the imagination with useful information, protecting it from an onslaught of detail that contains impertinent, as well as, unimportant, streams of stimuli.

For example, the autonomic nervous system performs a variety of operational functions that keep the organism alive, such as regulating heartbeat and respiration, while the rest of the mind can perform other duties. Similarly, the unconscious mind acts a preprocessor for the conscious mind, preparing information so that the conscious level can rapidly understand and use it.

To provide intelligence without getting any help from the unconscious portion of the brain would be like asking the president of a major corporation to run a profitable business, while answering the phones and fulfilling customer requests without assistance from the rest of the organization.

In this manner, the unconscious portion of the mind allows the conscious level to manage symbols more effectively, using the underlying management structure to conduct the various routine operations, gather information about the outside world, and bubble-up the appropriate items to upper management for their attention.

- - -

Neuron Story: *"Once the incoming streams of input have been organized, essential operational duties performed, and management reports generated, then what happens?"*

"The information is sent to the interpretive center, where hopefully it makes someone smile."

- - -

When symbols are received by the interpretive center, they are evaluated to determine whether they are qualified to enter the imagination. Since paradigms are the actual gatekeepers to all interpretation and understanding, symbols are evaluated based upon their ability to integrate with one of the paradigms that are presently active.

When there is a sharp rise in the number of symbols that cannot be integrated into an active paradigm, the interpretive center may evaluate other paradigms until it can locate one that most of the symbols can be integrated with. If an acceptable paradigm cannot be located, the interpretive center may begin to fail, thereby allowing all symbols to enter the imagination. This can result in a significant level of confusion.

Although the number of simultaneously active paradigms may vary among individuals, when multiple paradigms exist, the paradigm that can integrate the greatest number of important symbols is identified by the interpretive center as the dominant paradigm.

The imagination is the conscious level of the brain, and similar to an unconscious level of the mind, the conscious level consists of a number of functional components. The functional components that exist include functions that are related to sensory stimuli, such as the Language, Visual, and Tactile components; and functions not related to sensory stimuli, such as the Time Component, Numerical Processing component, and the Analogical and Metaphorical engines, essential to the more advanced levels of intelligence. There are also functions that are related to those found in the unconscious levels of the brain, such as the Imagination's Pattern Recognition, and Symbol Activation and Importance Determination components. Similar to their counterparts at the lowest level, these functions determine how the various segments of stimuli are packaged and ultimately utilized. The cognitive ability that results, however, is determined by the combined functional capabilities of all components.

Beginning with the functions that are related to those within the lowest level of the brain, where sensory organs provide stimuli into the brain, various functional components of the Imagination generate stimuli into the conscious workspace of the brain. The various functional components that operate within the Imagination, generating low level stimuli, are similar to the sensory devices present at the lowest level of the brain. Streams of stimuli that are generated from the functional components of the Imagination, in many respects, require the same treatment as stimuli generated by sensory organs. One of the differences, however, is that a number of additional functional components had to evolve in order to support a variety of advancements.

> For example, the ability of a bumblebee to track time, or of a migratory animal to remember its place of birth, requires functions of the mind that are unrelated to any of the sensory organs. Hence, the minds of simple organisms begin to show traces of capabilities that are unrelated to the functions associated with external sensory organs.

Although newly developed intellectual capabilities may assist animals in survival, capabilities of the mind can also evolve beyond the level needed to help the organism meet the challenges of survival in its natural environment.

For example, chimpanzees and apes in particular have developed a number of intellectual skills that their simple existences in the jungle do not require. "At the Language Research Center of Georgia Status University, in Atlanta, there is a monkey that, armed with a miniature joystick, can anticipate the complex movement of an object on a computer screen and ultimately 'capture' the object. Even for a human, the task is not easy. It requires concentration on, and predictions of, the object's likely trajectories, as well as fine manipulation of the joystick."

"In another part of the center are to be found chimpanzees that can accomplish even more demanding intellectual problems, often ones that require the ability to see three or four moves ahead in a sequential puzzle."
(Origins Reconsidered, Leakey and Lewin, 1977, pg. 284)

As such, functional capabilities within the mind can develop beyond a species' survival needs. Although some of these intellectual capabilities are directly related to the enhanced processing of sensory stimuli, other capabilities can also develop that have a somewhat distant relationship to the senses. As these additional intellectual capabilities develop, they remain available to the individual until such time that circumstances may allow them to eventually utilize them.

One such functional component of the Imagination is the Numerical Processing Component. Although mathematics and arithmetic are learned skills, the ability to perform calculations is absent when the left angular gyrus deep in the human brain is damaged, and with only one exception, there is no impact upon any other intellectual capabilities that are detectable.

For example, "Many patients... with dyscalculia also have an associated brain disorder called finger agnosia: They can no longer name which finger the neurologist is pointing to or touching. It is a complete coincidence that both arithmetic operations and finger naming occupy adjacent brain regions, or does it have something to do with the fact that we all learn to count by using our fingers in early childhood?" (Phantoms in the Brain, Ramachandran, M.D., Ph.D. and Sandra Blakeslee, 1998, pg.19)

Hence, whether the capability remains undeveloped does not matter, the intellectual capability exists to be developed, if circumstance allow the capability to be utilized.

Similar to the other functional components of the Imagination, the Numerical Processing Component accepts and generates stimuli. In the case of arithmetic operations, such as addition, subtraction, multiplication and division, the stimuli received include the values and the operation, while the stimuli returned includes the calculated result.

As for intellectual capabilities that are closely related to the senses, as long as 400,000 years ago, archaic *Homo sapiens* had developed the physiological capability to think in words. Whether circumstances permitted the capability to be utilized at that time, however, is unclear.

> For example, vocalization is dependent upon the position of the larynx and the pharyngeal cavity at the base of the skull, also called the basicranium. The basic pattern of the basicranium in mammals, including pre-Homo sapiens is flat. However, "the earliest time in the fossil record that you find a fully flexed basicranium is about 300,000 to 400,000 years ago, in what people call archaic Homo sapiens." (Origins Reconsidered, Leakey and Lewin, 1977, pg. 262)

It is well accepted that *Homo sapiens sapiens* have the ability to think using words, using a sort of inner ear within the mind, as well as, by using images, using a sort of inner eye within the mind, which is sometimes referred to as, the mind's eye. When the imagination uses symbols, which are words or visual images, it makes use of the characteristics associated with their particular symbols. Although, auditory languaging and visual imaging are the dominant sensory functions within humans, they represent only a small portion of the overall activities that occur within the Imagination Component.

Upon entering the imagination, symbols freely participate with the various functional components of the conscious level. Although the component that is responsible for management of the Imagination, which we call the Thought Management component, does not necessarily become conscious of every symbol that enters this level, if it does, the symbol, or any of its segments of stimuli may be intentionally manipulated or modified.

> For example, the manipulation of a symbol, means that the symbol's associated stimuli may be recombined or re-sequenced. During this process any combination of its segments of stimuli may be modified, the symbol's level of importance may be modified, and its relationships to other symbols may be altered.

The behavior of symbols can be willfully controlled by the imagination by altering the stimuli associated with it. Although the associated stimuli and relationships depict how a symbol should act, the imagination has the ability to substitute physical characteristics and rules of behavior. In fact, symbols within the imagination can be given any set of visual, auditory, olfactory, or tactile characteristics, and they can be made to adhere to the laws of nature and mankind, or their behavior can be modified in such a manner as to be completely unnatural.

23.1 Integrating Segments of Stimuli

As stimuli are returned from the various functional components of the Imagination, a number of segments of stimuli are combined like sensory stimuli from the sensory organs are formed at the lowest level.

For example, the segments from the Language, Visual and Tactile components are combined together as auditory, visual and tactile stimuli, the auditory segment containing a sound sequence, the visual segment containing a visual sequence, and the tactile components containing touch, texture and feelings of the body.

The Imagination contains the only workspace that can integrate sensory stimuli with stimuli from other functional components of the Imagination. Thus, the workspace of the Imagination is the only area of the brain that can bring information together into a single, unified view.

Similar to Symbol Generation at the unconscious level, new symbols are generated with the Imagination by combining segments of stimuli. Once generated, the new symbols become generally available to the functional components of the Imagination.

For example, the relationship that one symbol forms with another, may be associated with clusters of symbols in the Analogical and Metaphorical Engines. If a cluster of symbols, within the Analogical or Metaphorical engines, are enhanced with the addition of new symbol, then the memory of the new symbol may be retained relative to both functional components.

Using the Imagination's Symbol Activation component, memories can be recalled from their multiple locations, activating a sequence of symbols from past experience. However, using combinations of symbols including those recalled from memory, segments of stimuli can be recombined and re-sequenced in such a way as to create, or imagine, an experience that has never occurred.

23.2 Consciousness

According to our definition, an organism is conscious, and therefore has consciousness, when it is capable of creating the minimum representation of their environment within their brain. Consciousness, therefore, allows an organism to improve its chances of survival, even if the organism can only achieve a marginal understanding or its surroundings.

By this definition, an organism that can not represent its external environment internaliy within the mind, or that cannot become aware of it recreation of the environment within its mind, must necessarily be considered unconscious. Hence, the ability to understand one's environment requires at least one sensory organ and the ability to represent internally the stimuli that it generates as it interacts with the environment. Consciousness, however, is not equivalent to self-awareness. In order to be self-aware, the organism would have to be mindful of its body or thought process.

- - -

Neuron Story: *"Couldn't we be conscious if our sensory organs were removed?"*
"You could only imagine you were conscious."

- - -

23.3 Thought Management

"It is as if just a few places on the vast map of our mind were illuminated."

Immanuel Kant

Nearly all organisms must be conscious of their environment in order to survive. Many, however, are preprogrammed in how they respond to stimuli. Preprogramming, however, does not necessarily mean that the organism is unconscious. On the contrary, it means that there are predetermined behavioral responses, to predetermined symbols, which implies that a less sophisticated internal representation of the environment may be required.

Individuals that have a greater ability to learn are less dependent upon preprogramming. Since a greater level of intelligence is associated with greater ability to learn, individuals that are more intelligent are naturally less predictable.

> For example, flying insects will invariably travel toward light, even if the light source is a flame. Therefore, when a wasp or hornet is trapped inside an automobile, the process of covering the windows to prevent the sunlight from entering the windshield or rear window will often redirect the lost insect to an open door.

As the complexity associated with a greater intelligence makes for a large number of decision-making factors and possible outcomes, the predictability of an organism decreases with an increase of intelligence. While these factors affecting the predictability of humans is largely based upon cultural values, regardless of the considerations used, decisions that are not preprogrammed are made all the time.

Neuron Story: *"Am I preprogrammed?"*
　　　　　　　　"We've long determined that you couldn't be."

- - -

　　The decision making process using various considerations is managed by the Thought Management component. The Thought Management component is different than the other functional components of the Imagination because of the way it can look into the Imagination. The Thought Management Component looks into the conscious part of the Imagination in a manner similar to certain types of software products that are used for debugging.

　　For example, debugging software, which itself is software, is used by the software industry to search for problems. Debugging products have the ability to look into any area of memory and any process, including itself. In a similar manner, the Thought Management component can look into any of the functional components of the Imagination, in order to observe various processes. If, for argument sake, it were to look into the Numerical Processing Component, various aspects of arithmetic operations could be observed.

　　Although debugging software is typically directed by a software engineer to look at particular things, the Thought Management component would determine what to look at.

　　With a capability such as this, the Thought Management Component of an intelligent being can observe and direct numerous operations within the Imagination. Not only can it experience the combined stimuli of the various components of the brain, but it can also direct them.

　　Driven by the Importance Determination Component within the Imagination, the Thought Management Component evaluates everything it observes within the context of its active paradigms. In this sense, each paradigm is a small universe of rules.

　　For example, groups of symbols within the Analogical and Metaphorical Engines represent sets of rules that depict an analogical or metaphorical model. Paradigms are also groups of symbols, however they are more comprehensive than analogies and metaphors, providing a complete set of rules from which to direct the interpretation of all stimuli.

To understand paradigms better, let's first look at analogies and metaphors, and how they are represented within their respective components.

Summary & Questions

Using streams of stimuli from sensory organs, even the most rudimentary nerve bundles provides the organism an ability to understand some aspects about its environment. As organisms evolved, they developed increasingly advanced capabilities that extended beyond the limitations of their sensory organs.

Regarding the functionality referred to as 'The Imagination', briefly explain:
1. How do unconscious levels of the mind support the conscious level?
2. How do symbols gain entry into the imagination?
3. What is the role of a paradigm, and what can cause it to fail?
4. What are some of the components of the imagination?
5. What does the imagination have in common with the lowest level?
6. What perceptual capabilities are unrelated to sensory organs?
7. Have some functional components been influenced by others, and how?
8. What are some of the techniques available to the imagination to manipulate and evaluate the objects it perceives from the external world?
9. How can the imagination use these techniques to manipulate ideas imagined within its internal world?
10. What is the distinction between the imagination' s external and internal world?
11. How does the imagination provide a consolidated view of the environment?
12. What permits memories to be recalled and experienced?
13. What is consciousness, and how can it facilitate survival?
14. What is the distinction between consciousness and self-awareness?
15. What is thought management, and what is it similar to?

24 Analogical Engine

"Information, which is unrelated to any other information, is completely useless. Knowledge, regardless of the symbols used to record it, is no longer knowledge the moment its symbols can no longer be interpreted."

(The Neurons)

Analogies, similes, and metaphors form the foundation for understanding the meaning of all concepts that are built upon an individual's pre-wired knowledge. Just as the various things that are analogous to comfort and discomfort are generalized as desirable and undesirable, the learning process involves the generalization and categorization of new stimuli with respect to previously learned stimuli that they already have the capability to recognize.

The entire realm of cognition, which involves the process of thinking, encompasses the high-level capabilities of the intellect, such as perception, attention, judgment, reasoning, memory, imagining and speech, which are all highly dependent upon the ability to form analogies.

The ability to form analogies is essential to advanced levels of intelligence, especially those that exceed the minimum necessary to support basic survival. The ability to form analogies provides the foundation for generalization, learning, and to problem solving using inductive, as well as, deductive reasoning.

> For example, "in logic, analogy is the name of an inductive form of argument, which asserts that if two or more entities are similar in one or more respects, then a probability exists that they will be similar in other respects."
> (Microsoft Encarta 1997)

Analogies are also used in deductive reasoning to introduce stimuli when performing problem solving. As such, analogies can activate symbols, and their related segments of stimuli, which reveal relationships that are essential to the process of deductive reasoning.

> For example, in '<u>The Case of the Falling Woman</u>', a story from a series of children's mysteries, a young detective, known as Encyclopedia Brown, encountered the following set of circumstances:
>
> One late evening, Encyclopedia Brown and his friend, Sally, were sitting in their living room, when they both heard a sound from outside. Sally, at the instruction of Encyclopedia, turned off the only light in the room allowing them to see out the window, into the moon lit front yard. They were surprised to see a school friend of theirs, Scott, preparing to take a picture of them together.

When they questioned Scott, he explained that he desperately needed a photograph for a photography contest he was entering, where he would compete against the notorious cheater, Winthrop Ledbetter.

At the photography competition, Winthrop entered a single photograph. "It showed a teenage girl touching a flaming match to a Christmas candle. Beside the candle stood a pile of gifts ... lighted by two table lamps. What made the picture amazing, however, was the second figure ... a woman. She could be seen falling outside the large window behind the teenage girl. The picture was titled 'Christmas Miracle.' Beside it was pinned a white card on which was written, 'This photograph was taken December 16, at 9:30 P.M., by Winthrop Ledbetter, age 11, in the living room of his parents' apartment.' At the moment Winthrop snapped the picture of his teenage sister Mary, Miss Abigail Greer was toppling from the apartment house roof one story above..." blown off by a forty mile an hour wind.

As the judges were about to place the first prize blue ribbon on the photograph, Encyclopedia Brown declared that the photograph was a fake! (<u>Encyclopedia Brown Volume 6, The Case of the Falling Woman</u>, Donald J. Sobol, 1969, pg. 83-89)

Although the information necessary to solve the mystery was provided to the reader early in the story, the reader must first form an analogy with the preceding events of the story, when Encyclopedia Brown and Sally were sitting in the living room.

For example, as Encyclopedia Brown explained to the judges, "as the winds of '40 miles an hour' would have blown out the match and candle, 'the large window' behind Winthrop's sister must have been closed. Further, the room was lighted by 'two table lamps' and the flashgun of the camera, while outside, it was night." Therefore, the window should have acted as a mirror. However, the falling woman could be seen through the window. A physical impossibility! (<u>Encyclopedia Brown Volume 6, The Case of the Falling Woman</u>, Donald J. Sobol, 1969, pg. 109)

Although the ability of Encyclopedia Brown and Sally to see outside the living room window after the lights were turned off was analogous to the situation revealing that Winthrop Ledbetter's photograph was a fraud, our dependency upon analogies is far more extensive.

For example, as intelligent beings, we not only depend upon analogies to understand the circumstances in the story, but we also rely upon analogies to understand the meaning of each phrase, and of each word.

The first three words, 'One late evening' are rapidly associated, as the visual symbols, 'o', 'n', 'e', ' ', 'l', 'a', 't', 'e', ' ', 'e', 'v', 'e', 'n', 'i', 'n', 'g', ',', and then as 'one', 'late', and 'evening', delimited by spaces. The visual words are then associated as the sounds, 'one late evening' within the mind's inner ear, and then as the meaning analogous to 'one late evening', as in 'some particular day well after sunset.'

By the end of the first paragraph, most of us have formed a number of assumptions about how the living room looked, the general style of house, the outdoor surroundings, and potentially the type of interaction that Encyclopedia Brown and Sally were having. All of these assumptions, however, are formed by analogy. The analogies we form within our minds introduce sets of symbols that we use to imagine the unspecified details of the story.

Whether through imagined or experienced segments of stimuli, analogies convey the meaning of symbols in terms of other symbols, and their related segments of stimuli. The interpretation of the symbols determine which other symbols will be activated. Irrespective of the interpretation, the primary base of knowledge, from which all analogical meaning and understanding is derived, is the analogical engine.

24.1 Role of Analogies

Analogies depict the relationship between two or more things. The relationships may involve any type of characteristic, such as a relationship in time, sequence, physical characteristic, usefulness, structural design, psychological effect, or any intangible trait. Although many analogies are formed based upon the characteristics of the stimuli generated by the senses, analogies are also formed as a result of intellectual activities within the brain. These analogies are based upon the characteristics of the stimuli that were generated internally by the imagination.

For example, distinct from simple associations, such as the visual beauty of a flower with its scent, more advanced forms of analogy can be formed among the characteristics of the stimuli associated with previous sensory experiences.

In the story, 'The Case of the Falling Woman', there is a simple analogy between, the lighting conditions of the room that prevented Encyclopedia Brown and his friend, Sally from seeing into the dimly lit front yard, and the lighting conditions in Winthrop Ledbetter's photograph. From

Encyclopedia Brown's perspective, an analogy existed between the lighting conditions of the two situations, deducing that the results should have been the same.

On the other hand, more advanced analogies are formed among the characteristics of the stimuli associated with experiences generated from within the Imagination, such as with a logic problem and the approach used to determine its solution.

In solving how to make a light bulb emit light, there is a predictive analogy between heat causing metal to glow, and electricity causing heat, to make a light bulb light. From Thomas Edison's perspective, an analogy existed between the concepts of heated metals and electrical resistance, predicting that the results should produce light.

Analogies created by inventors, such as Thomas Edison, occur with stimuli generated from within the Imagination, as Mr. Edison could not have previously experienced a functioning light bulb with any of his five senses.

Analogies are the mechanism by which the brain performs a comparison of one set of characteristics and rules to another. As such, analogies facilitate the comparison of the knowledge represented by different sets of symbols with another. When new information is encountered, it is compared to previously recognized sets of symbols.

For example, sets of symbols include their segments of stimuli, and the rules by which they are know to behave. Comparisons are made between symbols, segments of stimuli, and the rules that depict their behavior.

The usefulness of the relationship formed by an analogy depends upon the accuracy of the level of importance that is placed upon the characteristics that form the analogy. The strength of an analogy is determined by the number and importance of the relationships, which are found to be analogous as well as the ones that are not.

For example, in an analogy between a human and an automobile, corresponding systems that are analogous would be the respiratory, digestive, and cooling systems, while a non-analogous system would be the reproductive system.

There are also analogies that are loosely formed, which are typically found in certain types of creativity, and humor.

For example, an android, which had received instructions from terrorists to blow up a bus, returned shortly afterwards with burnt lips.

An analogy exists between 'blowing up' a balloon using your lips, and 'blowing up' a bus using explosives. A loose analogy exists between the relationship of the results when you 'blow up a bus', in the same manner that you 'blow up a balloon'. The tail pipe on a bus can get extremely hot.

The sudden shift in paradigm, however, with a mildly sympathetic android victim, is capable of creating a humorous image.

Figures of speech, and multiple meanings of words and word phrases, are useful devices to misdirect an individual's interpretive process. There is a fine distinction, however, between an intentional misdirection of a loose analogy, and a misinterpretation. In the misinterpretation, the loose analogy is taken seriously as if it were not loose at all.

For example, the older model robot in the audience asked, 'Wasn't that a mean thing to do to a poor android?' and 'Didn't the android know that the tail pipe was hot?'

- - -

Neuron Story: *"Didn't she ask if robots should avoid running away from bears and holding deep breaths of highly compressed air?"*
"Those early robots, they all look alike."
"They don't look alike if they play with bears and compressed air."
"I suppose you are using the word 'play' as a loose analogy, where a shift in paradigm exists between harmless fun..."
"...and routine disfigurement?"
"...or complete destruction."

- - -

Whether analogies are tightly or loosely formed, for analysis purposes it is useful to categorize them by the general capabilities that they provide. As identified in 'Metaphor and Cognition', by Bipin Indurhkya, to be properly analyzed, analogies should be distinguished into at least three groups of usage.

24.2 Simple Analogies

Symbols, and their segments of stimuli, can represent any type of thing, action or circumstance. The segments of stimuli associated with a symbol portray its characteristics. Segments of stimuli that have originated at sensory organs can be categorized into as many categories as there are types of sensory organs.

> For example, stimuli originated from any of the sensory organs of a human are limited to the five categories of characteristics, which are smell, taste, touch, sight and sound.

Symbols originating from components of the Imagination also generate segments of stimuli. However, stimuli originating from the conscious level of the brain are not necessarily restricted to the categories associated with sensory organs.

> For example, symbols originating from the components of the Imagination also include segments of stimuli for abstract characteristics, which include level of importance, mathematical abstractions, and analogical and metaphorical relationships.

Analogies, therefore, may be formed from any combination of categories of stimuli, whether they are associated with sensory organs, or with the stimuli generated by the additional functional components of the brain. As such, analogies can exist among mathematical relationships, or any other form of abstraction.

In its simplest form, an analogy exists when the characteristics among one or more categories of stimuli share a resemblance. The degree of resemblance between the stimuli of two symbols is determined by the pattern recognition ability of the Analogical Engine.

Before an analogy has been completed, the similarities between the two symbols must be evaluated for their level of importance. The more important the areas of resemblance, the stronger the resulting analogical relationship will be.

24.3 Proportional Analogies

In a proportional analogy, there are two sets of simple analogies that are compared to one another. The resulting analogy is considered to be proportional when there is an analogous relationship between the two sets of analogies themselves.

> For example, in the proportional analogy, 'a Persian cat is to a Bengal Tiger, as a Toy Poodle is to an Alaskan Wolf', there are numerous proportional analogies between the two sets of simple analogies.

> Although the two sets of simple analogies share the fact that they are both mammals that are carnivores, the first

item in each pair is a significantly smaller, lighter weight, and relatively harmless version of the second item.

Hence, a proportional analogy exists between the two sets of simple analogies among the characteristics of relative size, weight, and harmlessness, as well as their propensity to be considered suitable house pets.

In summary, while a simple analogy may exist between a single set of symbols, such as 'A' and 'B', a proportional analogy exists between pairs of symbols, such that 'A' and 'B' are proportionally analogous to 'C' and 'D' along one or more sets of characteristics.

24.4 Predictive Analogies

A predictive analogy begins as a simple analogy between a set of symbols, where segments of stimuli, or characteristics, other than those involved in the simple analogy, can be predicted.

For example, a theory is a system of rules that makes assertions about what things are and how they behave. Hence, theories can be used to predict how objects will behave under specific circumstances.

Similarly, a predictive analogy asserts that the unknown characteristics of one symbol can be predicted by the known characteristics of another symbol, based upon the fact that the symbols form a simple analogy.

When a simple analogy is formed, the known characteristics and system of rules that define a symbol can often be used to fill in the unknown characteristics and system of rules that define another symbol. As such, identifying predictive analogies represents the capability to theorize and perform analogical reasoning.

- - -

Neuron Story: *"Do metaphors work the same as analogies?"*
"Metaphors are not analogous."

- - -

Summary & Questions

The meanings associated with symbols establish knowledge. Meanings may be determined in a variety of ways using paradigms. Although meaning may be directly interpreted by the paradigm, the meaning of a symbol may also be inferred through the use of an analogy.

James V. Luisi

Regarding the functionality referred to as 'The Analogical Engine', briefly explain:

1. What is the formal definition of an analogy as it pertains to logic?
2. How can analogies be used in deductive reasoning?
3. How are analogies used in everyday perception?
4. Are analogies restricted to particular types or sources of characteristics?
5. How can analogies be used to invent or predict an outcome?
6. How does importance determination participate in the identification of an analogy?
7. What is a simple analogy?
8. What are proportional analogies?
9. How are predictive analogies defined?

25 Metaphorical Engine

"An analogy between two objects having similar characteristics and rules can cause a shift to an unexpected paradigm. A metaphor, on the other hand, is when the stimuli of an object are intentionally interpreted using an alternate paradigm, which reveals useful characteristics and rules where none were necessarily expected."
(The Neurons)

More advanced than analogies, metaphors provide an another mechanism by which symbols can be interpreted. In order to convey meaning to an object, metaphors make use of paradigms that contain an alternate view of symbols and relationships, which can be used to drive the interpretive process. This paradigm, often referred to as a 'looking glass', provides an alternative method for attributing meaning to the stimuli and relationships of the object. As such, the alternate method for interpreting the object does not have to be complete. It just has to apply meaning to some aspect of the object.

For example, "Metaphor is the process of meaningfully interpreting something as something else, and in the process, the fact that some parts of the interpretation have been carried out successfully, does not justify in any way that other parts of the interpretation can be carried out as well." (<u>Metaphor and Cognition</u>, Bipin Indurkhya, pg.33)

To borrow the nomenclature from '<u>Metaphor and Cognition</u>', by Bipin Indurkhya, we will refer to the object being interpreted as the 'target', and the object characterizing the paradigm, whose characteristics and rules are used to reinterpret the target, as the 'source'. Hence, metaphors always require one object to be the source, which provides the paradigm for interpretation, and the other the target, which is the thing being reinterpreted. However, unlike analogies, the source and the target are not reversible.

For example, the analogy between an oxygen-breathing human and an automobile, share a number of reversible characteristics, such as respiration, cooling, fuel consumption, and the elimination of waste.

In the analogy, the characteristics of one object can lead one to the other, where analogous rules and characteristics may be borrowed back and forth.

In comparison, when the research group examined how to improve the effectiveness of the synthetic-bristle paintbrush to match the performance of the natural-bristle paintbrush, they eventually benefited from the symbols introduced by the paradigm of a pump. By evaluating the possibility that the natural-bristle paintbrush worked like a pump between its fibers, it became possible to design a synthetic-bristle paintbrush that would not smear or streak. However, let us consider the paradigm in reverse, where the source becomes the target and the target becomes the source.

Using the prevailing model of a paintbrush, where paint is smeared onto a surface with the ends of the bristles, it would be inconceivable to get to the model of a pump, never mind invent a pump.

In a metaphor, the characteristics of each object do not necessarily have the ability to lead to the other. The object that acts as the source provides the paradigm from which to reinterpret the target object, in order to represent a new meaning. In a metaphor, however, the paradigm of the target cannot be reversed analogously to the source. Once the rules of the source have been applied to the target, however, it is possible for the newly formed relationship to be analogous in both directions.

As such, analogies may share, or predict, characteristics back and forth, such as 'A' is to 'B' and 'B' is to 'A', while metaphors are non-reversible, where 'A' is not to 'B', even though 'B' is to 'A'.

While analogies use similarities of characteristics to determine other objects with which to form an analogous relationship, metaphors rely on other methods to determine source paradigms, potentially resulting in one that may have no recognizable characteristic in common, before applying the metaphor.

For example, the Thought Management component uses a number of strategies to determine a source paradigm for its interpretive system. These include trial and error, sequential searches, suggestions from other individuals, or just the pure desire for a relationship to exist. In any event, the source paradigm is chosen through non-analogical means.

Once a source paradigm is determined, the rules of the source paradigm are applied to the target, providing it new meaning. Once the new meaning of the source paradigm is learned, as through common usage, what was once a functioning metaphor, becomes a learned figure of speech, which may also referred to as a 'conventional' metaphor.

For example, the first time a metaphor is used the rules of the source paradigm are not analogically related to the target, hence it is a 'novel' metaphor. However, once a metaphor has been used and understood, it becomes a learned expression, providing an alternate meaning for what was once the source of the metaphor.

Hence, after the metaphor creates a relationship between the source and the target, the metaphor no longer functions as a metaphor. Once the phrase that represents the metaphor is recognized, it becomes reduced to a simple figure of speech, albeit with the same interpretation.

- - -

Neuron Story: *"Metaphors are here, and then they're gone?"*
"They no longer act like metaphors after you learn them."
"What if I refuse to learn them?"
"With you, refusal to learn is not an option... it just happens."

- - -

25.1 The Metaphorical Engine

The secondary base of knowledge, from which all metaphorical meaning and understanding is derived, is the Metaphorical Engine. As such, it differs from the Analogical Engine in both its identification and application of metaphors.

For example, the Analogical Engine does not make use of alternate paradigms in order to interpret the characteristics of either object involved in an analogy, whereas the Metaphorical Engine must shift to the paradigm of the source object in order to interpret the target.

Also, in order to identify an analogy, characteristics of one object are matched against the characteristics of another. A loose analogy results when the similarities among the characteristics are few and weak. Metaphors, on the other hand, do not rely upon analogical relationships.

The usefulness of using a metaphor as a figure of speech is not only determined by the depth of meaning that can be derived by interpreting the target using the source paradigm, but it is also dependent upon the probability that other individuals will interpret the metaphor properly. The choice of metaphor, therefore, requires a good degree of judgment, which is highly dependent upon properly assessing the intended audience.

The task of identifying the appropriate metaphor, therefore, requires particular abilities with paradigms. The better one can perceive and generate paradigms, the more capable they will be in choosing and creating metaphors.

James V. Luisi

- - -

Neuron Story: *"I can create metaphors with stories I've heard."*
"It's even easier if you can perceive multiple paradigms simultaneously."
"You mean like a Level Two or Three?"

- - -

Metaphors are dependent upon paradigms, as paradigms provide the key to interpreting the meaning of symbols represented by metaphors. This can be illustrated by analyzing how stories create paradigms within which metaphors can flourish.

For example, in the 1991 episode of 'Star Trek, The Next Generation', entitled, 'Darmok', the Enterprise and a Tamarian ship rendezvous at a planet named, El-Adrel. Although the Tamarians use English words, the meaning of their language is found to be incomprehensible.

The Tamarian Captain attempts to communicate to Captain Picard using phrases from a Tamarian story of 'Darmok and Jelad at Tenagra', which is about two heroes who traveled separately to a distant island, defeated a mighty beast, and left together.

When Captain Picard eventually understands the meaning of the Tamarian story 'Darmok and Jelad at Tenagra', he realizes that the Tamarian language is based upon Tamarian folklore and metaphor. Hence, when the Tamarian Captain uses the phrase, 'when the walls fell', he is reciting a part of the story when the two heroes befriend one another and combine their efforts.

As such, the story of 'Darmok and Jelad at Tenagra', provided a paradigm, from which phrases could be understood metaphorically. Hence, when the Tamarian Captain used the metaphor, 'when the walls fell', he meant that he and Captain Picard should act as friends and cooperatively combine their efforts. (Darmok, 'Star Trek, The Next Generation', episode story authored by Philip Lazebnik and Joseph Menosky, 1991)

However, metaphors are not the only thing dependent upon paradigms. Paradigms are essential for establishing a context in order to interpret the meaning of symbols. In summary, one must use at least one paradigm, in order to determine at least one meaning, for at least one symbol.

- - -

Neuron Story: *"You mean we need paradigms to understand everything?"*
"Even a paradigm, would have no meaning, without a paradigm."
"Where do paradigms begin?"
"They begin with meaning."

- - -

I dedicate the Metaphorical Engine to Bipin Indurkhya, for helping me conceptualize my understanding of metaphorical thinking. I also wish to extend my gratitude to him for personally providing me a copy of his book, 'Metaphor and Cognition', when I could not otherwise acquire one. Most of all, however, I wish to express my appreciation for his most sincere and stimulating correspondence.

Summary & Questions

Just as the meaning of a symbol may be inferred through the use of an analogy, the meaning of symbols may also be determined through alternative paradigms that direct the interpretive process with a different set of rules.

Regarding the functionality referred to as 'The 'Metaphorical Engine', briefly explain:
1. In what ways are analogies and metaphors different from one another?
2. How are metaphors identified?
3. What are novel versus conventional metaphors?
4. What are metaphors dependent upon?
5. What are the pros and cons to a language wholly dependent upon metaphors?

26 Paradigms

"Paradigms define what symbols mean and how they are to be interpreted. Intelligence, therefore, cannot exist without a paradigm, as information would have no meaning."

(The Neurons)

When we are born, we are equipped with basic paradigms, such as comfort, discomfort and the absence of comfort or discomfort. These paradigms are not comprised of advanced symbols, such as words. Instead they consist of symbols representing various sensory stimuli, which provide interpretations of either feeling good, bad or indifferent. Although it is difficult to study these early stages of brain development, occasionally scientists are provided the opportunity to get a rare glimpse into the recesses of the early mind

For example, in a study of an individual afflicted with synaesthesia, where the stimuli that are received by one sensory organ are simultaneously perceived across other senses, the result was a rare and powerful photographic memory that could penetrate early childhood. After that period, memories are typically built from verbalized word associations, often replacing the pre-verbal period, thereby making early memories scarce. This individual's memory was based on sensory stimuli, such that he was able to retain memories from his early childhood.

"S.'s extraordinary memory gave him one distinct advantage: he had recollections that dated back to infancy, memories others of us may simply never have formed or have lost because of the vast number of subsequent impressions that displaced them. Possibly, too, our impressions failed to settle at such an early stage of life because our basic tool of memory, speech, had not yet developed then."

"What recollections do we generally have of early childhood? Some picture, perhaps, pasted to the top of a toy chest? The steps of a staircase where we sat as a child? An impression of a quilt we had, the sense of what it felt like to be bundled in it?"

"It is no wonder that S.'s memories of early childhood were incomparably richer than ours. For his memory was never transformed into an apparatus for reshaping reminiscences into words, which is what happens to others of us at a fairly early age. Rather, his memory continued to summon up spontaneously images that formed part of an early period of awareness." (The Mind of a Mnemonist, A. R. Luria, pg. 75-76)

S.'s memories during infancy reveal his interpretations of his experiences believed to be before the age of one. In the Record of August 1934, S recalls the images from that time period in his life.

> For example, "I remember that the wallpaper in the room was brown and the bed white... I can see my mother taking me in her arms, then she puts me down again... I sense movement... a feeling of warmth, then an unpleasant sensation of cold." (The Mind of a Mnemonist, A. R. Luria, pg. 77)

As a result of evolution, interpretations from an early age are generated using basic, pre-wired paradigms. As new segments of stimuli are successfully incorporated into these simple paradigms, interpretations are generated when these symbols correspond to one of the previously existing paradigms.

> For example, at an early age, segments of stimuli regarded as pleasant would be successfully incorporated into the paradigm representing an interpretation of things that are good.

Beginning with an upside down view of their visual world, infants can only establish a simple understanding of their environment, delivering either comfort or discomfort. As the learning process progresses, however, new paradigms become created and existing ones evolve.

- - -

Neuron Story: *"How big can these simple paradigms get?"*
"Oh... just large enough to encompass an individual's entire reality, their understanding of the universe, who they are, and their purpose in life."

- - -

Although paradigms start off as basic structures of symbols, as learning occurs, the corresponding structure of symbols can grow substantially, or the structure of symbols may be used to generate a new paradigm. As such, paradigms grow as additional structures of symbols consistent with enhancing the interpretations, are learned and incorporated into the paradigm.

The structure of symbols for a given paradigm will always result in the same particular interpretation. If the incoming stimuli cannot be interpreted, or the interpretations that occur conflict with its corresponding observations, then a new paradigm must be created. Hence, new paradigms are required when existing paradigms cannot interpret incoming symbols effectively.

For example, every child has a paradigm whereby the activity of playing and making noise is associated with the concept of fun, which is ultimately interpreted as comforting. Parents encourage this paradigm of playing by providing positive reinforcement.

However, as the tolerance level of adults are eventually exceeded, each child will come to experience the circumstance when the same activity, of playing and making noise, is met with negative reinforcement. The initial shock on the child's face is usually the result of their inability to interpret the conflicting observations within their comfort paradigm.

When the child realizes the conflict in interpreting the concept of playing, such as when their parents were trying to speak on the telephone, watch television, or simply relax, they construct a new paradigm. Although the new paradigm contains the same symbols as when the activity of playing is interpreted as comforting, the new interpretation is that playing can cause discomfort.

Once the alternate paradigm is constructed, the child will have the ability to choose from the various paradigms that contain similar structures of symbols. This would then include the paradigm in which the activity of playing is interpreted as discomforting, as well as the other where playing results in an interpretation that is comforting.

As one can begin to see, successful paradigm selection is dependent upon one's ability to detect conflicts in interpretation and create new paradigms to resolve the conflicts.

For example, if the child discards the conflict in interpretation, by simply chucking the inconsistency, the child will continue to experience negative reinforcement for the same circumstances.

Whereas, if the child detects the specific distinction between the comforting form of playing and its discomforting counterpart, thereby learning the specific circumstances in which adults should not be disturbed, the child may only experience negative reinforcement for variations of the same behavior.

However, if the child remains unable to detect the distinction between the comforting form of playing and making noise, and repeatedly experiences negative reinforcement, the child may draw the unfortunate conclusion that playing is no longer an acceptable form of behavior.

As the individual creates and evolves their paradigms, they are expanding their understanding of the world. As their paradigms continue to develop, their interaction and interpretation of events also develops. Whether the paradigms that are considered accurate or flawed, they provide the only mechanism from which to interpret the meaning of symbols.

- - -

Neuron Story: *"What paradigm can I use to detect my own imperfect paradigms?"*
"Obviously not one of your own."

- - -

Paradigms determine how streams of stimuli are interpreted and the way that individuals interpret experiences, significantly influence their attitude. Individuals with imperfectly formed paradigms will generate interpretations quite differently from individuals possessing well-formed paradigms.

For example, the success rate of highly intelligent individuals is influenced by their paradigms, which affect the way that they understand and interact with others, often under particular circumstances.

As such, some individuals may be quite comfortable interacting with large groups of people, while others may have difficulty interacting with anyone at all.

The scope of an individual's paradigms may vary significantly. Paradigms can increase in complexity until their structures of symbols define an entire universe of how everything works.

For example, extensive religious training will result in significantly larger structures of symbols than an occasional exposure. However, religious doctrines and scientific theories are paradigms, such as the scientific theory of evolution, which is capable of explaining the universe, its origins and possibly its destiny.

A paradigm determines the meaning associated with every stream of stimuli, representing the context within which interpretations may be possible. This includes every culture, every discipline, and every point of view. When a given paradigm fails to provide an interpretation, another paradigm may. However, until an effective paradigm is identified or created, whatever information remains uninterpretable, is completely without meaning.

Summary & Questions

Any symbol does not have a particular number of meanings, if any. How the segments of stimuli associated with a symbol are interpreted is determined by the paradigms that are active when the symbol is either introduced or activated.

Regarding the functionality referred to as, 'Paradigms', briefly explain:
1. What are basic pre-wired or genetic paradigms, and why are they necessary?
2. What are the types of things that are incorporated into paradigms?
3. When are new paradigms created or modified?
4. Why is it important to detect interpretative conflict?
5. How is intelligence affected by the accuracy of one's paradigms?
6. How can the lack of an effective paradigm affect one's sanity?

27 Architecture of the Mind

27.1 System Architecture

Every organism is comprised of parts. Depending upon the organism, many of these parts may be related in functionality, and hence can be grouped together. Together these parts that support a particular capability may be considered to be a subsystem.

For example, mammals have parts that help to absorb oxygen into the bloodstream, as well as, release carbon dioxide from the bloodstream. These parts belong to the respiratory and circulatory systems.

As organisms increase in complexity, the number of systems that are required to make them function also increases. However, when we look at the organism from the perspective of it as an entire system, the various systems that comprise it, such as a respiratory system, would then be considered to be subsystems. The overview of the various subsystems, and how they interconnect to support the entire system is the architecture of the system.

- - -

Neuron Story: *"Each system is a subsystem of a bigger system!"*
"I'll never get you out of my system."

- - -

Hence, the system architecture pertains to a system, and the identification of the system is the first step towards defining its architecture.

For example, from the perspective of the increasingly larger system, the respiratory system of a mammal is a subsystem within the overall system of the beaver. Likewise, mammals are a part of their local ecological system, and their local ecological systems are part of a much larger ecological system.

Likewise, the respiratory system of a mammal consists of a set of subsystems, such as a pair of lungs, a diaphragm, thorax, intercostal muscles, bronchi, trachea, and nasal passages. The lungs, in turn, consist of alveoli and a capillary network.

Hence, the 'architecture' of a mammal includes a number of 'subsystems', such as a respiratory system, as well as, a skeletal, nervous, pulmonary and digestive system.

From the perspective of our mechanically intelligent brain, the system architecture is comprised of hardware, software, network, application and data architectures. Of these, we will focus mostly upon the software architecture, which itself, consists of an information system and a control system architecture.

For example, information systems and control systems represent distinct software paradigms. Although both paradigms deal with information, information systems involve a large variety of information, as is typical of business systems, while control systems involve a large quantity and rapid flow of signal data, as is typical of aircraft control software.

The distinctions among the paradigms, however, do not stop there. From a high-level perspective, the primary design objective of an information system is to protect the integrity of information, while the primary goal of a control system is to keep the mechanical system functioning, regardless of any information errors that may occur.

As such, a control system would not be designed to tell the pilot of a Stealth B2 Bomber that operation of his aircraft was temporarily suspended because data could no longer be recorded into the database.

27.2 Software Architecture

All software applications that have been developed may be categorized as either an information system, which is primarily concerned with managing data, or a control system, which is primarily concerned with managing mechanical devices. Since the brain is concerned with managing information, as well as, mechanical devices, our software architecture must include both information and control system software.

The intellectual components of the brain, which are responsible for thinking, must be supported by an architecture that is attuned to handling a large variety of data, which is typical of an information system. This information system, however, is somewhat unusual in that it does not follow the conventional design disciplines of an information system. As such, we will refer to it as an "hybrid information control" system.

For example, the intellectual components of the brain must process large amounts of signal data, and must tolerate data related problems in a manner more closely resembling a control system.

- - -

Neuron Story: *"So we should ignore our fatal errors?"*
"Might as well."

- - -

27.3 Hybrid Information-Control System

Although the electrochemical processes of the brain are slow, it supports a large number of processes that work in parallel to one another.

For example, the activity of the brain involves the release of chemical ions through a cell membrane along sequences of connecting nerve cells. The rate of signal transfer is limited to the speed at which this reaction can be propagated to adjoining nerve cells. Although this rate is slow when compared to the speed of an electric current through a conductor, it is offset by the fact that there are millions of processes working together at the same time.

Although it is not practical to match the degree to which the biological brain can support parallel activities, the fact that a non-biological mechanical brain has such an advantage in signal transfer rate, makes the two approaches comparable, at least from the perspective of speed. Hence, while the biological mind is a highly parallel system with slow moving signals, in comparison our non-biologically mechanical mind is barely parallel, but with high-speed signals.

In computer technology, however, there are at least two types of parallel processing. One type can be described as performing many different tasks at the same time, while the other performs an individual task by sharing it among multiple processors.

For example, if a company had a large order to fill, they may organize their employees such that each of them will fulfill all of the steps that are necessary to complete an order, thereby processing orders in parallel to one another. The company could also organize their employees in an assembly line, with each employee performing an individual step in the process, thereby working as many orders in parallel as there are steps in the assembly line. The company can also organize their employees in combinations of these two approaches, such as having multiple assembly lines, or multiple individuals working together to perform an individual task along any given assembly line.

Another type of labor distribution common to computer technology, which is more prevalent than parallel processing, is one that involves sharing an individual processor.

For example, an employee may have enough time, to be able to split their time up to perform multiple tasks. As a result, numerous tasks may proceed forward by performing a portion of work on each, in succession, rotating through each of them until they have all been completed.

In computer technology, these approaches to parallel and shared processing techniques are common to operating systems and operating system like environments. Hence, in order to process the vast quantity of signals, and provide the functional components of the brain at various levels, a hybrid information control system must also be integrated with an operating system paradigm, resulting in an information system control system operating system paradigm. We will refer to this conglomeration within our software architecture as an info-con-op system.

For example, an operating system provides an environment for programs to run in. It provides resources that the programs need in order to function, such as memory and processor time. Operating systems also provide an interface between functional programs and the computer's physical devices.

- - -

Neuron Story: *"Does intelligence exist in programs?"*
"No, the key is information."

- - -

Summary & Questions

Organizing functions, services and hardware into types of functions, services and hardware provides for a more manageable environment more readily allowing skill sets to be focused on the pertinent areas. Although it is important to specialize in one or more areas, it is equally important to understand the various architectures involved.

Regarding the 'Architecture of the Mind', briefly explain:
1. What is an 'architecture'?
2. What is the first step toward defining a 'system architecture'?
3. What is a 'system architecture' comprised of?
4. What is the distinction between a control system and an information system?
5. How many types of parallel processing are there, and how do they differ?

6. How does a mechanical form of intelligence compensate for the comparative lack of parallel processing?
7. What is an information control operating system, and why is it necessary to support a mechanically intelligent being?

James V. Luisi

28 Cognitive Database

One of the most significant hurdles in the study of cognitive science has been the representation of knowledge and a database that can support intelligence. The vast quantity of stimuli that the biological brain collects is no match for even the most robust databases previously used for business and research.

For example, databases with just one million records per table cannot support a five-table join on the most powerful modern computers if given weeks to complete the operation. A table join is when related records from separate tables are associated with one another, such as, associating an individual's credit card purchase, which is a record on a "transaction" table, with their credit limit, which is another record on a "customer account" table.

In order to support the data requirements of the brain, a database must be capable of performing massive joins among billions of records in seconds. However, such a database is unthinkable in terms of commercial technology, and would be a major departure from the current paradigm of database technology.

On May 12th 2000, such a database was unveiled at the "DAMA Data Warehouse" conference in New York City. Using a standard Intel server attached to a storage array, a variety of data analysis techniques, involving massive three table joins of more than 300 million records in 27 seconds was demonstrated.

This new database technology is at the center of our software architecture as the first cognitive database. As we progress past the trillion record level, this remarkable relational database will house the masses of stimuli that have been generated from external sensory devices, as well as our internal functional components of the brain. Database capabilities such as these should be able to support the data requirements of our various functional components, including the Imagination. ('DP DBMS, DataPulse and MailWizard', Web-site addresses: www.LMLabs.com and www.DataPulseDB.com, 1/1/2001, DataPulse, Inc.)

- - -

Neuron Story: *"Wouldn't that be a great place to store my thoughts?"*
"Why would you need something so powerful?"

"My mind wonders a lot."

- - -

One of the key architectural differences of cognitive database technology is that it relies upon a completely different set of database internals. The way that data is organized and stored in previously existing database products has not changed from the inception of database technology, over twenty years ago. In summary, data is stored on pages, usually 4K-bytes in length (4,096 characters), with each page having a header and a footer record. In the old paradigm, the data belonging to a table is physically stored as a group of attributes that belong to an occurrence of a specific row. Depending upon the width of the tables and the number of tables that are stored within the particular address space, the number of times that a given attribute may be stored within a 4K-byte page may vary significantly. Hence, in order to retrieve a handful of occurrences of a particular attribute, it may be necessary to retrieve a large number of 4K-byte pages.

In cognitive database technology, on the other hand, even the bits that comprise a given attribute need not be stored contiguously on a page.

Another important distinction of cognitive database technology is that it relies upon an advanced form of data compression, achieving a higher compression ratio. Unlike the older technologies, which compress only the non-key attributes, cognitive database technology compresses key data as well, and can perform queries and arithmetic expressions without decompressing the data.

While some of the more proprietary features of cognitive databases involve the way that various types of joins are supported, the end result is a product with the look and feel of a standard commercial database, with performance commensurate with the new breeds of technological advancements.

Summary & Questions

Intelligence is an information intensive process to support. When one considers the knowledge that is accumulated in a lifetime, the experience necessary to educate an intelligent being represents quite a vast quantity of sensory stimuli.

Regarding a 'Cognitive Database', briefly explain:
1. What is a Cognitive Database?
2. What is a table join?
3. Why are cognitive databases required to support artificial intelligence?

29 Conclusion

29.1 Chance and Probabilities

In the world of the infinitesimally small, the laws of quantum mechanics are completely dependent upon chance and probability. However, the macroscopic world is not altogether different. The events that have led to the development of molecules, and the evolutionary forces that have led to the development of *Homo sapiens sapiens* are all dependent upon chance.

For example, "As most people are aware, sixty-five million years ago marked the end of the Age of Dinosaurs, terminated by some link of natural catastrophe, almost certainly the collision of Earth with a large asteroid or comet. For 150 million years, dinosaurs were the major terrestrial group, occupying niches that in nature and number were about the same as mammals fill today. The mass extinction that put an end to this group, also devastated other groups, including various forms of mammal. In all, about 60 to 80 percent of all terrestrial species perished in the Cretaceous extinction." (Origins Reconsidered, Leakey and Lewin, 1977, pg. 347)

"Mammals had existed almost as long as the dinosaurs, but they remained a relatively insignificant part of terrestrial life, occupying a small-bodied, insectivorous niche. Being small, mammals had a better chance of surviving mass extinction (a general rule of the history of life), and many did. Among them was a primitive primate, ancestor to all the six thousand primate species that had existed since that time (about 183 live now). One of the properties of mass extinction is that many of the normal rules of biology are briefly suspended, principally those relating to everyday competition and survival. Species that survive mass extinction do so for reasons having to do with geographic distribution, body size, and plain luck. Had that primitive primate been less lucky at the Cretaceous extinction, there is no reason to expect that animals like primates would ever have evolved again, no prosimians, no monkeys, no apes – no humans." (Origins Reconsidered, Leakey and Lewin, pg. 348)

The living organisms of this planet have experienced five periods of mass extinction. The first was the Ordovician extinction, 430 million years ago, when primitive life existed in the sea. The second was the Devonian extinction, 350 million years ago, when the first air-breathing arthropods (e.g., spiders and mites) and fish with fins lived. The third was the Permian extinction, wiping out 96 percent of all marine species and more than 50 percent of all species around 225 million years ago. The fourth was the Triassic extinction, 200 million years ago, where seventy-five percent of invertebrate species were obliterated. And then the most recent, the Cretaceous extinction, only 65 million years ago, when dinosaurs completely disappeared from the face of the earth.

Aside from chance survival of catastrophic events, other events worked in favor of the evolution of hominids, propelling life toward the evolution of *Homo sapiens*.

> For example, "...what of the environmental and climatic changes associated with the formation of the Great Rift Valley, some ten million years ago and onward? I think it likely that the highland, mosaic environments generated by these events were important in the origin of the hominids in the first place. Had there been no such tectonic events in East Africa at that time, leaving the forests intact, perhaps hominids would not have evolved then; perhaps not at all."
>
> "What for instance might have happened if the drastic global cooling around 2.6 million years ago had not taken place? This cooling, remember, correlates with the origin of new australopithecine species (the robust boisei) and the evolution of the enlarged brain, the beginning of Homo. With no cooling, and without the ecological modifications resulting from it, perhaps Homo would not have appeared then; perhaps not at all."
>
> "Homo sapiens was one of a range of possibilities in the evolution of the hominid group, not an inevitable product of that process."
>
> (<u>Origins Reconsidered</u>, Leakey and Lewin, pg. 347)

As we continue deeper into our future, chance and probability will continue to play a role involving everything from technological discoveries to the eventual certainty of future mass extinctions. Since all change, even the ones that cause mass extinctions, occur over a number of years, it becomes possible for our advancements in technology to play a crucial role in determining whether we succeed as a species or not. It is perhaps, a way to tilt the odds of survival and proliferation in our favor.

29.2 Intelligence Born

Neuron Story: *"Do our lives have meaning?"*
"That depends completely on our paradigms."

James V. Luisi

Throughout the history of life, consciousness and intelligence have served as tools for survival. Just as organisms and their biological intelligence advance, non-biological forms of intelligence will advance as well. Many individuals will either fear or disbelieve the possibilities of an advanced form of non-biological intelligence for a number of reasons, supported by both scientifically and non-scientifically based paradigms. Although this can be minimized to some extent, there is nothing that anyone can do to prevent it. After all, diversity of thought and opinion is one of the greatest strengths of our species. The key is that we understand our past and agree on our objectives for the future.

- - -

Neuron Story: *"So just as Leakey helped to discover the past, we will help discover the future."*
"It gives us meaning."

- - -

29.3 Credit to the Leakey Legacy

More has been discovered about the evolution of our species in the last fifty years than in the previous hundred million. When we consider how long it took for life to evolve, and how long the forces of nature have had to destroy and hide the evidence left by the evolutionary process, it is a marvel that Louis and Mary Leakey have achieved so much success, in so little time. During almost thirty years of research beginning in 1931, they have uncovered many examples of ancient stone tools used by the elusive successors of *Ramapithecus*, and to this day, their children continue to unlock the past using a shovel and brush.

Mary Leakey found the first, *Zinjanthropus boisei*, later to be grouped with *Australopithecus boisei*, at Olduvai Gorge, East Africa, in 1959. One year later, in 1960, Mary Leakey found a partial cranium of *Homo habilis* at Olduvai Gorge. While Mary was visiting the Koobi Fora camp at Lake Turkana in 1969, team members Kimeu, Mutwiwi and Muoka each found a fragment of a boisei jaw and later at Lake Turkana they found *Homo habilis*.

When Louis Leakey analyzed the fragments of the cranium in Olduvai in 1959, he determined that it was sufficiently different from the South African *bosei* to separate it into a new species and genus, *Zinjanthropus boisei* (East African man). He found that the East African bosei were so much larger than their South African cousins. "The East African animals are now called *Australopithecus boisei*, that is, the same genus as their South African cousins but a different species." (People of the Lake, Leakey and Lewin, p66-7)

Louis Leakey died in October 1972 and Mary Leakey still lives as of the writing of this book, with her son Richard having assumed the task of research.

By following in his parent's footsteps, Richard Leakey has gained a deep and thorough understanding, which makes him stand out from among his peers. I have not only been inspired by his writings, but it has been an honor for me to quote his work in order to present the background of our past.

30 Epilogue

Even though there were many titles that were more appealing, few seemed to ring a chord as strongly as the title, 'Sensitive By Nature'. It could be due to the fact that every reader's mind is the subject of the discussion, or that the assertions contained in the book generally run counter to existing belief systems.

- - -

Neuron Story: *"The presentation of ideas is riddled with opportunities to offend groups or individuals without the least intention to do so."*
"Only as you violate their paradigms."

- - -

Controversy can be found where individuals have well rooted paradigms, especially when the mind is naturally compelled to defend its paradigms. The contents of this manuscript, for example, run contrary to the mainstream artificial intelligence community in academia, government and industry, as well as, to the broad foundation involving the field of psychology, comprising numerous psychologists, psychiatrists and behavioral scientists.

Ideas themselves should not offend people. In a world of reason, when individuals present their point of view, others should be able to express why they agree or disagree. Unfortunately, when an individual's belief systems are involved, the debate may be passionate, albeit somewhat less than intellectual.

For example, Charles Darwin, who originally studied to become a clergyman, outraged scientists, clerics and the general public with the notion of natural selection and genetics because it contradicted the book of Genesis. When Darwin's friend, Thomas Henry Huxley, debated Bishop Samuel Wilberforce, the bishop asked him whether it was on his grandmother's or his grandfather's side that he was descended from an ape, Huxley replied, "I would much rather be descended from an ape, sir, than a bishop."

Although Charles Darwin never learned the underlying mechanisms of genetics that Mendel discovered, his intuition drove him to observe the characteristics of so many species, that he was moved in the right direction.

There were many prevailing theories on genetics during Darwin's lifetime, one popular theory asserted that the offspring resulting from sexual reproduction took on the characteristics midway between each parent.

Another theory stated that all future generations of an organism were encapsulated microscopically inside the sperm or egg, with every generation's characteristics already predetermined.

However, when scientists evaluated Mendel's new paradigm of dominant and recessive traits driven by statistical probabilities, every possible result occurred. Scientists embraced, refuted and even plagiarized it.

> For example, a biometrician named Darbishire, used metrics to show exceptions to Mendel's genetic inheritance as a disproof of its concepts. Although he could not produce the details of his experiments to support his research when asked.

> Whereas, without crediting Gregor Mendel, Hugo De Vries represented Mendel's discoveries as his own, including the monk's terminology for dominant and recessive characteristics.

Similarly, in order to address the scope of mechanical intelligence, however, a number of barriers must be overcome. Scientists should agree to a common set of terminology, such as what major functions exist, and upon a model depicting how these functions relate to one another, such as the generation of symbols before determining the corresponding level of importance. One benefit of such an approach is the possibility of integrating the results between efforts. Of course, others would argue that the absence of standards is necessary to succeed.

- - -

Neuron Story: *"Would technology be more advanced if there were no standards for software, electronics and mechanical devices?"*

"Did the Bohr model of the atom help scientists advance their understanding of physical chemistry?"

- - -

Although everyone will not agree on a common model, when presenting ideas it would be helpful if ideas were generally presented in the context of a defined model. However, the lack of standardization is not the only barrier to the advancement of technology.

Whether he lived in the 1800's or the year 2000, Mendel was ahead of his time. Regardless of the year, or whether it was within the academic community or the commercial sector, Mendel would learn that there are many barriers to creating an awareness of a breakthrough. In his era, his was merely the first paradigm to change.

30.1 Content

Volumes of literature have been written in the past two hundred years about the topics discussed in the Requirements Section. Many great minds have expressed numerous intellectual insights into these topics, such as love, God, and psychology.

Regardless of their time in history, these intellectuals approached the subject matter and their particular point of view using language as an art form. The result of using this art form, however, is that ideas are expressed using a variety of techniques to express ideas and explore the various aspects of their subject matter. The manner, in which they express their ideas, are dependent upon their capabilities and choices in their use of language, similar to the way an artist uses their brush to express ideas and feelings. As a result, the free and artistic use of language may express many ideas in a rather non-standard form, thereby making it difficult to compare the ideas of individuals expressed in unrelated terms.

- - -

Neuron Story: *"The way they expressed their ideas were not implementable."*
"Back then, who would have thought of that?"

- - -

The purpose of the Requirements Section is to characterize some of the most difficult topics in a manner that lends itself to being implemented. To determine this characterization required an iterative process, one where functional components are identified to implement the requirements, and then the requirements that are unimplementable are re-defined. The result is a paradigm of defining requirements that evolves as the conceptual design develops.

30.2 Presentation

The importance of the paradigm that I was creating was to define requirements so that they were implementable. To develop that paradigm, I felt that diverting the reader's attention by highlighting the controversial aspects of each idea and presenting alternatives make it difficult to stay focused on the main points of the story. In addition, in order to give each controversial position the appropriate level of consideration, one must make an earnest effort to bridge the difference in terminology, explain the other perspective within the context of this book, and then demonstrate why the other perspective was not chosen.

For example, the philosophy of Nelson Goodman, outlined in 'The Problem of Counterfactual Conditions', 'The

Passing of the Possible', 'The New Riddle of Induction', and 'Prospects for a Theory of Projection', debate many aspects of cognition with respect to the mind making generalizations and distinguishing among them. The concepts and terminology put forth by Goodman are quite interesting as a philosophical topic. Although many feel that questions raised by Goodman cannot be answered, when his ideas are placed into our paradigm of stimuli, the questions that Goodman raises can be addressed.

Without oversimplifying too much, using the paradigm of our functional components, such as symbol generation, pattern recognition, importance determination, and so on, it becomes readily apparent that the intellectual process of generalizing from experience, in some ways and not in others, is determined by combinations of these components. The generalizations that are formed, are themselves, symbols that are generated from the combinations of stimuli from an individual's experiences. The symbols that are activated due to similarities with existing symbols, and their relative levels of importance, not excluding the symbols that have been activated by the analogical and metaphorical engines, determine which generalizations are made.

If we were also to consider the various points of view that contrast with Nelson Goodman, such as the views of Noam Chomsky, Jerrold Katz and Jerry Fodor, the same considerations apply. To do justice, one must painstakingly define the paradigm that they employ to characterize their concepts, and if possible, explain why.

- - -

Neuron Story: *"Research that doesn't define its base paradigm provides such freedom of expression and interpretation."*
"That is certainly one philosophy."

- - -

30.3 Philosophy

The research of language and how the mind works can get quite involved in matters of philosophy. When researchers evaluate how the mind can determine the meaning of sentences and whether the meaning is potentially valid, they must consider the construction of the sentence, the assertions that the sentence makes, and usually some set of information that existed before the sentence was introduced. The field of philosophy has also researched whether the validity of the assertion of a sentence can be determined with an individual sentence, without previously asserted facts.

For example, in summarizing his lecture on 'Counterfactual Conditionals', Nelson Goodman addresses the issue of how to validate standalone sentences, writing "...our problem to the question how to define the circumstances under which a statement is acceptable independently of the determination of any given instance. But this question I do not know how to answer." (Fact Fiction and Forecast, Nelson Goodman, p27)

- - -

Neuron Story: *"I can make standalone sentences that are independently true, such as 'I think, therefore I have a reason to believe that I somehow exist'."*

"and my favorite is... 'No matter where I go, I am here... with you'."

- - -

I must say that I am not qualified to state whether Nelson Goodman would have accepted self-referential sentences. However, the pursuit of such issues, such as analyzing how the mind deals with assertions and then determines their subsequent validity while outside a comprehensive paradigm for thought, is an example of how one may engage in creating paradigms that will lead to unanswerable questions. The choice of framework for analyzing any complex subject matter will always determine whether the resulting discussion is a scientific one, or one that is based in religion.

The foundation that philosophy is built upon is pure logic and reasoning. To quote Susanne K. Langer, "...general logic is to philosophy what mathematics is to science; the realm of its possibilities, and the measure of its reason." (An Introduction To Symbolic Logic, Susanne K. Langer, p334)

30.4 Logic and Reason Revisited

As we know, nearly an equal number of individuals voted for Bush in the race for president during election 2000, as for Gore. In contesting the results of the vote count in Florida, the Gore side made a logical argument supporting their interests. Likewise, in defending the machine counts and the certification of the results by the Florida legislature, the Bush side made a logical argument supporting their interests.

What happened next was a contest over the results of an election, where nearly all the supporters on the Bush side and nearly all the supporters on the Gore side disagreed on the interpretation of laws that defined the process. However, the important aspect for understanding the topic of logic and reasoning is not which side ultimately won the contest, but what happened to the exercise of logic and reasoning of each side.

We shall begin by identifying our basic assumptions, which are that the individuals on each side of the contest consisted of reasonable, well-intentioned, law-abiding individuals. Additionally, from the perspective of one's ability to exercise logic and reasoning, we should concede that both sides are well endowed intellectually. And lastly, that both sides have ample legal knowledge to support whatever claims they make. Hence, it is clear that both sides are comprised of well-motivated, intelligent and knowledgeable individuals.

What then, could explain how these individuals, including State and Federal Justices, could interpret the same laws and events to reason that only the sides that they are affiliated with should prevail? Is there any reasonable probability that such a large proportion of voters, legislators and judges could be so unreasoning?

Since it is rather far fetched that such an overwhelming majority of voters, legislators and judges would be using anything other than logic and reasoning to evaluate the circumstances and the laws, we should realize that there is a strong probability that each side employed a different paradigm. Although the individuals of each side may not have a strong preference when they initially voted, they had increasingly strong emotions regarding the outcome of the election.

Each side had a preferred outcome, which had a critical influence in determining how individuals would interpret the laws and principles involved. As such, the paradigm of each side not only determined how individuals would interpret the law, but it also prevented them from perceiving the viewpoint of the other side.

> Although both sides used the same laws, one side adopted a strict interpretation of the law, while the other incorporated the general principles of natural law. Although natural law is unwritten, it protects fundamental rights of people to life, liberty, the pursuit of happiness, and includes the right to vote. Whether one agrees with the application of natural law, using logic and reasoning it has frequently been applied in a philosophical way towards problem solving and decision making.

The outcome of logic and reasoning is not only determined by one's political preferences. Logic and reasoning can be used to achieve different results in science as well.

For example, while the arithmetic expression zero divided by zero is generally considered as an undefined expression, mathematicians may employ it creatively.

If we recall a few basic rules about division, we encounter three potentially conflicting rules: 1) A number divided into itself equals one. 2) A number divided into zero equals zero. 3) A number divided by zero is equal to infinity.

The result is that zero divided by zero can be interpreted by the first rule as equaling one, the second rule equaling zero, and the third rule equaling infinity.

In practice, therefore, mathematicians and politicians alike, adopt the rules that contribute the most toward achieving their objectives. Hence, the use of logic and reasoning does not guarantee that only one possible outcome exists, and it cannot guarantee that one outcome is any more correct than another outcome. Although, logic and reasoning is good a tool, it is by no means infallible.

- - -

Neuron Story: *"Can we find a topic more sensitive than politics?"*
"Wait! I'm still busy counting votes."

- - -

30.5 Religion Revisited

In discussing the topic of religion I wanted to point out that I could have selected any religion as a reference point, however, I chose to adopt a Christian perspective only for the purpose of personal convenience. While I made that choice because I happen to be most familiar with it, my intention was to challenge beliefs regarding artificial intelligence and its treatment of religion, and not religion itself. I can only hope that I was successful in challenging the way that individuals think about religion from the perspective of artificial intelligence, and not come away with the impression that any particular religion or system of belief is inferior to any other.

As a result, no one should feel that their personal beliefs have been challenged, although perhaps some individuals may now be better able to share ideas about their beliefs and the beliefs of others. If anyone found that they were particularly emotional during the discussion of beliefs, they may find it helpful to pause briefly and inquire as to why. Just note that while it is true that many individuals have died for their beliefs, it is clear that too many individuals have also killed for their beliefs, as well.

- - -

Neuron Story: *"After reading 'Sensitive By Nature', I'm ready to experience any beliefs."*
"Does that make you a believer of all beliefs, or a non-practicing non-believer?"

- - -

30.6 Next Steps

"Rather than trying to build costly, clumsy physical robots, researchers should concentrate their efforts entirely on computer simulations – that's the key to unraveling the nature of intelligence."
Marvin Minsky

The difficulty in implementing a mechanically intelligent being has not stifled the design and manufacture of robots. Robots have been used to perform physical tasks for industry, albeit usually for an assembly line to execute mindless activities. Increasingly, robotic devices have been used for tasks that are difficult or dangerous for humans. Regardless of the role that was chosen for them, however, robots have usually been designed in very specific ways, to be preprogrammed or to be controlled remotely by humans.

Among the few exceptions, it is worth mentioning some robots that have been designed to perform a portion of their activities, dynamically by the robot depending upon what it encounters, rather than externally by a human.

Of the least advanced robots are robotic pets provided by a variety of manufacturers. These robots are generally priced below fifty dollars.

The intelligence of these robots and others like them are limited to the intellectual processing that supports locomotion. Although robots with wheels do not generally require much sophistication, robots with four, and particularly two legs, have to be much more advanced to cope with balance issues, such as avoiding accidentally tipping over and righting themselves when they do. Although software to enable walking should not be taken lightly, these robots lack any other form of intelligence.

For example, Sony Corporation manufactures a small mechanical dog, called AIBO. Although it is described by its manufacturer as a robot that has the ability to exhibit learning, it actually only exhibits a form of time-released programming, which permits it to roam and behave autonomously the longer it is turned on.

At first, this $2,500 plastic dog from Sony appears to lack the ability to stand up, never mind walk. After a certain amount of time, however, "AIBO" decides that it is ready to stumble forwards and backwards, scratch for imaginary fleas, and yawn excessively.

James V. Luisi

- - -

Neuron Story: "And since yawning is so contagious, the consumer yawns too."
"Yes, but that depends on who yawns first."

- - -

There are also a variety of robots that are not yet available to consumer market, which would be in a considerably more expensive price range.

For example, Honda Motor Corporation manufactures the "P3", a humanoid robot that has two arms with hands that can hold things, two legs that can walk and climb stairs, a head, and of course a torso which all of these parts are attached to. As for scale, in a standing position these robots are five feet three inches high, and can walk at a top speed of 1.2 mph, which is approximately about one fourth the speed of a human. Although Honda is unwilling to reveal the price tag, industry experts estimate that cost of each P3 exceeds one million dollars.

The disappointment, however, is that the P3 is not autonomous, as its every movement, excluding the process of balancing its 130 kg body (nearly 300 lbs.), must be carefully programmed. The P3 must be carefully positioned at some predetermined starting point, usually marked by tape on the floor, before executing each preprogrammed movement.

Even though it would be a monumental programming effort, one of the objectives identified by Honda was for their robot to participate in the RoboCup games.

- - -

Neuron Story: "Did you know RoboCup is a soccer match for robots?"
"I thought it was an article of robot protective clothing."

- - -

The reason that I have chosen the name of Quantum Series One for our robot is that like quantum theory and the uncertainty principle, its very basis and explanation is founded in the effects of chance and probability. The aspect of Series One within the name reflects my hope and expectation that several versions will be based on this technology.

On that note I wish to thank those that have found reading '<u>Sensitive By Nature</u>', a stimulating experience, as well as those who have persevered through it. I look forward to reading your comments and criticisms. JimLuisi@worldnet.att.net

James V. Luisi

Bibliography

1. James Allen, 1987, "Natural Language Understanding", The Benjamin / Cummings Publishing Company, Reading, MA, U.S.A., Menlo Park, CA, U.S.A., Don Mills, Ontario, Canada, Wokingham, England, Amsterdam, Sydney, Singapore, Tokyo, Madrid, Bogota, Santiago, San Juan, ISBN 0-8053-0330-8
2. Thomas Armstrong, Ph.D., 1999, "7 Kinds of Smart: Identifying and Developing Your Multiple Intelligences", Plume, Penguin Putnam Inc., N.Y., New York, U.S.A.; London, England; Victoria, Australia; Toronto, Ontario, Canada; Auckland, New Zealand, ISBN 0-452-28137-7
3. Isaac Asimov, (in one of his early short stories about robots, 1941), "Robot Visions", ROC Science Fiction) (paperback)
4. Avron Barr and Edward Feigenbaum, 1981, "The Handbook of Artificial Intelligence, Volume 1", Addison Wesley Publishing Company Inc., Reading, MA, U.S.A., Menlo Park, CA, U.S.A., Don Mills, Ontario, Canada, Wokingham, England, Amsterdam, Sydney, Singapore, Tokyo, Madrid, Bogota, Santiago, San Juan, ISBN 0-201-11811-4
5. Avron Barr and Edward Feigenbaum, 1982, "The Handbook of Artificial Intelligence, Volume 2", Addison Wesley Publishing Company Inc., Reading, MA, U.S.A., Menlo Park, CA, U.S.A., Don Mills, Ontario, Canada, Wokingham, England, Amsterdam, Sydney, Singapore, Tokyo, Madrid, Bogota, Santiago, San Juan, ISBN 0-201-11813-0
6. Gareth Brawyn, 1998, "Pumping Plastic", Wired Magazine, April 1998 issue
7. Encyclopedia Britannica CD Multimedia Edition 1998 (Version 98.0.0.9) Fifteenth Edition, Encyclopædia Britannica, Inc.
8. Kenneth W. Church, 1987, "Phonological Parsing in Speech Recognition", Kluwer Academic Publishers, Boston, MA, U.S.A., Dordrecht, Netherland, Lancaster, United Kingdom, ISBN 0-89838-250-5
9. Paul R. Cohen and Edward Feigenbaum, 1982, "The Handbook of Artificial Intelligence, Volume 3", Addison Wesley Publishing Company Inc., Reading, MA, U.S.A., Menlo Park, CA, U.S.A., Don Mills, Ontario, Canada, Wokingham, England, Amsterdam, Sydney, Singapore, Tokyo, Madrid, Bogota, Santiago, San Juan, ISBN 0-201-11815-7
10. Dr. Howard Gardner, 1993, "Frames of Mind, the Theory of Multiple Intelligence", Basic Books, New York, U.S.A.

11. Gertner D. and Jeziorski M., 1989, "Historical Shifts in the Use of Analogy in Science," in B. Gholson et al. (eds.) The Psychology of Science: Contributions to Metascience, Cambridge University Press, London, U.K.
12. Dr. Daniel Goleman, 1995, "Emotional Intelligence", Bantam Books, New York, U.S.A.
13. Nelson Goodman, 1979, 1983, "Fact Fiction and Forecast", Harvard University Press, Cambridge, Massachusetts, U.S.A. and London, England, ISBN 0-674-29071-2
14. Nelson Goodman, 1976, "Languages of Art", Hackett Publishing Company, Inc., Indianapolis, U.S.A. and Cambridge, London, England, ISBN 0-915144-34-4
15. John Gribbin, 1985, "In Search of the Double Helix", McGraw-Hill, 1987 Bantam Books, New York, U.S.A., ISBN 0-553-34432-3 (paperback)
16. Stephen Grossberg, Daniel Bullock, Gail A. Carpenter, Michael A. Cohen, William Gutowski, Daniel Levine, Ennio Mingolla, Nestor A. Schmajuk, Gregory O. Stone, Dejan Todorovic, 1988, "Neural Networks and Natural Intelligence", Bradford Books - The MIT Press, Cambridge, MA, U.S.A., London, England, ISBN 0-262-07107-X
17. John Hallam, Chris Mellish, Andy Clark, John Kelly, Alexander Nakhimovsky, Han Reichgelt, Edward Tsang, Tony Morgan, Mauro di Manzo, Emanuele Trucco, Roddy Cowie, Steve Reeves, Lincoln Wallen, Gregory Wilson, David Frost, Roman Jansen-Winkeln, Roger Evans, Bo Zhang, Ling Zhang, Sam Steel, Anne de Roeck, Paul Brna, Alan Bundy, Helen Pain, Laim Lynch, Afzal Ballim, Allan Ramsay, 1987, "Advances in Artificial Intelligence", John Wiley and Sons, Chichester, New York, Brisbane, Toronto, Singapore, ISBN 0-471-91549-1
18. Derek J. Hatley and Imtiaz A. Pirbhai, 1988, "Strategies for Real-Time System Specification", Dorset House Publishing, New York, N.Y., U.S.A., 0-932633-11-0
19. Robin Marantz Henig, 2000, "The Monk in the Garden – The Lost and Found Genius of Gregor Mendel, the Father of Genetics", Houghton Mifflin Company, Boston and New York, U.S.A., ISBN 0-395-97765-7
20. Douglas Hofstadter and The Fluid Analogies Research Group, 1995, "Fluid Concepts and Creative Analogies", Basic Books/Perseus Book Group, (paperback) New York, U.S.A., ISBN 0-465-02475-0
21. Douglas R Hofstadter, 1989, "Godel, Escher, Bach: An Eternal Golden Braid", Vintage Books/Random House Inc., (paperback) New York, U.S.A., ISBN 0-394-75682-7

22. Bipin Indurkhya, 1992, "Metaphor and Cognition," Kluwer Academic Publishers, The Netherlands. ISBN 0-7923-1687-8
23. Philip C. Jackson, Jr., 1985, "Introduction to Artificial Intelligence", Dover Publications Inc., New York, U.S.A., ISBN 0-486-24864-X (paperback)
24. Immanuel Kant, Translated by Victor Lyle Dowdell, 1978, "Anthropology From a Pragmatic Point of View", Southern Illinois University Press, Carbondale & Edwardsville, U.S.A., ISBN 0-8093-2060-6
25. Ray Kurzweil, 1999, "The Age Of Spiritual Machines", Penguin Putnam Inc., Harmondsworth, Middlesex, England ISBN 0-670-88217-8
26. Susanne K. Langer, 1967, "An Introduction to Symbolic Logic", Dover Publications Inc., New York, N.Y., U.S.A., ISBN 0-486-60164-1
27. Susanne K. Langer, 1979, "Philosophy in a New Key", Harvard University Press, Cambridge, Massachusetts and London, England, ISBN 0-674-66503-1
28. Richard E. Leakey and Roger Lewin, 1977, "Origins," E.P.Dutton, Inc., New York, U.S.A., ISBN 0-525-48013-7 (paperback)
29. Richard E. Leakey and Roger Lewin, 1979, "People of the Lake", Avon Books, (paperback) New York, U.S.A., ISBN 0-380-45575-7
30. Richard E. Leakey and Roger Lewin, 1993, "Origins Reconsidered", First Anchor Books / Random House, Inc., New York, U.S.A., ISBN 0-385-46792-3 (paperback)
31. Aleksandr Romanovich Luriia, 1968, "The Mind of a Mnemonist", translated from Russian by Lyn Solotaroff, Harvard University Press, Cambridge, Massachusetts and London, England, ISBN 0-674-57622-5
32. James Martin, 1982, "Computer Database Organization", Prentice Hall Inc., Englewood Cliffs, NJ, U.S.A., ISBN 0-13-165423-3
33. Peter Menzel and Faith D'Aluisio, 2000, "Evolution of a New Species Robo sapiens", The MIT Press, Cambridge, Mass, U.S.A., London, England, ISBN 0-262-13382-2.
34. Microsoft Encarta, 1997, 1998, Encyclopedia CD, Microsoft Corporation Inc., U.S.A.
35. Oxford English Dictionary, 1994, Oxford University Press, CD-ROM (Version 1.13), Walton Street, Oxford, England
36. Dr. Maria Paschitti, 1998, "IQ and EQ: How They Impact On The Success We Achieve In Our Chosen Careers", Summer Institute For The Gifted, North Carolina Association For The Gifted (NCAGT) Newsletter

37. Pearl, Nau and Beal, 1980, "Heuristics" (Out of Print)
38. James Rumbaugh, Michael Blaha, William Premerlani, Fredrick Eddy, William Lorenson, 1991, "Object Oriented Modeling and Design", Advanced Concepts Center - Martin Marietta, Prentice Hall Inc. a division of Simon & Schuster, Englewood Cliffs, NJ, U.S.A., ISBN 0-13-110439-X
39. Stuart C. Shapiro, Editor-in-Chief, 1992, "Encyclopedia of Artificial Intelligence", Volumes 1 & 2, John Wiley & Sons, Inc., New York, Chichester, Brisbane, Toronto, Singapore, ISBN 0-471-50305-3
40. Everett L. Shostrom and Dan Montgomery, 1967, "The Manipulators", Abingdon Press, Nashville, TN, U.S.A., ISBN 0-687-23075-6 (paperback)
41. Donald J. Sobol, 1969, "Encyclopedia Brown Volume 6, The Case of the Falling Woman", Bantam Book, published by arrangement with Thomas Nelson Inc., Publishers, U.S.A., ISBN 0-553-15735-3 (paperback)
42. The Wall Street Journal, 1989, "Olive Tasters", Wall Street Journal, April 20 1989 issue)
43. Philip Wegener, 1885, "Untersuchungen uber die Grundfragen des Sprachlebens", Halle, out of print
44. Ludwig Wittgenstein, 1953, 1958, 1997, "Philosophische Untersuchungen - Philosophical Investigations", translated by G. E. M. Anscombe, Blackwell Publishers, Oxford, U.K., Malden, MA, U.S.A., ISBN 0-631-20569-1 (paperback)
45. Ludwig Wittgenstein, 1969 "Uber Gewissheit - On Certainty", edited by G. E. M. Anscombe and G. H. von Wright, translated by Denis Paul and G. E. M. Anscombe, Harper Torchbooks, Harper and Row, New York, Grand Rapids, Hagerstown, Philadelphia, St. Louis, San Francisco, London, Singapore, Sydney, Tokyo, Toronto, ISBN 0-06-131686-5 (paperback)
46. Dean Wooldridge, 1968, "Mechanical Man – The Physical Basis of Intelligent Life", McGraw Hill, (paperback), New York, U.S.A.
47. Carl Zimmer, 2000, "Parasite Rex", The Free Press, Simon & Schuster, Inc., New York, U.S.A., ISBN 0-684-85638-7

Index

Age of Mammals, 36
Agriculture, 50
analog, 93, 94, 215, 216, 222, 257, 314
analogy, 68, 73, 74, 102, 171, 193, 220, 221, 263, 270, 279, 329, 331, 358, 372, 373, 374, 375, 376, 377, 378, 379, 380, 382, 383, 385
ape, 20, 41, 61, 129, 409
Armstrong, Thomas, 294
artificial intelligence, 10, 315, 316, 317, 408, 416, 428
Asimov, Isaac, 278, 289
Australopithecus, 40, 44, 45, 61, 62, 405, 407

Babbage, Charles, 66
belief system, 235, 236, 243, 249
body-kinesthetic intelligence, 294
Bohr atom', 24
Bohr, Niels, 24
Bongard, 218
Broca's, 60, 129
Bubble-up Importance, 137

carotid sinus, 62
cerebral cortex, 60
Chomsky, Noam, 412
chunking, 54, 133, 168, 171, 301, 357
common sense, 179, 180, 181, 182, 183, 184, 301
conceptual design, 11, 12, 13, 306, 307, 308, 319, 343, 344, 411
conductive plastic, 82
conscious, 30, 31, 65, 78, 98, 99, 101, 123, 126, 135, 136, 137, 138, 139, 140, 172, 188, 201, 202, 203, 204, 205, 206, 215, 240, 257, 288, 290, 301, 323, 348, 349, 350, 351, 357, 361, 362, 363, 364, 366, 368, 369, 370, 378
consciousness, 102, 350, 351, 368, 406
Darmok, 386
Darwin, Charles, 18, 20, 408, 409
decision making, 100, 210, 212, 213, 221, 228, 237, 294, 302, 319, 355, 369, 415
deductive reasoning, 101, 171, 181, 182, 213, 223, 224, 225, 226, 233, 245, 372
degree of certainty, 173, 174
digital, 93, 94, 216, 222, 257, 258, 334, 338
DNA, 19, 25, 26, 28, 47, 222
Doppler, Christian, 248
Dryopithecus, 39

Einstein, Albert, 18, 73
Eliza effect, 318
emotional intelligence, 298, 299

finite loop, 141
Fodor, Jerry, 412
formal system, 70, 73, 74
Fouts, 52
Freud, 57, 361
full language system, 255, 256, 258, 260

gatherer/hunter, 57
gatherers and hunters, 51
Generalizations, 174
genetic programming, 136, 159, 160, 161
Gigantopithecus, 39
Goodman, Nelson, 153, 197, 226, 322, 411, 412, 413
Gregor Mendel, 18, 248

hippocampus, 127
Hofstadter, Douglas, 318
holistic, 219, 220, 302
Holloway, Ralph, 61
hominids, 29, 39, 40, 41, 42, 44, 45, 46, 54, 62, 97, 405
Homo erectus, 45, 46, 47, 48, 62
Homo habilis, 45, 407
Homo sapiens, 37, 42, 45, 46, 47, 48, 50, 51, 52, 54, 55, 56, 57, 62, 65, 157, 187, 247, 249, 366, 404, 405
Homo sapiens sapiens, 47, 48
humor, 2, 112, 188, 189, 190, 197, 199, 266, 267, 272, 293, 301, 376
hunter/gatherer, 50

imagination, 74, 121, 122, 123, 124, 125, 126, 130, 133, 152, 213, 301, 319, 320, 323, 326, 328, 343, 346, 348, 354, 359, 362, 363, 366, 375
Imagination Component, 343, 348, 349, 363, 364, 365, 366, 367, 369, 370, 375, 376, 378, 401
Immanuel Kant, 115, 116, 140, 305, 368
implementation phase, 310
Importance Determination, 136, 343, 352, 354, 355, 356, 357, 358, 359, 360, 361, 363, 370
Indurkhya, Bipin, 217, 263, 264, 329, 330, 382, 387
Infinite Loop, 142
infinite loops, 143
informal system, 73
integration testing, 311, 312
isomorphism, 221, 222

Kanzi, 53
Katz, Jerrold, 412
Koko, 52, 129

Langer, Susanne K., 413
Laws of Robotics, 289
Leakey
Louis, 11, 50, 407
Mary, 11, 46, 50, 407
Richard, 11, 29, 37, 42, 43, 46, 47, 48, 52, 53, 54, 57, 61, 130, 247, 365, 366, 404, 405, 406, 407
learning, 11, 20, 42, 43, 52, 112, 119, 124, 132, 133, 155, 157, 158, 160, 161, 162, 163, 165, 167, 168, 169, 170, 174, 176, 178, 182, 192, 193, 201, 231, 239, 258, 259, 260, 268, 276, 290, 291, 299, 301, 325, 326, 328, 335, 336, 347, 357, 358, 360, 372, 390, 391, 392, 417
Level One, 111, 112, 113, 114, 117, 118, 119
Level Three, 117, 118, 119, 120, 121, 128
Level Two, 114, 115, 116, 117, 118, 120, 121, 207, 232, 233, 386
logical design, 308, 309, 312
Lucy, 40, 52
Luria, 390

Maslow, Abraham, 191
Matata, 53
Mendel, Gregor, 409
messenger RNA, 25
metaphor, 112, 186, 260, 261, 263, 264, 329, 330, 370, 372, 380, 382, 383, 384, 385, 386, 387
Minsky, Marvin, 417
mitochondrian DNA, 47

naked, 43
Nakedness, 43
Napp, Abbot, 18, 19
Neanderthals, 45
Neuman, John Von, 66

Pangaea, 36, 37, 38
paradigm, 10, 12, 106, 107, 108, 109, 110, 111, 112, 113, 114, 115, 116, 117, 118, 120, 121, 145, 146, 148, 155, 188, 189, 199, 224, 227, 232, 263, 304, 305, 318, 320, 329, 343, 346, 347, 354, 363, 370, 377, 382, 383, 384, 385, 386, 387, 389, 390, 391, 392, 393, 399, 401, 402, 409, 410, 411, 412, 413, 414
paradox, 245, 269, 280
Paschitti, Maria, 298, 299

pattern recognition, 160, 204, 218, 307, 332, 334, 336, 337, 338, 339, 343, 344, 379, 412
perception, 37, 56, 78, 102, 104, 106, 107, 129, 130, 155, 173, 192, 193, 200, 301, 319, 331, 339, 351, 372
personality, 107, 194, 197, 199, 201, 207, 239, 301, 360
phonetic languages, 258
physical design, 309, 310
pictographic languages, 255, 258
polypyrrole, 82
Premack, 52
problem solving, 151, 161, 182, 183, 212, 213, 214, 215, 219, 220, 221, 233, 252, 291, 294, 295, 299, 302, 329, 372, 415
programming language, 69

Quantum Mechanics, 23, 233

Ramapithecus, 39, 40, 41, 45, 407
recursion, 140, 319
recursive loop, 141
reductionistic, 219, 220, 302
requirements, 10, 11, 12, 13, 15, 33, 68, 69, 75, 76, 78, 79, 83, 84, 87, 89, 95, 98, 121, 124, 152, 155, 158, 161, 178, 191, 278, 297, 299, 301, 302, 303, 304, 305, 306, 307, 308, 309, 310, 311, 312, 315, 316, 317, 319, 331, 401, 410, 411
RNA, 25, 26, 28
Rumbaugh, 52

Segment Integration Component, 342, 343
self-esteem, 196, 199, 200, 201, 207, 301
sharing, 44, 55, 56, 211, 390
spoken language, 52, 54, 153, 186, 215, 260, 275, 322, 323
Stendhal syndrome, 104
subliminal, 140, 203, 204, 205, 206, 301
success, 10, 12, 31, 39, 57, 160, 215, 248, 275, 290, 297, 298, 299, 320, 393, 407, 423
superstitious beliefs, 241, 242, 243
Susanne K. Langer, 242, 274, 275
Symbol Activation, 343, 345, 346, 348, 350, 357, 363, 367

thalmus, 127
theory of multiple intelligences, 294
Thinking Roller Coaster, 131, 132
tools, 12, 43, 45, 46, 50, 65, 66, 79, 89, 97, 121, 161, 213, 220, 247, 279, 290, 296, 309, 316, 406, 407
unconscious, 99, 106, 107, 134, 137, 139, 140, 203, 204, 237, 348, 350, 351, 352, 357, 361, 362, 363, 367, 368, 369

Washoe, 52
Watson and Crick, 19
Weizenbaum, Joseph, 318
Wernicke's, 61
Wittgenstein, Ludwig, 107, 125, 166, 210, 235

James V. Luisi

The Inside Jacket

'Sensitive By Nature', is a thought provoking approach toward the development of true AI.
A book written for the 21st Century
'Sensitive By Nature', challenges the reader to evaluate:
- Why intelligence exists
- What intelligence is
- How intelligence evolved
- What is our relationship to other life
- What thinking is
- How thinking is performed
- Why people believe the things they do
- What logic and reasoning is
- How we determine our purpose
- How to interact with others
- How misunderstandings occur
- How to negotiate
- How to measure intelligence
- …and many more

An easy to understand 'guided tour' of biological intelligence, and a glimpse into the making a mechanical form of intelligence.
© 2001
For a Nondramatic Literary Work
United States Copyright Office
TXu 1-001-086
Effective 20 April 2001

James V. Luisi

The Author

Jim Luisi is a graduate of Brooklyn College and currently participates in the management of two software companies, inventing new ways of looking at things and designing leading edge business solutions. Having lived previously New York and California, Jim is a now resident of New Jersey. Jim still enjoys the area in California that his mom lives in, and enjoys visiting his sister, Marie, as she periodically relocates to new and interesting locations throughout the United States.

Jim is grateful to his sister and the various elves for their tremendous contribution to the book with their skillful proof reading and relentless, yet always, constructive criticism.

Jim has worked in database technology for over twenty years, participated in every aspect of the software development life cycle for large information systems on Wall Street, and large control systems regarding defense work, and performed as a management consultant in extremely large automation efforts. He has also managed a research effort into artificial intelligence for a major aerospace company, and co-developed 'Process Normalization', which is a process that normalizes millions of lines of code to tens of thousands.

As to specific accomplishments, Mr. Luisi was the chief architect of the *DataPulse database* technology, the first cognitive database system, and the Business Intelligence applications that have been developed using it.

Most importantly, Jim's pride and joy is his daughter, born in San Diego on the 21st of August 1990, whose welcome interruptions, along with those of the rest of his family, helped influence Jim's decision not to change his career to become a writer.

Printed in the United States
727700001B